Digital Transformation and Artificial Intelligence for Operational Excellence in Healthcare

ADVANCES IN DIGITAL TECHNOLOGY AND DATA-DRIVEN BUSINESS PRACTICES

Series Editor: Nripendra Singh – Pennsylvania Western University, USA

Digital technology in marketing is dynamic and continually evolving, providing marketers with innovative tools and strategies to connect with audiences in an increasingly digital-centric world. Adopting and adapting to these technologies is essential for staying competitive and effectively reaching target audiences. Businesses that leverage digital marketing effectively are better positioned to connect with their audience, drive business growth, and stay competitive in the digital age. Beyond the technical and ethical, *Advances in Digital Technology and Data-Driven Business Practices* exhibits real-world applications of digital marketing and data-driven practices. Through compelling case studies, it demonstrates its efficacy in areas such as market research, competitor scrutiny, and gleaning customer insights, traversing various channels, encompassing the likes of social media, e-commerce, and email marketing.

Forthcoming Volumes

Destination Data: Charting the Course for Transformative Travel Experiences
Edited by Gautam Shandilya, Nripendra Singh, Praveen Srivastava and Niraj Mishra

Sustainable Futures: Integrating Technology and Responsible Decision Making
Edited by Nandita Mishra, Tanusree Chakraborty, Mahesh Luthia, Manjula Shastri, and Nripendra

Intelligent Retail: Artificial Intelligence Strategies for a New Era of Shopping
Edited by Heather Morgan, Nripendra Singh, and Tanuj Singh

Immersive Wellness: Journey Beyond the Senses
Edited by Tanusree Chakraborty and Nripendra Singh

The Data-Driven World of Academic Publications: Citations, Indexing and Impact Factors
Edited by Tanuj Singh, Shakhil Ahmad, and Nripendra Singh

Mindful Unplugging: The Power of Digital Detox Retreats
Edited by Tanusree Chakraborty and Nripendra Singh

Generative Creations: Harnessing AI for Advertising, Design, and Marketing
Edited by Robert J. Thompson, Nripendra Singh, and Heather Morgan

Digital Transformation and Artificial Intelligence for Operational Excellence in Healthcare

EDITED BY

ANAND JAISWAL
TERI School of Advanced Studies, India

VINAYTOSH MISHRA
Gulf Medical University, UAE

AND

NRIPENDRA SINGH
Pennsylvania Western University, USA

emerald PUBLISHING

United Kingdom – North America – Japan – India – Malaysia – China

Emerald Publishing Limited
Emerald Publishing, Floor 5, Northspring, 21-23 Wellington Street, Leeds LS1 4DL

First edition 2026

British Library Cataloguing in Publication Data
A catalogue record for this book is available from the British Library

ISBN: 978-1-83662-315-1 (Print)
ISBN: 978-1-83662-314-4 (Online)
ISBN: 978-1-83662-316-8 (Epub)

Printed and bound by CPI Group (UK) Ltd, Croydon, CR0 4YY

INVESTOR IN PEOPLE

Contents

About the Editors

Anand Jaiswal is an Assistant Professor in the Department of Policy and Management Studies at TERI School of Advanced Studies, New Delhi. He holds a Ph.D. in Industrial Management from IIT (BHU) Varanasi and has over 17 years of academic and industry experience. His expertise spans Sustainability Management, Life Cycle Assessment, ESG Compliance, and Operations & Supply Chain Management. A certified professional in Blockchain, Lean Six Sigma, and Project Management, Dr. Jaiswal has led various research and consultancy projects, published in reputed journals, and serves as a reviewer for ABDC- and SCOPUS-indexed publications.

Vinaytosh Mishra is working as the Director for Thumbay Institute for AI in Healthcare at Gulf Medical University, Ajman, UAE. He has done his B-Tech and Ph.D. from the Indian Institute of Technology (BHU), India, and Post Doc from the University of Arizona, USA. He has more than 18 years of industry and academia experience and was the CEO of a multi-specialty hospital between 2012 and 2018. His research interests include healthcare delivery, supply chain management, and digital health. He has more than 50 publications in reputed journals.

Nripendra Singh is a tenured Full Professor of Marketing in the Department of Business, Economics, and Communication, College of Science, Technology, and Business at Pennsylvania Western University. He is a recipient of Fulbright scholarship, a flagship program of the United States Department of State, Bureau of Educational and Cultural Affairs. He completed Fulbright research at The Pennsylvania State University. As a visiting research scholar, Dr. Singh visited renowned institutions such as the University of California at Berkley, CA and Technology University, NJ. He is a postdoc fellow of the Global Institute of Flexible Systems & Technology and "Campus-2-Capitol Fellow" of Bard College, NY. He earned two doctorate degrees and two MBA degrees. As a certified professional, he completed the Preparing Future Faculty program at Iowa State University. Dr. Singh is an avid researcher and is on the editorial board and reviewers committee of several reputable journals. He has published and presented more than a 100 research articles in reputable journals and conferences. He is the President and Director of 'International Association of Technology and Management', a nonprofit to promote research of Clarion Consulting Center, which provides consulting services to businesses and helps students gain real-world project experience. He mentors and advises young faculty members, research scholars, and undergrad students globally.

About the Editors

About the Contributors

Moumita Acharyya is the faculty of Human Resource Management & Organizational Behavior. She is a recipient of the prestigious Dr. S. Radhakrishnan postdoctoral fellowship in Humanities and Social Sciences. She completed her doctoral studies from the Faculty of Management Studies, University of Delhi. She is UGC NET-JRF qualified, and with more than 16 years of teaching and research experience, she has published in various national and international journals and presented papers in various conferences of repute. Her research interests focus on corporate social responsibility (CSR), human resource management, organizational commitment, sustainability, among others. Her teaching interests include human resource management, organizational behavior, training and development, employee performance management, and talent management.

Nishtha Agarwal is an Assistant Professor at Symbiosis Institute of Business Management (SIBM), Pune. Her teaching portfolio includes warehouse management, production management and service operations management. She has also served reputed institutions like Indian Institute of Public Administration (IIPA), PHD Chamber of Commerce and Industry (PHDCCI) as research Officer and New Delhi Institute of Management (NDIM) as Assistant Professor. She obtained her PhD from Indian Institute of Foreign Trade (IIFT), New Delhi where she researched towards enhancing resilience of Indian automobile supply chains. Her research interest includes supply chain risk management and resilience, green supply chain, supplier selection, to name a few.

Kumar Chokalingam, Head of International Business, Turtle Shell Technologies Private Limited, Bangalore, India. Dr. Chokalingam is a seasoned clinical researcher with over 15 years of experience in healthcare innovation and clinical trials. Currently serving as the Head of Clinical Research, he has been instrumental in leading clinical validation studies of Dozee's AI-based remote patient monitoring system across India and the United States. His efforts have been pivotal in securing key regulatory approvals, including USFDA 510K clearance and CDSCO approval. Dr. Chokalingam's expertise lies in developing and executing clinical research protocols, with a focus on improving patient outcomes through continuous, contactless monitoring solutions. He holds a Ph.D. in Biomedical Engineering from the University of Cincinnati and has extensive experience in both human and animal clinical studies, with a strong background in regenerative medicine and tissue engineering. His contributions to healthcare technology and clinical research have helped advance innovations in noninvasive patient care and AI-driven monitoring systems.

Jannatul Ferdous, an Associate Professor at the Department of Public Administration, Comilla University, Bangladesh, has a diverse academic background and extensive research contributions. Dr. Ferdous holds a Master's degree, an MPhil in Public Administration, and a Ph.D. in Development Studies from Dhaka University. Her research interests include population migration, governance, trust, gender, public policy, climate change, and development. Dr. Ferdous has made significant contributions to scholarly discourse through her publications in reputable refereed journals and chapters in books. She has authored several books on governance, gender, contemporary issues, and migration, published by renowned publishers such as Springer, Routledge, and Cambridge University Press. Furthermore, Dr. Ferdous has actively engaged in national and international academic conferences by presenting her research findings, chairing sessions, and serving as a keynote speaker.

Nidhi Gupta is an Assistant Professor in the field of Commerce and Business Management with nearly 10 years of teaching experience. She holds a Ph.D., an MBA, and an M.Com and is UGC NET qualified in both Commerce and Management. Her research interests include digital marketing, sustainability, and business process management. She has published in Scopus and ABDC-indexed journals and actively contributes to academic research and teaching.

Mohd Junaid Akhtar is currently working as an Assistant Professor at the New Delhi Institute of Management, India. He has 8 research papers in various reputed journals (indexed in Scopus WoS and ABDC) and presented papers in international and national conferences. His research interest lies in social media marketing, E-commerce, and consumer behavior.

Rajbeer Kaur is an Assistant Professor in Finance at NDIM. She has completed her graduation from the University of Delhi and her postgraduation from Jamia Millia Islamia. She received her Ph.D. in Management from Jamia Millia Islamia. Her research interests include portfolio management, financial markets, and sustainable investing. She has taught as a guest faculty at the National Institute of Technology, Kurukshetra, and the University of Delhi.

Vinod Kumar is a Professor of Marketing in New Delhi Institute of Management. He has 12 years of Industry experience and 14 years of academic experience. His area of interest includes: digital marketing, social media marketing, search engine optimization and affiliate marketing.

Meenal Kulkarni is with the Symbiosis Institute of Health Sciences, Symbiosis International (Deemed University), Pune, India as an Associate Professor. She has been in the field of academics for the last 15 years. Kulkarni has earned her Ph.D. in Healthcare Management. She has to her credit more than 35 research papers/book chapters and conference proceedings. Her interests include healthcare operations, quality and accreditation, and healthcare technology.

Sharif Mohd is an Assistant Professor in Finance and Accounting at New Delhi Institute of Management New Delhi. He has done M.Phil. and Ph.D. from Himachal Pradesh University, Shimla. With over 7 years of academic experience, he has published 2 books and 13 research papers. He has organized many conferences and Faculty Development Programmes. His research interests include Green Finance, Microfinance, and Personal Finance.

Angad Munshi, a faculty member and researcher, is committed to advancing knowledge in marketing management through innovative research. His current work delves into the complexities of online start-up evolution, examining the critical role of service quality and best practices in driving operational success within the F&B sector. With over a decade of experience collaborating with India's leading start-ups, he brings a unique blend of academic rigor and industry insight. His scholarly contributions include publications in esteemed peer-reviewed journals, presentations at prestigious international conferences, and the authorship of a well-received book.

Subhransu Nag, Head of International Business, Turtle Shell Technologies Private Limited, Bangalore, India. He is an industry thought leader with extensive international sales and marketing experience spanning over two and half decades in the Medical Devices MedTech & Pharma sector alongside managing C-suite client relationships. Previous engagements cover business development, product management, and market segmentation strategy. He has numerous success stories showcasing his ability to drive revenue growth, increase sales margins, and nurture high-performing teams. He has won several accolades in professional journey like APAC President Club, Excellence award, People Manager award, and many more. He has completed the Executive Program in Business Management from IIM Calcutta and recently completed Master's in Business Management from Savitribai Phule Pune University. He is currently a scholar pursuing Ph.D. in Marketing from the New Delhi Institute of Management

Sarita Nagvanshi is an Assistant Professor at New Delhi Institute of Management in the Department of Marketing. She has published and presented several research papers in Scopus journals and international and national conferences. Her research interests include consumer behavior, social media marketing, health care, etc.

Pushpa Negi is presently working as an Associate Professor at New Delhi Institute of Management in the Finance Department. Her research interests are in the areas of Stock Market, Accounting, Entrepreneurship, Sustainability, etc. She has been actively involved in research since 2004 initially as a part of doctoral program and subsequently focused on commerce and management–related issues.

Monika Nijhawan has presented many articles in national and international conferences. She received an award on the best paper presentation at the International Conference on Computer, Cybernetics and Education (iccce-2023) at Jakarta, Indonesia. She is currently working in the New Delhi Institute of Management in the Data Analytics Department.

Pinki Paul is a research scholar in Department of Commerce and Management, Banasthali Vidyapith, Rajasthan. Her area of expertise is Human Resource Management and published 4 Scopus-indexed articles. She participated in various national and international conferences, workshops, etc. She has experience in SPSS, AMOS, etc.

Jennifer A. Pope is an Associate Professor of International Business and Marketing at Grand Valley State University in Michigan, USA. She is also a Visiting Professor at the DHBW in Baden – Württemberg, Germany and IEDC – Bled School of Management in Slovenia. She has published numerous articles and books/book chapters in several areas throughout her career, primarily focusing on marketing for nonprofits and international marketing. She has lived in England, Germany, Taiwan, and Slovenia and has traveled to over 30 countries. She has consulted with multiple companies and NGOs often working with students on the projects. She is a US Fulbright Scholar and spent the 2016–2017 school year at IEDC – The Bled School of Management in Slovenia for her Fulbright.

Partha Protim Bora is a dedicated research scholar at the School of Law, ICFAI University, Tripura. With a strong academic foundation in legal studies, he has consistently pursued excellence in the field of law. He completed his Master of Laws (LLM) from Gauhati University, Guwahati, Assam, where he developed a deep understanding of advanced legal concepts and honed his research skills. Before this, he earned his Bachelor of Arts and Bachelor of Laws (BA. LLB) degrees from Jorhat Law College, Assam, where his journey began in the legal profession. His academic pursuits reflect a commitment to legal education, and his work as a research scholar signifies his dedication to contributing to legal scholarship and jurisprudence.

Ashim Raj Singla, a distinguished academic and industry expert with over two decades of experience, specializes in Information Systems, Data Analytics, Big Data Analytics, ERP (SAP), DBMS, and Web Technologies. As a Professor and the Head of IT & Knowledge Management and Controller of Examination, he plays a pivotal role in shaping academic and technological advancements. His expertise extends to process design, data modeling, technology planning, and the development of cutting-edge Network Management Systems, driving impactful research and innovation in the field.

Moumita Sharma is currently associated with the School of Business (PG) MIT World Peace University, Pune. She has handled roles of the Area Chair for Human Resource Management, the Head of Student Welfare, and a faculty for MBA-HR specialization. She is passionate about teaching and leaves no stone unturned to deliver latest quality knowledge to her students and mentor them to excel in their life and careers. Dr. Moumita has a combined work experience of 15+ years. Dr. Moumita has completed her Doctorate of Philosophy in the area of Quality of Work Life and Employee Performance. She has publications and book chapters which are indexed in Scopus and UGC-CARE. Her research interests include innovative HR practices and employee behavioral challenges at the workplace, technology and HR in the healthcare sector, and general management.

Pooja Sharma is an Assistant Professor in the field of Management with nearly six years of teaching experience. She holds a Ph.D. degree and is UGC NET qualified in Management. She has published chapters in various Scopus-indexed books and ABDC-indexed journals and actively contributes to academic research and teaching.

Balgopal Singh is an Associate Professor in Faculty of Management Studies, Banasthali Vidyapith, Rajasthan. His area of research is branding and aviation management. He has published 40+ articles in national and international journals of repute. A few of his articles have been published in the *International Journal of Consumer Studies, Asia Pacific Journal of Marketing and Logistics, Journal of Air Transport Management, Indian Journal of Marketing,* and *The TQM Journal.*

Teena Singh, Teena Singh been working as a Professor and Registrar at NDIM since June 2009, demonstrating long-standing dedication and leadership at the institute. She has over 22 years of experience in the fields of HR, Academics, Strategic Management and Consultancy both for the Corporate and Academia. She has organized many Conferences, Summits, Management Development Programmes, and panel discussions on futuristic topics. Her papers have been published in national and international journals. Student Engagement, Employee Engagement, and Psychological Well-Being are her current areas of research. She is responsible for establishing international linkages and leading new strategic initiatives. She has authored a book on People Management in 21st century published by McGraw Hill. She is a certified POSH Trainer and an external member of POSH Committee of CDAC, Ministry of Electronics and Information Technology. She is a member of CII's HR-IR Committee and a member of Academic Council of NHRD Network Delhi NCR Chapter.

Monica Verma has written articles and papers in many national and international journals and presented papers at international conferences. Prof. Monica received the Best Paper Award at the 2nd International Conference on Redefining Human Resources and Management Perspective organized by the School of Commerce, Jain (Deemed-to-be-University), Bengaluru on April 8, 2021. In 2019, she presented a paper at the prestigious Academy of Management Conference in Boston, USA. She is a reviewer of many international journals. Her research interests include gender studies, ethical leadership, governance, and CSR. She is currently working as a Professor (OB/HR) at the New Delhi Institute of Management.

Editorial: Digital Transformation and AI Innovation Redefining Healthcare Excellence

Anand Jaiswal[a], *Vinaytosh Mishra*[b] *and Nripendra Singh*[c]

[a]TERI School of Advanced Studies, India
[b]Gulf Medical University, UAE
[c]Pennsylvania Western University, USA

The healthcare industry is on the verge of a transformative era in which digital technologies and artificial intelligence (AI) are fundamentally changing how care is delivered, managed, and experienced. This convergence of digital transformation and AI innovation has enormous potential for achieving operational excellence and improving patient outcomes, but it also presents significant challenges that must be managed with caution. As editors of this volume, we intend to investigate the complex impact of these technologies on healthcare, drawing on latest research and real-world applications to provide a comprehensive overview.

Digital transformation in healthcare refers to the integration of digital technologies into all domains of healthcare delivery, from clinical care to administrative processes. This transformation is driven by the need to address longstanding inefficiencies, rising costs, and the growing demand for personalized, patient-centric care. Electronic Health Records (EHRs), telemedicine, wearable devices, and the Internet of Medical Things (IoMT) are just a few examples of how digital tools are reshaping the healthcare landscape. According to a study by Topol (2019), the digitization of healthcare data has enabled more accurate diagnoses, reduced medical errors, and improved coordination among care providers. For example, the adoption of EHRs has been shown to improve the patient safety surveillance, as highlighted by Adler-Milstein et al. (2017).

The COVID-19 pandemic served as a catalyst for digital transformation, accelerating the adoption of telemedicine and remote monitoring technologies. A study by Hollander and Carr (2020) found that telemedicine visits increased by 154% in the United States during the early months of the pandemic, demonstrating its potential to enhance access to care, particularly in underserved areas. Similarly, IoMT devices, such as wearable glucose monitors and remote cardiac monitors, have enabled continuous patient monitoring, reducing the need for

Digital Transformation and Artificial Intelligence for Operational Excellence in Healthcare, 1–4

doi:10.1108/978-1-83662-314-420251003

in-person visits and improving chronic disease management. These advancements underscore the transformative potential of digital technologies in addressing some of healthcare's most pressing challenges.

However, the true power of digital transformation lies in its synergy with AI. AI, particularly machine learning and deep learning, is revolutionizing healthcare by enabling faster, more accurate diagnostics, personalized treatment plans, and predictive analytics. AI algorithms can analyze vast amounts of medical data, identifying patterns and insights that would be impossible for humans to discern. For example, Esteva et al. (2017) demonstrated that a deep learning algorithm could classify skin cancer with a level of accuracy comparable to board-certified dermatologists. Similarly, AI-powered diagnostic tools have shown remarkable success in radiology, with studies indicating that AI can detect abnormalities in medical images with accuracy rates exceeding 90% (McKinney et al., 2020).

AI is also transforming drug discovery, a traditionally time-consuming and costly process. Companies, like Insilico Medicine, are leveraging AI to identify potential drug candidates in a fraction of the time required by conventional methods. A study by Stokes et al. (2020) highlighted how an AI model identified a novel antibiotic compound, halicin, which was effective against drug-resistant bacteria. This breakthrough underscores the potential of AI to address global health challenges, such as antimicrobial resistance, by accelerating the development of new therapies.

In addition to diagnostics and drug discovery, AI is enhancing operational efficiency in healthcare. Predictive analytics, powered by AI, is being used to optimize hospital resource allocation, reduce wait times, and improve patient flow. For instance, a study by Shickel et al. (2017) demonstrated how AI algorithms could predict patient deterioration in intensive care units, enabling early interventions and reducing mortality rates. Similarly, AI-driven supply chain management systems are helping hospitals reduce waste and ensure the timely availability of critical medical supplies.

Despite these advancements, the integration of digital transformation and AI in healthcare is not without challenges. Data privacy and security remain paramount concerns, as healthcare data are highly sensitive and vulnerable to breaches. The implementation of robust data protection frameworks, such as the General Data Protection Regulation (GDPR) in Europe and the Health Insurance Portability and Accountability Act (HIPAA) in the United States, is essential to safeguarding patient information. However, compliance with these regulations can be complex and resource-intensive, particularly for smaller healthcare providers.

Another significant barrier is the resistance to change among healthcare professionals. The adoption of new technologies often requires a cultural shift, as well as training and upskilling of the workforce. A study by Sittig and Singh (2016) highlighted the importance of addressing these human factors to ensure the successful implementation of digital health solutions. Additionally, regulatory hurdles can slow down the deployment of innovative technologies, particularly in highly regulated fields like healthcare.

Ethical considerations also play a critical role in the adoption of AI in healthcare. Bias in AI algorithms, for example, can lead to inequitable outcomes, particularly for marginalized populations. A study by Obermeyer et al. (2019) revealed that a widely used healthcare algorithm exhibited racial bias, resulting in Black patients receiving less care than White patients with similar health conditions. Addressing these ethical challenges requires a multidisciplinary approach, involving not only technologists but also ethicists, policymakers, and healthcare providers.

Looking ahead, the future of healthcare lies in the continued integration of digital transformation and AI. Emerging technologies, such as blockchain, 5G networks, and quantum computing, hold the potential to further enhance data security, interoperability, and computational power. Blockchain, for instance, can provide a secure and transparent framework for managing healthcare data while 5G networks can enable faster and more reliable telemedicine services. Quantum computing, though still in its infancy, promises to solve complex medical problems that are currently beyond the reach of classical computers.

AI will also play a critical role in pandemic preparedness and response. During the COVID-19 pandemic, AI was used to track the spread of the virus, develop vaccines, and optimize resource allocation. A study by Naudé (2020) highlighted how AI models were instrumental in predicting the spread of the virus and identifying high-risk areas. As the world continues to grapple with the aftermath of the pandemic, the lessons learned from these applications will be invaluable in shaping future responses to global health crises.

Global collaboration will be key to harnessing the full potential of digital transformation and AI in healthcare. Initiatives like the Global Partnership on Artificial Intelligence (GPAI) and the World Health Organization's (WHO) Digital Health Technical Advisory Group are fostering international cooperation to address common challenges and share best practices. By working together, stakeholders can ensure that the benefits of these technologies are equitably distributed and that no one is left behind.

In conclusion, the convergence of digital transformation and AI innovation is reshaping the healthcare landscape, offering unprecedented opportunities for enhanced patient care and operational excellence. However, realizing this potential requires addressing challenges related to data privacy, workforce adaptation, and ethical considerations. As editors of this volume, we hope to inspire and inform stakeholders – policymakers, healthcare providers, technologists, and researchers – to collaborate in creating a future where technology and healthcare are seamlessly integrated. The possibilities are limitless, and the impact on global health will be profound.

References

Adler-Milstein, J., Holmgren, A. J., Kralovec, P., Worzala, C., Searcy, T., & Patel, V. (2017). Electronic health record adoption in US hospitals: the emergence of a digital "advanced use" divide. *Journal of the American Medical Informatics Association, 24*(6), 1142–1148.

Esteva, A., Kuprel, B., Novoa, R. A., Ko, J., Swetter, S. M., Blau, H. M., & Thrun, S. (2017). Dermatologist-level classification of skin cancer with deep neural networks. *Nature*, *542*(7639), 115–118.

Hollander, J. E., & Carr, B. G. (2020). Virtually perfect? Telemedicine for COVID-19. *New England Journal of Medicine*, *382*(18), 1679–1681.

McKinney, S. M., Sieniek, M., Godbole, V., Godwin, J., Antropova, N., Ashrafian, H., Back, T., Chesus, M., Corrado, G. S., Darzi, A., Etemadi, M., Garcia-Vicente, F., Gilbert, F. J., Halling-Brown, M., Hassabis, D., Jansen, S., Karthikesalingam, A., Kelly, C. J., King, D., ... Shetty, S. (2020). International evaluation of an AI system for breast cancer screening. *Nature*, *577*(7788), 89–94.

Naudé, W. (2020). *Artificial intelligence against COVID-19: An early review* IZA Discussion Paper No. 13110.

Obermeyer, Z., Powers, B., Vogeli, C., & Mullainathan, S. (2019). Dissecting racial bias in an algorithm used to manage the health of populations. *Science*, *366*(6464), 447–453.

Shickel, B., Tighe, P. J., Bihorac, A., & Rashidi, P. (2017). Deep EHR: A survey of recent advances in deep learning techniques for electronic health record (EHR) analysis. *IEEE Journal of Biomedical and Health Informatics*, *22*(5), 1589–1604.

Sittig, D. F., & Singh, H. (2016). A new socio-technical model for studying health information technology in complex adaptive healthcare systems. *BMJ Quality and Safety*, *25*(3), 1–6.

Stokes, J. M., Yang, K., Swanson, K., Jin, W., Cubillos-Ruiz, A., Donghia, N. M., MacNair, C. R., French, S., Carfrae, L. A., Bloom-Ackermann, Z., Tran, V. M., Chiappino-Pepe, A., Badran, A. H., Andrews, I. W., Chory, E. J., Church, G. M., Brown, E. D., Jaakkola, T. S., Barzilay, R., & Collins, J. J. (2020). A deep learning approach to antibiotic discovery. *Cell*, *180*(4), 688–702.

Topol, E. J. (2019). *Deep medicine: How artificial intelligence can make healthcare human again*. Basic Books.

Chapter 1

Digital Transformation in Healthcare: Analysing the Current State, Challenges and Future Research Agenda

Jannatul Ferdous

Comilla University, Bangladesh

Abstract

More and more people in the healthcare industry and academia are considering how digital transformation (DT) can impact patient care. The demand for chronic disease management is rising due to an ageing population, new technologies and individuals more involved in healthcare decisions. In this chapter, the author aimed to investigate the literature on the ubiquity of digital technology in healthcare and to pinpoint how the COVID-19 epidemic compelled all systems to adopt new digital technology in a manner that was both disruptive and influential for management and business. To gain an understanding of the role of digital technology in the healthcare sector and how it is being revived as a result of the pandemic, the authors conducted a structured literature study on the current level of DT in healthcare. To achieve this objective, the underlying information technologies must be adaptable to each organisation's digitalisation maturity level while being secure, dependable, reasonably priced and easily expandable. Researchers should focus on three main topics: the impact of DT on healthcare stakeholders, the role of digital technology in enabling digital healthcare services and how stakeholders can participate in digital healthcare services. They bridge the gap between the many domains, illuminating how digital technology facilitates the delivery of digital services, the improvement of operational efficiency and the production of value within the healthcare system. At the end of this chapter, the authors outline some potential avenues for further study, together with inevitable consequences for management and practice.

Digital Transformation and Artificial Intelligence for Operational Excellence in Healthcare, 5–21

Published under exclusive licence by Emerald Publishing Limited
doi:10.1108/978-1-83662-314-420251006

Keywords: Digital transformation; healthcare; digitalisation; COVID-19; AI; technology

Introduction

Since March 2020, the first wave of the COVID-19 pandemic has begun to affect economies and enterprises worldwide. These impacts are predicted to last for decades (Miao et al., 2020; Saarikko et al., 2020). The pandemic has caused significant changes in the healthcare sector. Agarwal et al. (2010), Raimo et al. (2023) and Kraus et al. (2021) all note that COVID-19 has generated a great deal of interest in the healthcare sector. While medical and technological progress is improving healthcare globally, governments, healthcare providers and citizens are concerned about growing prices (Dieleman et al., 2017). The traditional doctor–patient relationship and its associated private environment are becoming less commonplace in modern medicine. A vast web of human and nonhuman entities is involved in healthcare distribution. Examples include databases, hospital information systems, electronic medical records, digital health cards, online patient communities, health-related applications and smart homes with ambient assisted living technology. When networks adhere to standards like authenticity, transparency, participation, flow of information and connectedness, they function most efficiently. These standards govern the creation and application of health-related knowledge. Belliger and Krieger (2018) define how health-related knowledge might improve care quality and efficiency. Patients' increasing need for accessible point-of-care alternatives and added services such as remote testing and health information exchange motivates them to take a more active role in treatment decisions. This further strains the healthcare system (Cordina et al., 2018). Regulations and compliance requirements heavily influence the research and treatment of drugs due to the high stakes involved in human life. However, there is an added expense and effort associated with these standards, which could slow down the digitisation of healthcare (Dissanayake et al., 2018).

Kraus et al. (2021) and others have studied all healthcare ecosystems for potential solutions that involve the unprecedented adoption of digital technologies. The widespread adoption of technology is mainly driven by the hope that state-of-the-art resources, like as Electronic Health Records, e-health platforms, blockchain and Internet of Things (IoT) sensors, can simplify the incredibly intricate healthcare industry (Massaro, 2023; Ritala & Karhu, 2023; Spanò et al., 2021). Many fresh prospects have emerged for scientists and medical professionals due to digital technologies, which can enhance diagnostic and therapeutic procedures (such as telemedicine systems for patient consultations and monitoring, Artificial Intelligence [AI] for diagnostic tasks, surgical decision-making, etc.). These technologies also improve administrative and organisational processes, leading to more cost-effective services through redesign (Biancone et al., 2023; Loftus et al., 2020).

There is a trend toward more secure and high-quality healthcare that can be described as digital transformation (DT), which encompasses all of these factors (Haggerty, 2017). The widespread usage of digital technology has given rise to several new issues since the beginning of the epidemic (Xiang et al., 2020). For instance, social media platforms like Twitter and WeChat, which are digital technologies (Massaro, 2023; Wang et al., 2020), can improve public health communication and education (Nadkarni & Prügl, 2021). Modern operating robots and other instruments have improved surgical planning and safety, benefiting everyone involved: the patient, the surgeon, the healthcare facility and society (Dal Mas et al., 2023). The advent of 3D printing and automation has brought new tools to the medical field, and the utilisation of big data has made it possible to gather helpful information that can be utilised for medical education purposes as well as to improve current healthcare methods in the face of the COVID-19 pandemic (Balch et al., 2023). To address the current and future healthcare sector challenges, as well as those caused by the pandemic, researchers and practitioners must work together to comprehend the capabilities of the sector and to determine how these capabilities define the dynamics, determinants, processes and possible outcomes. Considerations of sector dynamics include figuring out how to maximise the use of these cutting-edge innovations, which have both immediate and distant benefits, the latter of which could call for a significant shift in organisational strategy (Cobianchi et al., 2020). This chapter examines DT's efficacy, issues and healthcare applications. The research questions addressed here concern the evolution of the theme, its uses, benefits, drawbacks, prospects and hazards faced by the health sector. Additionally, we hope to study how these ubiquitous technologies might enhance and revolutionise healthcare sector operations, management and performance after a pandemic by bringing together the literature on DT and healthcare.

Methodology

A structured literature review (SRL) was employed in this section by the author. According to Massaro et al. (2023), SLRs are best used to help "experienced scholars [in developing] new and interesting research paths by accessing and analysing a considerable volume of scholarly work". They also contribute to developing "research paths and questions by providing a foundation" for future research avenues. This SLR was conducted by analysing research from a variety of reputable sources, including Taylor & Francis, the World Economic Forum, Elsevier B.V., Springer, Nature, Wiley, BMJ, Edward Elgar Publishing, Pew Research Center, Emerald, MIT and MDPI. The review focused on literature from the last 10 years, covering key themes related to DT in healthcare. The selection criteria included studies that addressed topics such as transformation, healthcare innovation, DT, the health sector, digital technology and AI. The strategic importance of pre-existing digital technologies has been the focus of multiple research assessments. Research in this area has included studies that have examined healthcare organisations' DT (van Velthoven et al., 2019). This chapter's overarching goal is to forward a research agenda that, drawing from disciplines as diverse as sociology, psychology, engineering, business management and marketing, presents a fresh perspective on the potential uses of digital technology in healthcare. In this chapter, the author examines articles published in different scholarly journals using content analysis.

Digital Transformation

When an entity's qualities are improved by using various forms of information, computers, collaboration and networking technology, it can be said to have undergone DT (Vial, 2021). DT has far-reaching effects on businesses, influencing internal organisational structure changes, metric and target development, digital resource acquisition and digital growth strategy creation (Verhoef et al., 2021). Information, computers, communication and networking technologies are all part of DT, a process that tries to make something better by altering its qualities significantly (Hermes et al., 2020).

Information systems, marketing and strategy are just a few of the business fields that have made this phenomenon a popular topic of study because of its profound impact on the corporate sector. The healthcare industry has been a long-standing site of DT. Health Care includes all the services doctors and other medical professionals offer to keep people physically and mentally healthy (Marques & Ferreira, 2020). In medical practice and value generation, new business opportunities and models are rising due to the digital revolution in healthcare. This transformation assists in resolving numerous societal problems, such as those related to the ageing population (Elton & O'Riordan, 2016; Kraus et al., 2021). Shukla et al. (2022) referred to healthcare systems as the "fundamental weave in the fabric of human society" since they enable all populations to stay healthy through the efforts of medical professionals, support staff, hospitals and other related entities. Modern technologies like AI, big data and the creation of more efficient algorithms – all made possible by ever-increasing computer capacity – are causing a massive upheaval in the Healthcare sector 4.0 (Piccialli et al., 2021).

Digital Transformation Insights for the Healthcare Sector

The healthcare industry is experiencing a significant shift due to DT, which profoundly impact the industry. Despite this, there needs to be more empirical data on the efficacy, issues and uses of digital healthcare advances in the existing literature, which is surprising given the rapid development and widespread acceptance of these technologies. There has yet to be a comprehensive study of DT in healthcare systems even though there's a lot of literature on healthcare IT in general (Dionisio et al., 2023). Several businesses have instituted remote work practices (COVID-19) to contain the coronavirus epidemic, which has just broken out globally. Customers' buying habits have swiftly shifted to online media as they avoid face-to-face interaction. This means several sectors have been able to speed up their digital infrastructure development due to the pandemic (Kim, 2020). Businesses have created cloud-based IT systems to experiment with new methods for delivering seamless, contact-free services through mobile apps, video calls, advanced telemedicine, online learning, remote work and mobile payment solutions (Xiao & Fan, 2020). It is logical to argue that the "contactless" era has already arrived given the global resurrection and variations of COVID-19, its impact on consumer behaviour and the rising tide of advancements in digital technology (Zeng et al., 2020).

Many modern healthcare facilities have pursued contactless services and operational process advancements to increase organisational adaptability and efficiency (Lee & Lee, 2020). A multitude of touchless services have been enabled by advanced information and communication technologies (ICTs) like AI, the web, the IoT, big data, 3D printing, virtual reality (VR), augmented reality (AR), smart sensors, drones and more. Telemedicine, which has been a part of remote healthcare since the 1990s, long before the COVID-19 pandemic, is just one facet of these services. However, in today's digital age, touchless healthcare services extend far beyond telemedicine (Marin, 2020). A paradigm shift is occurring in healthcare systems, which is changing traditional methods of management and organisation (Schwab et al., 2016). This shift calls for fresh ideas about how health services will be designed and delivered in the future, which could lead to improvements on a global scale (Hospodková et al., 2024). Digitally driven care delivery models are being developed by healthcare companies using cloud-based computing, 5G telecommunications, interoperable data and analytics and more. These models aim to expand availability, encourage self-sufficiency and independent living, reduce healthcare expenditures and use outpatient virtual care appointments. These technologies may substantially improve health systems (Allen, 2022; Kim et al., 2021). According to Dionisio et al. (2023), the healthcare industry has been most transformed recently. Still, healthcare's heavily regulated and policy-driven character and the inherent caution in an industry where users' lives are on the line are two of the reasons that slow down DT's uptake (Latif et al., 2017; Montero-Cuadrado et al., 2020).

Prior research on the topic of DT in healthcare has shown that, from a small number of studies published between 1973 and the late 1990s, the primary goal of this field's written literature has been to investigate how computers can facilitate healthcare operations as well as the data storage and retrieval needs of different types of patients, medical records and digital imaging of the body (Marques & Ferreira, 2020). As digital technologies advanced and DT became more widely utilised in healthcare around the turn of the century, researchers mainly concentrated on two areas: how DT affected healthcare performance and problems associated with DT adoption (Agarwal et al., 2010). When looking at healthcare performance, researchers mainly focused on effects on patients, like reduced mortality rates (Amarasingham et al., 2009), or outcomes, like decreased costs, more significant revenues and improved productivity (Dionisio et al., 2023). However, there needs to be more empirical data on the efficacy, issues and applications of digital healthcare advances, which is surprising given the rapid development and widespread adoption of these technologies (Dionisio et al., 2023).

A total of 24,46,008 people have lost their lives to COVID-19 so far, with 110,384,747 cases confirmed as of February 20, 2021 (WHO, 2021). It is reasonable to expect a proliferation of contactless services in most countries during this uncertain and frightening moment. After the epidemic, when individuals are ready to break out of their social isolation, some famous wireless services may bring back in-person contacts (Zeng et al., 2020), while others may stay or even see expanded practices. One possible solution to the challenges of healthcare inefficiency and high medical expenditures is telemedicine (Akiyama & Yoo, 2016). Amidst the unknown COVID-19 climate, patients have been satisfied with virtual medical care, which does not include in-person doctor visits. Thus, it is safe to assume that telemedicine's present growth trajectory will carry over into the post-pandemic future. There are only a few systematic reviews of DT in healthcare systems even if there is a rapidly expanding corpus of work on healthcare IT. By examining the current state of these deployments and their influence on healthcare systems via the prism of applications, advantages, possibilities and dangers, this SLR aims to fill the void.

The healthcare business has made great strides in the 4IR period, implementing numerous technologies that have expanded access to healthcare beyond geographical and temporal constraints (Yoon et al., 2020). Wearable devices have become increasingly popular for health monitoring and illness prevention thanks to advancements in AI and IoT, Cloud Computing, Big Data, Mobile (ICBM) in the cloud (Yoon et al., 2020). Additionally, AI has been finding more and more applications in healthcare diagnostics and therapy. Healthcare services that are centred on the patient are made possible by AI, which also helps hospitals run more efficiently (Yoon & Lee, 2018). Furthermore, the healthcare business spearheads innovation efforts with competent healthcare that integrates advanced IT (e.g., AI and ICBM). For instance, a lot of hospitals have implemented intelligent healthcare systems that enable medical professionals to diagnose and treat patients both online and offline. Patients' post-treatment health is also monitored with wearable scanners or other medical devices, and applications made specifically for use in particular hospitals allow for round-the-clock monitoring of patients' situations. By using AI-enabled solutions for storing and preserving patient data, The Mayo Clinic and Google have transformed the delivery of healthcare services and opened the door for digital innovation that improves sickness detection and treatment (Anastasijevic, 2019).

Telemedicine was one of the contactless healthcare systems before the COVID-19 pandemic. Among the many examples of contactless healthcare systems, one stands out as an Radio-Frequency IDentification-based system for vital sign monitoring (e.g., BP, HR, temperature, etc.) (Hui & Kan, 2018). A reading device and connectivity to other systems are necessary for this automated method to monitor patients' vital signs, yet it is successful. Consequently, this system has been limited to adoption (Ukkonen & Sydänheimo, 2017). Robots powered by AI have found many uses in healthcare, such as aiding with inpatient rounds, organising patient records, processing payments and providing information about treatments (such as waiting times and estimated examination times) (Yoon et al., 2020). Thanks to the convergence of cutting-edge information technologies like AI and ICBM, competent healthcare has already started to develop at the beginning of the fourth industrial revolution (Lee & Lee, 2020), prior to the

COVID-19 pandemic. Telemedicine, AI in healthcare, staff and patient safety management (e.g., using chatbots and mobile platforms), and administrative tasks are among the many areas that have made use of contactless services during the COVID-19 pandemic (Lee & Lee, 2020). For instance, South Korean hospitals use video conferences for staff training, and patients are required to use a mobile app to complete a self-check-up questionnaire, which they must bring to their appointments (Lee & Lee, 2020). Modern contactless services have many potential uses, including AI for COVID-19 virus analysis, robots controlled from a distance to help enforce indoor and outdoor quarantine regulations, and robots to aid in the disinfection of large areas (Manyika, 2022). Before the pandemic, healthcare ICTs were extensively used. Since the epidemic, their use has rapidly increased throughout many healthcare services (Lee & Lee, 2021).

Opportunities and Challenges for Healthcare Services

It is imperative that public health and the healthcare industry effectively manage the current epidemic while also preparing for possible future outbreaks, which are expected to inflict far more extensive devastation.

Developing an Innovative Healthcare Delivery Infrastructure

The global proliferation of the COVID-19 pandemic has placed healthcare systems under extraordinary pressure. To keep healthcare operations running and decrease in-person contacts, the rapid spread of COVID-19 has necessitated immediate measures and the expansion of services to digital form (Keesara et al., 2020). There has been a proliferation and diversification of digital health services in the decade preceding the pandemic. However, some anticipate that the COVID-19 pandemic will radically impact these models (Taylor et al., 2020). While the goal of digital healthcare is to ensure services remain accessible and uninterrupted throughout the pandemic, not everyone has the same opportunity to gain from digitisation. Rapid health service digitisation could result in digital inequality and a number of unfavourable outcomes, including worse health outcomes, increased vulnerability to COVID-19 if essential services are not accessible remotely and social isolation (particularly for those who are already disadvantaged) (see Table 1.1) (Beaunoyer et al., 2020). Some people are worried that people who don't have the same opportunities, skills or means to utilise digital services haven't had the medical care they require (Dai et al., 2020; Farkas & Romaniuk, 2020).

Innovative digital device applications have proliferated across numerous industries thanks to the technological underpinning of the 4IR era (Yoon & Lee, 2019). Several healthcare companies have begun using AI and machine learning to create wearable gadgets and vaccinations to combat diseases at an early stage (Manyika, 2022). Some contactless services, which saw significant growth during the pandemic, may recoup to their levels before the epidemic, provided that

Table 1.1. Systematic Literature Review on Healthcare, Digitalisation and Public Health.

No.	Authors	Journal	Year	Key Themes	Methodology	Key Findings
1	Agarwal et al. (2019)	*Journal of the Academy of Marketing Science*	2019	Technological advances, healthcare transformation, value-centred marketing (VCM), digital data, AI integration	The paper develops a framework for value-centred marketing in healthcare, emphasising preferences, precision and process.	Emerging technologies (digital health data, analytics, AI) create opportunities for VCM strategy. Unintended consequences discussed.
2	Beaunoyer et al. (2020)	*Computers in Human Behavior*	2020	Digital access gaps, COVID-19 vulnerabilities, social determinants of health, inequality mitigation strategies	Discusses reciprocal impacts of COVID-19 on digital inequality and its health implications. Offers solutions for mitigation.	Digital inequalities worsen COVID-19 vulnerabilities; multi-layered strategies needed for mitigation.
3	Bhattacharyya et al. (2021)	*Journal of Medical Internet Research*	2021	Healthcare innovation, value-based care, virtual care, COVID-19 impact, new business models in healthcare	Explores innovation centres in healthcare and their structures for success, focusing on value-based care.	Health systems can drive innovation through structured innovation centres and digital tools post-pandemic.
4	Buljac-Samardzic et al. (2020)	*Human Resources for Health*	2020	Team training, communication tools, organisational redesign, simulation-based training, team performance improvement	Systematic review	Evidence supports principle-based training and simulation for improving healthcare team performance.

5	Xiang et al. (2019)	*Artificial Intelligence in Medicine*	2019	Public perceptions, AI receptivity, AI in healthcare applications	Survey	High receptivity and demand for AI in medical imaging, pathology and surgery.
6	Wang et al. (2019)	*Globalization and Health*	2019	Evolution of China's public health system, prevention-focused reforms	Retrospective review	Key stages identified in public health reforms, focusing on prevention and system flexibility.
7	Verhoef et al. (2019)	*Journal of Business Research*	2019	Stages of digital transformation (DT), growth strategies for digital firms	Literature review	Identified stages of DT and organisational strategies.
8	Van Velthoven et al. (2019)	*International Journal of Medical Informatics*	2019	Healthcare digitalisation, competition, interoperability	Thematic analysis	Identified key success factors for digital health organisations.
9	Mishra and Sharma (2024)	*The TQM Journal*	2024	Enablers of digital lean, HRM factors, leadership, technology	Mixed-method approach	Identified key enablers like practice factors, leadership and technology.
10	Mishra (2022)	*International Journal of Healthcare Management*	2022	Systemic versus behavioural barriers, awareness, trust	Systematic literature review, MCDM	Behavioural barriers are more critical than systemic barriers.

Source: Adapted by author.

appropriate cures and vaccines are available (Minor & Bevins, 2020). Face-to-face methods of personnel recruitment will be reinstated. Regarding healthcare, remote medical service could not be enough to address a patient's issue if an examination is necessary because of medication side effects. Yet, since telemedicine enables the efficient and timely delivery of healthcare treatments, these services will keep expanding. To prevent the transmission of infectious diseases, numerous healthcare providers are currently making significant efforts to provide safer environments for patients and medical staff (Lee & Lee, 2020). Consumers used to use ICT will likely seek more convenient options, including contactless services, in the post-COVID age, and technical innovation is predicted to pick up speed. Therefore, modern technology should be used appropriately for face-to-face and contact-free interactions. Buljac-Samardzic et al. (2020) state different operational techniques are needed in healthcare collaboration so that patients and medical personnel can co-create value in a one-to-many approach instead of a one-to-one one. To deliver top-notch care to patients, healthcare providers should apply the knowledge and skills they gained before and during the pandemic (Lee & Lee, 2020). The COVID-19 pandemic led to a rapid increase in the utilisation of telemedicine as many countries relaxed regulations regarding its use.

Distribution of Healthcare Resources via Online and Offline Services

The need for alternative care delivery models is urgently needed, as evidenced by the rising trends in healthcare spending, doctor visits and the percentage of the general population that is 65 and older. Additionally, there is a scarcity of workers and healthcare facilities and equipment. If the current scarcity of resources, especially human resources, persists, it will have a devastating effect on the provision of healthcare services in the future. Because of the recent COVID-19 epidemic, healthcare resources must be appropriately managed by implementing a plan to combine traditional and contact-free services (Lee & Lee, 2021). In the years to come, hospital resource management is likely to be heavily influenced by the insights gained from the COVID-19 pandemic and the creative application of existing technologies. In their shared efforts to stem the spread of the COVID-19 pandemic, people realise the importance of communal wisdom in fostering solidarity, justice and accountability rather than opportunistic and individualistic actions (Napier et al., 2020). To stop COVID-19 epidemics in communities, people must follow government regulations and voluntarily fulfil their civic responsibilities (Lee & Lee, 2020). Patients with respiratory illnesses, for example, can be served in a designated drive-through area, apart from the general public (Lee & Lee, 2021). The emotional and mental health of those infected with COVID-19 and their loved ones must be closely monitored throughout the pandemic (Lee & Lee, 2020). After a patient has recovered, the medical team should work together to offer therapies (such as counselling or psychiatric care) to allow the patient and their family to return to their regular routines. They can return to their regular lives faster using these supporting psychological services (Lee & Lee, 2020). Maintaining an open line of contact with the patient is critical for promoting collaborative treatment. Virtual care, FaceTime, Zoom or wearable gadgets can also be used as contactless communication methods while providing healthcare to patients (Lee & Lee, 2021).

The growing intricacy of the healthcare setting is another factor contributing to the increasing significance of efficient healthcare resource management (Kabene et al., 2006). Online care services, AI-based diagnoses and digital medical information systems are just a few examples of how healthcare delivery systems have changed with the rise of advanced digital technology (Yoon et al., 2020). On the other hand, patients' requirements changed, healthcare resources became more diverse and the healthcare environment grew due to these developments. The healthcare business faces new challenges due to current social and medical trends. These include an ageing population, fast urbanisation, the demand for speedy medical treatments, a tendency toward preventative healthcare, patients' more significant understanding of medicine and the spread of undiscovered diseases (Kabene et al., 2006; Lee, 2018). As a result of the COVID-19 scenario, there has also been a tremendous surge in contactless services. In addition to helping with COVID-19 mitigation, these remote and online services should help with the difficulties of insufficient healthcare funding (Lee & Lee, 2021). During the pandemic, many governments enforced the social distancing mandate, which led to the widespread adoption of contactless healthcare services, such as telemedicine. When providing health care services across international borders, there needs to be global standardisation to account for variations in regulations, insurance coverage and the potential for medical mistakes caused by language and cultural barriers (Engel et al., 2014).

A Future Research Agenda

Every nation places a high value on healthcare. Some argue that health is one of the most critical issues nations face today, right up there with poverty and climate change. Healthcare consumes a large portion of national resources and has a decisive impact on a nation's development and growth (Agarwal et al., 2010). The necessity for an efficient system of connection between online and offline service types has grown in recent years, and this applies to the healthcare industry; many other sectors face a similar dilemma. When it comes to the service sector, for instance, brick-and-mortar shops have the advantage of letting clients try out things in person.

In contrast, online shops have the advantage of collecting data on customers and developing strategies based on their unique traits (Lee, 2018). Companies can provide clients with personalised services, thanks to online interaction. Creating a two-way strategy that considers consumers' demands and limitations is essential, mainly because digital detox services are also available to help people limit their usage of digital gadgets. The term "digital detox" is derived from the idea of physically avoiding sophisticated ICT and returning to a more analogue setting (Basu, 2019). One possible sector to use this service is healthcare, given its purpose-built nature.

Many atypical enterprises are venturing into different healthcare services delivery market areas, drawn by abundant available capital and an industry experiencing significant disruption. These businesses are banking on a new business model to meet the needs of healthcare consumers who are getting more educated. As a countermeasure, established healthcare providers would do well to study the stories of other industries hit hard by technological upheaval, such as the film, music and publishing industries. Meanwhile, these established players need to start reimagining their areas of healthcare delivery (Healey, 2014; Healey & Marchese, 2012). The epidemic has spurred a dramatic expansion of 4IR across many sectors. The healthcare business is transforming from its traditional concentration on diagnosis and treatment to a consumer-oriented smart industry that prioritises illness prevention through cutting-edge technologies. The public, medical professionals and patients are thus increasingly able to access personalised, innovative healthcare services that use ICTs. The utilisation of digital devices, information systems and platforms by healthcare organisations is undergoing a rapid transformation due to these services (Lee & Lee, 2020; Liang et al., 2019; Petropoulos, 2020). However, our research showed that numerous healthcare facilities had already used AI for diagnosis, patient management and administrative tasks before the pandemic. As this gradual transition continues, it is essential to develop strategic plans for expanding contactless (untact) services in the healthcare sector. These services include telemedicine, health management and disease prevention. The provider–user perspective, along with considerations of efficacy, security and ease of use, should ideally inform the development of such solutions. Healthcare organisations should consider these tendencies when they use applicable technology, such as AI, Remote Monitoring, blockchain, Big Data and platforms. Building an effective medical organisation is critical to prepare for the time after the epidemic. In addition to utilising online and offline smart technologies, this organisation should fortify its alliances with other players in the healthcare business, including those involved in developing healthcare devices and systems, personal information security, pharmaceuticals and insurance (Lee & Lee, 2021).

When effective COVID-19 vaccinations and cures are widely accessible, the "new normal" will emerge despite the many opportunities and threats posed by the pandemic. Uncertainty, exacerbated by additional complicating variables, including climate change, other contagious diseases, trade disputes and regional warfare, will pose the greatest threat in the post-COVID-19 age (Poushter & Huang, 2020, pp. 1–37). Healthcare providers and other organisations must so be ready for the post-COVID-19 normal.

Conclusion

The COVID-19 pandemic response has elevated innovation from a marketing tool to a fundamental necessity, notwithstanding the pervasiveness of the terms improvement and innovation in healthcare. Fundamental differences exist between the two despite their shared problem-solving goals, improved outcomes and cost reduction. Progress is made little by little, iteratively. It entails optimising service reliability by testing and measuring the effects of minor modifications (Bhattacharyya et al., 2022). At its core, improvement is about improving a system by fixing its perceived flaws and then seeing how that changes things. Research on the effects of DT on healthcare has progressed over time, and this study seeks to catalogue that evolution as well as the most critical uses, advantages, opportunities and dangers previously found. The growing popularity of telemedicine should not be surprising. But contactless healthcare services cover much more than telemedicine diagnostics; they include automated vital sign monitoring, preventative medicine education programmes, team communication among medical staff, patient counselling and more. Therefore, all potential healthcare services that can be rendered using the contactless approach should be covered by future study. Next time, researchers should compile a list of everyone interested in cashless healthcare services. The development of smart healthcare organisations capable of diagnosing, treating and preventing infectious and other diseases is contingent upon the results of this and comparable research on contactless healthcare services.

References

Agarwal, R., Dugas, M., Gao, G., & Kannan, P. K. (2019). Emerging technologies and analytics for a new era of value-centered marketing in healthcare. *Journal of the Academy of Marketing Science*, *48*, 9–23.

Agarwal, S., Srivastava, A., & Kumar, S. (2010). Urban health in developing countries. In M. C. Gibbons, R. Bali, & N. Wickramasinghe (Eds.), *Perspectives of knowledge management in urban health* (pp. 61–94). Springer.

Akiyama, M., & Yoo, B. K. (2016). A systematic review of the economic evaluation of telemedicine in Japan. *Journal of Preventive Medicine and Public Health*, *49*(4), 183.

Allen, L. N. (2022). Primary health care is not just a service delivery platform. *Lancet Global Health*, *10*(8), e1092–e1093.

Amarasingham, R., Plantinga, L., Diener-West, M., Gaskin, D. J., & Powe, N. R. (2009). Clinical information technologies and inpatient outcomes. *Archives of Internal Medicine*, *169*(2), 108. https://doi.org/10.1001/archinternmed.2008.520

Anastasijevic, D. (2019). *Mayo Clinic selects Google as strategic partner for health care innovation, cloud computing*. Mayo Clinic News Network.

Balch, J. A., Ruppert, M. M., Loftus, T. J., Guan, Z., Ren, Y., Upchurch, G. R., Ozrazgat-Baslanti, T., Rashidi, P., & Bihorac, A. (2023). Machine learning–enabled clinical information systems using fast healthcare interoperability resources data standards: Scoping review. *JMIR Medical Informatics*, *11*, e48297.

Basu, R. (2019). Impact of digital detox on individual performance of the employees. *International Journal of Research and Analytical Reviews*, *6*(2), 378–381.

Beaunoyer, E., Dupéré, S., & Guitton, M. J. (2020). COVID-19 and digital inequalities: Reciprocal impacts and mitigation strategies. *Computers in Human Behavior*, *111*, 106424.

Belliger, A., & Krieger, D. J. (2018). The digital transformation of healthcare. In *Knowledge management in digital change: New findings and practical cases* (pp. 311–326). Springer International Publishing.

Bhattacharyya, O., Shapiro, J., & Schneider, E. C. (2022). Innovation centers in health care delivery systems: Structures for success. *Journal of Medical Internet Research, 24*(2), e33961.

Biancone, P., Secinaro, S., Marseglia, R., & Calandra, D. (2023). E-health for the future. Managerial perspectives using a multiple case study approach. *Technovation, 120*, 102406.

Buljac-Samardzic, M., Doekhie, K. D., & van Wijngaarden, J. D. (2020). Interventions to improve team effectiveness within health care: A systematic review of the past decade. *Human Resources for Health, 18*, 1–42.

Cobianchi, L., Dal Mas, F., Peloso, A., Pugliese, L., Massaro, M., Bagnoli, C., & Angelos, P. (2020). Planning the full recovery phase: An antifragile perspective on surgery after COVID-19. *Annals of Surgery, 272*(6), e296–e299.

Cordina, J., Kumar, R., Martin, C. P., & Jones, E. P. (2018). *Healthcare consumerism 2018: An update on the journey*. McKinsey & Company.

Dai, R., Spector, A., & Wong, G. (2020). e-Mental health care for people living with dementia: A lesson on digital equality from COVID-19. *Alzheimer's & Dementia: Diagnosis, Assessment & Disease Monitoring, 12*(1).

Dal Mas, F., Massaro, M., Rippa, P., & Secundo, G. (2023). The challenges of digital transformation in healthcare: An interdisciplinary literature review, framework, and future research agenda. *Technovation, 123*, 102716.

Dieleman, J. L., Campbell, M., Chapin, A., Eldrenkamp, E., Fan, V. Y., Haakenstad, A., Kates, J., Li, Z., Matyasz, T., Micah, A., Reynolds, A., Sadat, N., Schneider, M. T., Sorensen, R., Abbas, K. M., Abera, S. F., Kiadaliri, A. A., Ahmed, M. B., Alam, K., & Murray, C. J. (2017). Future and potential spending on health 2015–40: Development assistance for health, and government, prepaid private, and out-of-pocket health spending in 184 countries. *The Lancet, 389*(10083), 2005–2030.

Dionisio, M., de Souza Junior, S. J., Paula, F., & Pellanda, P. C. (2023). The role of digital transformation in improving the efficacy of healthcare: A systematic review. *The Journal of High Technology Management Research, 34*(1), 100442.

Dissanayake, S., Pitipana, H., Lanka, S., & Jayamanne, D. (2018, August). HealthXStream: A privacy focused doctor meetup solution for the general public. In *1st international conference on business innovation* (p. 153).

Elton, J., & O'Riordan, A. (2016). *Healthcare disrupted: Next generation business models and strategies*. John Wiley & Sons.

Engel, N., Van Hoyweghen, I., Krumeich, A., & Van Hoyweghen, I. (Eds.). (2014). *Making global health care innovation work: Standardization and localization*. Springer.

Farkas, K. J., & Romaniuk, J. R. (2020). Social work, ethics and vulnerable groups in the time of coronavirus and Covid-19. *Society Register, 4*(2), 67–82.

Haggerty, E. (2017). Healthcare and digital transformation. *Network Security, 2017*(8), 7–11.

Healey, B. J. (2014). Leadership solutions to health care problems. In *Introduction to health care services: foundations and challenges* (p. 323). Wiley.

Healey, B. J., & Marchese, M. C. (2012). *Foundations of health care management: Principles and methods*. John Wiley & Sons.

Hermes, S., Riasanow, T., Clemons, E. K., Böhm, M., & Krcmar, H. (2020). The digital transformation of the healthcare industry: Exploring the rise of emerging platform ecosystems and their influence on the role of patients. *Business Research, 13*(3), 1033–1069.

Hospodková, P., Klubarská, I., Mašek, M., & Budil, M. (2024, June). M-health in prostate cancer: Professional and patient perspectives. In *European medical and biological engineering conference* (pp. 111–121). Springer Nature.

Hui, X., & Kan, E. C. (2018). Monitoring vital signs over multiplexed radio by near-field coherent sensing. *Nature Electronics, 1*(1), 74–78.

Kabene, S. M., Orchard, C., Howard, J. M., Soriano, M. A., & Leduc, R. (2006). The importance of human resources management in health care: A global context. *Human Resources for Health, 4*, 1–17.

Keesara, S., Jonas, A., & Schulman, K. (2020). Covid-19 and health care's digital revolution. *New England Journal of Medicine, 382*(23), e82.

Kim, J. H., Choi, W. S., Song, J. Y., Yoon, Y. K., Kim, M. J., & Sohn, J. W. (2021). The role of smart monitoring digital health care system based on smartphone application and personal health record platform for patients diagnosed with coronavirus disease 2019. *BMC Infectious Diseases, 21*, 1–8.

Kim, S. (2020). South Korea bets on 'intact for the post-pandemic economy. *Bloomberg Businessweek*.

Kraus, S., Schiavone, F., Pluzhnikova, A., & Invernizzi, A. C. (2021). Digital transformation in healthcare: Analyzing the current state-of-research. *Journal of Business Research, 123*, 557–567.

Latif, S., Qadir, J., Farooq, S., & Imran, M. A. (2017). How 5G wireless (and concomitant technologies) will revolutionize healthcare? *Future Internet, 9*(4), 93.

Lee, D. (2018). Strategies for technology-driven service encounters for patient experience satisfaction in hospitals. *Technological Forecasting and Social Change, 137*, 118–127.

Lee, S. M., & Lee, D. (2020). Lessons learned from battling COVID-19: The Korean experience. *International Journal of Environmental Research and Public Health, 17*(20), 7548.

Lee, S. M., & Lee, D. (2021). Opportunities and challenges for contactless healthcare services in the post-COVID-19 era. *Technological Forecasting and Social Change, 167*, 120712.

Liang, H., Tsui, B. Y., Ni, H., Valentim, C. C., Baxter, S. L., Liu, G., Cai, W., Kermany, D. S., Sun, X., Chen, J., He, L., Zhu, J., Tian, P., Shao, H., Zheng, L., Hou, R., Hewett, S., Li, G., Liang, P., … Xia, H. (2019). Evaluation and accurate diagnoses of pediatric diseases using artificial intelligence. *Nature Medicine, 25*(3), 433–438.

Loftus, C. A., Soler, Z. M., Koochakzadeh, S., Desiato, V. M., Yoo, F., Nguyen, S. A., & Schlosser, R. J. (2020, February). Revision surgery rates in chronic rhinosinusitis with nasal polyps: meta-analysis of risk factors. *International Forum of Allergy & Rhinology, 10*(2), 199–207.

Manyika, J. (2022). Getting AI right: Introductory notes on AI & society. *Dædalus, 151*(2), 5–27.

Marin, A. (2020). Technology feature | Telemedicine takes center stage in the era of COVID-19. *Science*, *370*(6517), 731–733.

Marques, I. C., & Ferreira, J. J. (2020). Digital transformation in the area of health: Systematic review of 45 years of evolution. *Health Technology*, *10*(3), 575–586.

Massaro, M. (2023). Digital transformation in the healthcare sector through blockchain technology. Insights from academic research and business developments. *Technovation*, *120*, 102386.

Miao, R., Xiang, X., Wu, Q., & Jiang, Z. (2020). Evaluation method of medical service system based on DEMATEL and the information entropy: A case study of hypertension diagnosis and treatment in China. *PLoS One*, *15*(12), e0243832.

Minor, L., & Bevins, F. (2020). *Virtual, equitable, and precise: The dean of Stanford's medical school talks about what healthcare could be*. McKinsey & Company.

Mishra, V. (2022). Analysis of systemic and behavioral barriers to COVID-19 vaccination in rollout phase. *International Journal of Healthcare Management*, *17*(1), 131–140. https://doi.org/10.1080/20479700.2022.2157934

Mishra, V., & Sharma, M. G. (2024). Factors affecting implementation of digital lean in healthcare in the post-COVID world – Mixed-method approach. *The TQM Journal*, *36*(6), 1651–1664. https://doi.org/10.1108/tqm-08-2023-0251

Montero-Cuadrado, F., Galán-Martín, M. Á., Sánchez-Sánchez, J., Lluch, E., Mayo-Iscar, A., & Cuesta-Vargas, Á. (2020). Effectiveness of a physical therapeutic exercise programme for caregivers of dependent patients: A pragmatic randomised controlled trial from Spanish primary care. *International Journal of Environmental Research and Public Health*, *17*(20), 7359.

Nadkarni, S., & Prügl, R. (2021). Digital transformation: A review, synthesis and opportunities for future research. *Management Review Quarterly*, *71*, 233–341.

Napier, L., Curry, J., Libert, B., & de Vries, K. D. (2020). Modern business models will drive the post-pandemic world. *MIT Sloan Management Review*.

Petropoulos, G. (2020, March 23). *Artificial intelligence in the fight against COVID-19*. Bruegel.

Piccialli, F., Giampaolo, F., Prezioso, E., Camacho, D., & Acampora, G. (2021). Artificial intelligence and healthcare: Forecasting of medical bookings through multi-source time-series fusion. *Information Fusion*, *74*, 1–16.

Poushter, J., & Huang, C. (2020). *Despite pandemic, many Europeans still see climate change as greatest threat to their countries*. Pew Research Center.

Raimo, N., De Turi, I., Albergo, F., & Vitolla, F. (2023). The drivers of the digital transformation in the healthcare industry: An empirical analysis in Italian hospitals. *Technovation*, *121*, 102558.

Ritala, P., & Karhu, K. (2023). Capturing value from data complementarities: A multi-level framework. In *Research handbook on digital strategy* (pp. 273–288). Edward Elgar Publishing.

Saarikko, T., Westergren, U. H., & Blomquist, T. (2020). Digital transformation: Five recommendations for the digitally conscious firm. *Business Horizons*, *63*(6), 825–839.

Schwab, P., Saundankar, V., Bouchard, J., Wintfeld, N., Suehs, B., Moretz, C., Allen, E., & DeLuzio, A. (2016). Early treatment revisions by addition or switch for type 2 diabetes: Impact on glycemic control, diabetic complications, and healthcare costs. *BMJ Open Diabetes Research and Care*, *4*(1), e000099.

Shukla, P., Lee, M., Whitman, S. A., & Pine, K. H. (2022). Delay of routine health care during the COVID-19 pandemic: A theoretical model of individuals' risk assessment and decision making. *Social Science & Medicine*, *307*, 115164.

Spanò, R., Massaro, M., & Iacuzzi, S. (2021). Blockchain for value creation in the healthcare sector. *Technovation*, *120*, 102440. https://doi.org/10.1016/j.technovation.2021.102440

Taylor, C. B., Fitzsimmons-Craft, E. E., & Graham, A. K. (2020). Digital technology can revolutionize mental health services delivery: The COVID-19 crisis as a catalyst for change. *International Journal of Eating Disorders*, *53*(7), 1155–1157.

Ukkonen, L., & Sydänheimo, L. (2017). *Contactless health-care sensing. Nature*, *551*(7682), 572–573.

van Velthoven, M. H., Cordon, C., & Challagalla, G. (2019). Digitization of healthcare organizations: The digital health landscape and information theory. *International Journal of Medical Informatics*, *124*, 49–57.

Verhoef, P. C., Broekhuizen, T., Bart, Y., Bhattacharya, A., Dong, J. Q., Fabian, N., & Haenlein, M. (2021). Digital transformation: A multidisciplinary reflection and research agenda. *Journal of Business Research*, *122*, 889–901.

Vial, G. (2021). Understanding digital transformation: A review and a research agenda. *Managing Digital Transformation*, 13–66.

Wang, L., Wang, Z., Ma, Q., Fang, G., & Yang, J. (2019). The development and reform of public health in China from 1949 to 2019. *Globalization and Health*, *15*, 1–21.

WHO. (2021). *Coronavirus: Dashboard.* https://covid19.who.int

Xiang, Y., Zhao, L., Liu, Z., Wu, X., Chen, J., Long, E., Lin, D., Zhu, Y., Chen, C., Lin, Z., & Lin, H. (2020). Implementation of artificial intelligence in medicine: Status analysis and development suggestions. *Artificial Intelligence in Medicine*, *102*, 101780.

Xiao, Y., & Fan, Z. (2020). Technology trends to watch in the COVID-19 pandemic. *World Economic Forum*, Industry Agenda, COVID-19, Tech for Good, *10*.

Yoon, S. N., & Lee, D. (2018). Artificial intelligence and robots in healthcare: What are the success factors for technology-based service encounters? *International Journal of Healthcare Management*, *12*(3), 218–225.

Yoon, S. N., Lee, D., & Shin, Y. (2020). Innovative healthcare wearable device usage and service enhancement. *Global Business & Finance Review (GBFR)*, *25*(2), 1–10.

Zeng, Z., Chen, P., & Lew, A. (2020). From high-touch to high-tech: COVID-19 drives robotics adoption. *Tourism Geographies*, *22*(3), 724–734.

Chapter 2

Employee Engagement in Healthcare Using IoT: A SEM Approach

Pinki Paul and Balgopal Singh

Banasthali Vidyapith, India

Abstract

Employee engagement is essential for every organization to perform better in a competitive and rapidly expanding industry like the healthcare industry. It refers to commitment to the work, which can be measured using physical, cognitive, and emotional aspects. Embracing global digital advancement and meeting human resource management (HRM) issues are made easier with the help of Internet of Things (IoT) integration. This study evaluates the effectiveness of IoT on employee engagement. To determine how IoT relates to the factors influencing employees' emotional, cognitive, and physical engagement in the healthcare industry. It employed Structural Equation Modeling (SEM) to test the hypotheses. The study involved 370 healthcare professionals in total. A quantitative exploratory structural equation modeling-based investigation was carried out. Using the structured questionnaire and Likert scale, the authors examined relationships between variables and their underlying constructs through multivariate data analysis between IoT and employee engagement. Statistical Package for the Social Sciences (SPSS) and Analysis of Moment Structures (AMOS) software were used to evaluate the data. The findings demonstrate the correlation between engagement and productivity when utilizing IoT devices to amplify worker efficiency and foster organizational expansion. The SEM established connections between the many components of employee engagement. Confirmatory Factor Analysis (CFA) indicated that the scales used in the instrument effectively captured the latent constructs. Path analysis demonstrated IoT positively correlates with individual productivity (IP) and organizational productivity (OP). The research addresses the significance of the effectiveness of IoT in the healthcare industry, particularly focusing on

Digital Transformation and Artificial Intelligence for Operational Excellence in Healthcare, 23–43

Published under exclusive licence by Emerald Publishing Limited
doi:10.1108/978-1-83662-314-420251009

employee engagement influencing physical, cognitive and emotional impact in the workplace.

Keywords: Employee engagement; Internet of Things (IoT); human resource management (HRM); structural equation modeling (SEM); exploratory factor analysis (EFA); confirmatory factor analysis (CFA); path analysis; individual productivity (IP); organizational productivity (OP); healthcare sector

Introduction

Kahn (1990) defines the phrase "engagement at work" as the belief that employee engagement is essential to an industry's continuous growth and prosperity. Over the last two eras, the subject of engagement has increased attention from academic researchers as well as corporate sectors. It is defined as "the level of commitment and involvement of the employees toward their organization and its value which is contemplated by employee's mindset which includes physical, cognitive, and emotional engagement for an organization" (Saks, 2022). It is distinguished by deep emotional bond with one's work that inspires people to give their all at work and aim for more significant results. This emotional connection motivates employees to put their all into their work, which raises performance and productivity levels (Kossyva et al., 2023).

Employee engagement is defined as the degree to which an individual shows a preference for their job responsibilities, thereby fostering a relationship between themselves and their work. This relationship can improve job performance by incorporating cognitive, emotional, and physical commitment from the individual (Huang et al., 2022). This study defines cognitive engagement (CE) as the degree of mental concentration, absorption, and intensity of focus on a task. Emotional engagement (EE) is characterized by experiencing joy in one's job and having a strong emotional connection to the organization. Physical engagement (PE) refers to the level of work activity and the amount of energy expended during work. Additionally, the research considers categories of engagement: human resource management (HRM), productivity, and employee engagement, classifying engagement outcomes at both the individual and organizational levels. Engaging the employees in an organization is challenging for the human resource (HR) department to understand the employee's needs, well-being, attitude, and performance (Bailey et al., 2017). Researchers observed that employees' work strategies are as important as organizational practices. HR procedures should properly handle employee engagement and provide possibilities for them according to their individuality (Luu et al., 2019). Industry can demonstrate their appreciation for their workers' efforts by funding their professional growth, development and enhancing their overall performance. An engaged workforce cares deeply about the success of their employer to achieve its goals. HR practices indicate that engagement affects other crucial HR objectives, such as recruitment, selection, training, development, performance appraisal, retention, relationship, and compliance (Gibbons & Schutt, 2010).

Apart from this, employee engagement has increased from 2011 to 2020, and it is projected to reach up to 67% by 2023 (Statistia, 2024). In 2021, the United States faced a shortage of healthcare staff, admitted by 83% of the survey hospitals (Statistia, 2023a). A similar problem related to employee engagement is faced by the Indian healthcare industry, which is one of the largest sectors in India in terms of direct jobs and revenue (Mageswari, 2023). According to Statistia (2023b), healthcare industries need to adopt the global digital transformation to maintain service quality and accessibility to meet employee engagement challenges. The Internet of Things (IoT) advancements help to improve employee engagement in health care (Gryncewicz et al., 2023).

This study focused on the impact of physical, cognitive, and emotional engagements that influence employee productivity and HRM practices in the healthcare industry (Sultana et al., 2020). The existing studies were mainly focused on teamwork, work environment (Canavesi & Minelli, 2022), training, and performance (Sendawula et al., 2018). Therefore, the present study explores the various drivers and sub-factors like decision-making, problem-solving, technology-oriented training, the effectiveness of IoT for individual and organizational productivity (OP), data security and visibility, etc. which impacts employee engagement in health care has been investigated using exploratory study design. Healthcare organizations are seen to benefit from a positive work environment and proactive workplace behavior (Maassen et al., 2021). However, the working environment and circumstances in the healthcare industry are frequently marked by difficulties, including interprofessional disputes, hierarchy, high stress, and expectations (Holm et al., 2023). According to Christensen Hughes and Rog (2008) study, an organization's performance is significantly impacted by the actions of its engaged workforce. Cultivating a culture of engagement and cooperation in healthcare organizations requires effective communication and positive teamwork. Problems with cohesive cooperation, poor communication, and disagreement among team members can all harm employee engagement. The healthcare industry leads to challenges, like all other organizations, regarding proper engagement, employee retention, capacity, trust and satisfaction, and many more related to OP. Information security breaches are most commonly caused by negligence, which occurs when individuals within the industry disclose information without proper authorization or human error (Mikuletič et al., 2024). Healthcare facilities may increase retention rates and foster a more positive and productive workplace culture by addressing the root causes of poor employee engagement. The utilization of the IoT in this industry has the potential to minimize human errors.

Application of IoT in Health Care

One of the most inventive and quickly developing sensor-based technologies of the current day is IoT. It can drastically improve social and organizational connections positively (Haitaamar et al., 2023). A significant transformation that is changing society is the IoT, the online exchange of data from physical items. Taking inspiration from Khan (1990), Manonmani et al. (2013) claimed that employee engagement includes feelings about the job description, the organization, and the individuals' reputation and work experience. This technical framework connects everyday things and gadgets to the internet so they may gather, exchange, and transmit data. The sensors are essential for monitoring various environmental conditions. According to Javed et al. (2023), technology makes things easier for all administrators and medical practitioners to optimize procedures for increased productivity and efficiency, it has permeated the industry's growth. IoT technologies are already employed in the healthcare industry to enhance patient outcomes and care, providing new avenues for remote monitoring (Mohammed & Hasan, 2023). The study primarily examines the level of employee engagement and the significant role played by the IoT in rapidly adapting the workplace to match the evolving job market. These concerns include the organization's reliance on IoT, its potential benefits and drawbacks, drivers, and work engagement (Ceipek et al., 2021) for a new strategic plan (Rose et al., 2015). This technology can automate administrative chores to expedite healthcare operations and HRM practices, performance appraisal, tracking and management, communication, productivity tracking, monitoring, reporting, and sustainability compliance to overcome all administrative challenges. IoT technologies can transform administrative work by streamlining repetitive processes, optimizing resource utilization, and facilitating data-driven decision-making (Li et al., 2024). In terms of long-term career development goals, researchers concentrate on the relationship between career development and job satisfaction. IoT applications to make the workplace more intelligent and friendly can improve job performance, retention and help employees to learn new skills.

Productivity has emerged as a crucial aspect of the work culture within the organization. Productive employees do tasks faster and more skillfully. The IoT is bringing about a fundamental shift in the healthcare sector that will provide significant advantages to the effectiveness of IoT for individual productivity (IP) and OP outcomes.

Problem Statement

This research created the bridge built upon the previous studies through a comprehensive analysis and profound understanding of the utilization of IoT in health care. The study emphasizes the significance of specific types of sensors, communication methods, and highlights such as customized treatment plans, remote patient monitoring, and accelerated healthcare delivery. Another study investigates the distinct security and privacy features required for smart health care (Nissar et al., 2024). This study focused on employee engagement, linking it with IoT, and ultimately achieving goals related to individual and OP. This is assessed through physical, cognitive, and emotional dimensions.

Conceptual Framework and Hypothesis Development

The field of research is constantly evolving, and the outcome can be influenced by modification of conceptual frameworks and hypotheses. By utilizing theoretical structure centered on employee engagement, organizations can enhance both their success and the well-being of their employees through systematic method of comprehension, evaluation, and administration of individuals. Employee engagement is currently the main theoretical concept in HRM. Through an analysis of the leading definitions of employee engagement, researchers have found that engagement has the potential to positively impact human motivations (Pincus, 2022). It is the strategic approach to employee management that successfully and efficiently accomplishes organizational goals. Recruitment, training, performance management, employee relations, work–life balance, and organizational culture are just a few of the areas where HRM practices and strategies directly impact employee engagement. HR managers must provide employees in their organizations a great deal of attention since empowered workers make better decisions, enhancing the organization's excellence. According to the JD-R model (Schaufeli & Bakker, 2004), there are two categories of job characteristics: job demands and resources. Workplace demands have an impact on one's body and mind and are linked to organizational, social, physical, and psychological components of the job (Tripathi et al., 2021). According to Bakker et al. (2014), in the JD-R theory, there is an interaction effect between work demands and job resources that influences employee motivation and job strain. This theory can be utilized as a foundation for perceiving disruptive HRM technologies as favorable to alleviate the adverse impacts of workplace conflicts on employee engagement (Priyashantha et al., 2022). By strongly emphasizing employee engagement and applying sensible HRM practices, organizations may foster employee satisfaction, productivity, and retention. Skilled employee involvement is the utmost priority for HRM to efficiently carry out management operations. Based on a review of the research, it can be concluded that there is a positive relationship between employee engagement and HRM practices (Chughtai, 2013). An organization's productivity depends on employees' commitment to their work (Albdour & Altarawneh, 2014). The role of IoT is crucial in improving communication among employees and end users (Ratta et al., 2021). The healthcare sector produces massive amounts of data on employees, including the in-depth details of healthcare professionals. It has become highly challenging for healthcare workers to analyze the data manually every time. IoT is inclined toward connected devices as they facilitate efficient data tracking, decision-making, capacity management, and selection of appropriate communication and coordination methods for administrative tasks (Subrahmanya et al., 2022).

The best conceptual framework for the below-mentioned hypotheses was formulated:

Ha1. IoT for teamwork improves healthy communication positively associated with organizational productivity.

Ha2. IoT positively associated with decision-making effectiveness.

As stated by Nor et al. (2018), IoT-facilitated awareness is essential for employee engagement to understand the various aspects associated with employees. Higher employee engagement improves job satisfaction, performance, and loyalty of the employees in an organization (Veleva et al., 2017). IoT awareness helps the healthcare industry to understand the employees' commitment level and provide better administrative work (Saovapakhiran et al., 2022). Monitoring employee performance is crucial for evaluating their effectiveness, and IoT helps alleviate the workload of the HR department in delivering fair performance assessments to committed staff members (Moyeenudin & Anandan, 2021). Further, the HRM also worked to raise the performance of the employees by introducing training programs in the healthcare sector (Sendawula et al., 2018). IoT applications can offer direction that improves performance reviews and promotes worker well-being to increase retention. The implementation of learning-centered training programs is believed to enhance performance by positively influencing organizational learning (Aragón et al., 2014).

Ha3. IoT-enabled awareness positively associated with performance appraisal for employee retention.

Ha4. The technology-oriented training is positively associated with success in performance tracking.

The advantages of IoT-based digital assistants have been found transparency in communication to positively correlate with job satisfaction. Several researchers have examined the data security concerns associated with human error and transparency. Similar to the healthcare sector, large amounts of data from patients and employees are being stored on the cloud, necessitating the need for robust security measures and clear visibility. The implementation of efficient strategies and solutions to mitigate security risks and safeguard user privacy in cloud computing is successfully employed (Dwivedi et al., 2019). The IoT applications process huge amounts of raw medical data and convert it into useful information, improving privacy, and scalability (Li et al., 2022).

Ha5. IoT-enabled data security positively associated with organizational transparency.

IoT-based feedback tools can improve problem-solving for medical professionals (Onoue et al., 2017). The chapter suggested that constructive criticism-based feedback gives an idea to organizations on how to improve their work, giving them a sense of control over how their assignments turn out going forward. On the other hand, compliments indicate the possibility of future success. Through consistent data monitoring, IoT-based feedback also aids professionals in comprehending and offering possible solutions for organizational issues. However, several existing studies revealed the effectiveness of the IoT in the healthcare sector, which also improves employee engagement (Paul & Singh, 2023). However, it is also revealed the effectiveness of IoT-driven training enhances the capacity of employees that support performance monitoring, offering accurate feedback to increase overall performance and address errors more strategically (Li et al., 2022; Wan Ahmad et al., 2022). The following hypothesis is formulated:

Ha6. IoT-based feedback positively associated with problem-solving.

Methodology

Research methodology is the structured and scientific approach utilized to conduct research, investigate issues, and gather data for specific objectives. Research serves as a valuable contribution to the existing pool of knowledge, contributing to its advancement. It entails the pursuit of truth through study, observation, comparison, and experimentation.

Data Collection Procedures

- Primary data: A survey questionnaire was utilized in offline survey platforms. The questionnaires were designed to gather responses on a Likert scale ranging from 1 to 5, where 1 indicated "Strongly Disagree" and 5 indicated "Strongly Agree".
  The main tool for data gathering was a survey instrument. This technique utilized structured questionnaires distributed to a sample from the target population (Kothari, 2017). The process involved preparing a structured questionnaire and asking questions in a predetermined order. Primary data were collected through a survey that distributed physical copies of questionnaires to the selected sample group. A standardized method for gathering primary, ensuring comparability. Primary data for this study were collected from selected regions in the Eastern and Northeastern parts of India, specifically cities like Kolkata, Bhubaneswar, Guwahati, and Shillong.
- Secondary data: Secondary data also contributed information and facts relevant to the study. Therefore, secondary data were gathered from sources such as journals, reports, books, records, theses, etc.

Sampling

Sampling refers to the process of selecting a subset from a specific population, and this process is guided by a sample design. The sample design outlines the approach, method, or procedure that the researcher will use to choose the elements for the sample. This study utilizes snowball sampling to gather data. The researcher distributed questionnaires to over 400 healthcare professionals to test hypotheses and meet objectives. A total of 384 respondents responded. Ultimately, 370 responses were valid. The focus was on individuals who currently use or are interested in using IoT applications in their professional roles. Each survey consisted of 26 questions that were analyzed through Structural Equation Modeling (SEM).

Data Analysis

The reliability examination used Cronbach's alpha to validate the internal consistency of survey items. Further, the validation of factor analysis and model fitness has been evaluated using Confirmatory Factor Analysis (CFA).

Result and Discussion

Reliability Analysis

Cronbach's alpha tests assess the consistency and reliability of results. Table 2.1 shows reliability analysis for the study's construct scales. It indicates that PE (4 items; $\alpha = 0.926$), CE (5 items; $\alpha = 0.905$), EE (4 items; $\alpha = 0.70$), IP (6 items; $\alpha = 0.881$), and OP (6 items; $\alpha = 0.947$) items are reliable.

Exploratory Factor Analysis

EFA was using Varimax rotation to validate the questionnaire scales. Factor loadings near 0 are less valid than those near 1. The research had all factor loadings over 0.5, indicating strong validity. Kaiser–Meyer–Olkin sampling adequacy is 0.917, i.e., above the recommended 0.7. All Bartlett's test of sphericity scores were significant [$\chi^2(210) = 6{,}695.073$, $p < 0.05$], verifying the sample's eligibility for factor assessment and questionnaire validity. The factors, namely, PE, EE, CE, IP and OP conducted on distinct elements, have a cumulative variance of 79.718%. Table 2.2 shows the cumulative variance.

Confirmatory Factor Analysis

CFA, one of the recommended methods for testing validity, was employed to test the construct validity of the measurement scales used in the questionnaire.

Table 2.1. Reliability.

	Cronbach's Alpha	N of Items
PE	0.929	4
CE	0.905	5
EE	0.861	4
IP	0.881	6
OP	0.947	6

Source: Author's own.

Table 2.2. Variance.

Variables	% of Variance	Cumulative %
PE	44.846	44.846
CE	11.397	56.244
EE	9.629	65.872
IP	7.871	73.743
OP	5.975	79.718

Source: Author's own.

The researcher used Statistical Package for the Social Sciences–Analysis of Moment Structures (SPSS–AMOS) software.

CFA for PE, CE, EE, O1 (IP), O2 (OP)

Fig. 2.1 illustrates the constructs related to the five factors. Table 2.3 details the model fit indices associated with the factors incorporated in the model (PE, CE, EE, IP, OP). The Chi-Square (CMI/DF) value recorded was 2.182, which is within the range. CFI (0.970), NFI (0.936), RFI (0.945), IFI (0.970), TLI (0.963), and RMSEA (0.057) were all recommended ranges. Therefore, the scales employed in the instrument successfully captured the latent constructs, as demonstrated by the Model fit indices. From CFA model, researchers found different variables under different constructs (Table 2.4).

Convergence and Discriminant Validity

CFA results were conducted to assess latent factors (CE, PE, EE, IP, OP). High CR values defined strong internal consistency within each latent factor. The AVE values exceeded 0.5, suggesting strong convergent validity. Maximum shared variance (MSV) values indicate acceptable limits, thus suggesting a reliable measurement model for the latent factors under consideration (Table 2.5).

Path Analysis

In Fig. 2.2, the path model illustrates the effectiveness of IoT for IP and the effectiveness of IoT for OP based on engagement (PE, CE, EE). Table 2.6 represents the model fit indices for the factors used in the model (PE, CE, EE, IP, OP). The Chi-Square (CMI/DF) value was 1.901, which was within range. CFI (0.953), NFI (0.907), RFI (0.877), IFI (0.954), TLI (0.937), and RMSEA (0.049) were also found within limits. Hence, the instrument effectively measured the latent constructs, as evidenced by the model fit indices.

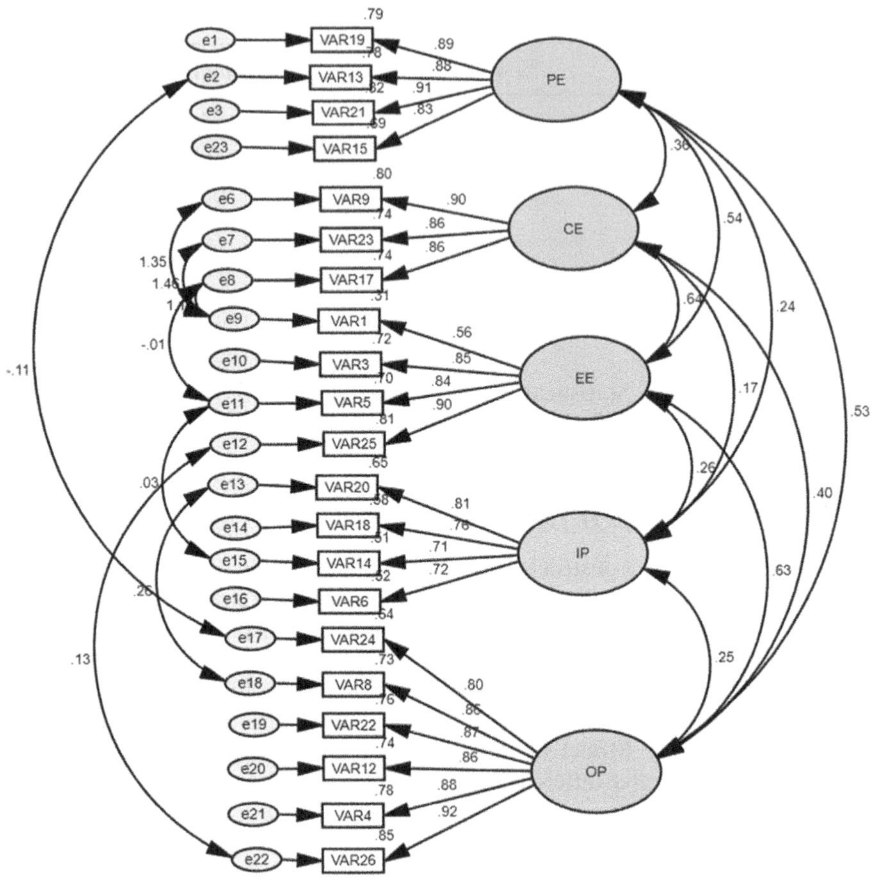

Fig. 2.1. CFA for PE, CE, EE, O1, and O2. *Source:* Author's own.

Hypothesis Testing

In Table 2.7, researchers examine the relationship between employee engagement and the IoT in health care through the analysis of three aspects: PE, CE, and EE.

The path model (Fig. 2.2) utilized Standardized Estimates to assess the connection between the observed and underlying latent constructs. The CR plays a significant role in hypothesis testing by assessing the statistical significance of the difference between two means. A higher CR means that the evidence for the hypothesis is stronger. It is important for testing hypotheses because it can tell us how significant the differences we see are and give us a standard way to compare things. In Fig. 2.3, the CR values exceeded 1.96 and were statistically significant at $p < 0.05$, indicating an impact of PE on IP and OP, EE on IP and OP, and CE on IP and OP.

Table 2.3. Variables Extracted.

PE	CE	EE	O1	O2
VAR19	VAR9	VAR1	VAR20	VAR24
VAR13	VAR23	VAR3	VAR18	VAR8
VAR21	VAR17	VAR5	VAR14	VAR22
VAR15		VAR25	VAR6	VAR12
				VAR4
				VAR26

Source: Author's own.

Table 2.4. Model Fit Indices.

Fit Measure	Good Fit	Excellent Fit	Goodness Fit Indices (Measurement model)	Remarks
χ^2/df (CMIN/df)	$0 \leq \chi^2/\text{df} \leq 2$	$2 < \chi^2/\text{df} \leq 3$	2.182	Excellent fit
RMSEA	$0 \leq \text{RMSEA} \leq 0.05$	$0.05 < \text{RMSEA} \leq 0.08$	0.057	Excellent fit
p-value for test of close fit (RMSEA < 0.05)	$0.10 < p \leq 1.00$ (RMSEA < 0.05)	$0.05 \leq p \leq 0.10$ (RMSEA < 0.05)	0.000	Excellent fit
NFI	$0.95 \leq \text{NFI} \leq 1.00$	$0.90 \leq \text{NFI} < 0.95$	0.945	Excellent fit
CFI	$0.97 \leq \text{CFI} \leq 1.00$	$0.90 \leq \text{CFI} < 0.95$	0.970	Good fit
FMIN		FMIN closer to 0	0.01	Excellent fit

Source: Author's own.

Key Findings

This study identifies factors that drive healthcare professionals to engage more through IoT applications. The researcher found that physical, cognitive, and emotional engagement significantly affected the effectiveness of the IoT on IP and OP, with values of 4.206 ($p < 0.01$), 2.507 ($p < 0.05$), and 3.853 ($p < 0.01$) for IP

Table 2.5. Computation of CR, MSV, and AVE.

Factors	CR	AVE	MSV
CE	0.907	0.765	0.411
PE	0.948	0.832	0.295
EE	0.903	0.734	0.411
IP	0.863	0.643	0.066
OP	0.953	0.78	0.402

Source: Author's own.

Table 2.6. Model Fit Indices.

Fit Measure	Good Fit	Excellent Fit	Goodness Fit Indices (Measurement model)	Remarks
χ^2/df (CMIN/df)	$0 \leq \chi^2/\text{df} \leq 2$	$2 < \chi^2/\text{df} \leq 3$	1.901	Excellent fit
RMSEA	$0 \leq \text{RMSEA} \leq 0.05$	$0.05 < \text{RMSEA} \leq 0.08$	0.049	Good fit
p-value for test of close fit (RMSEA <0.05)	$0.10 < p \leq 1.00$ (RMSEA < 0.05)	$0.05 \leq p \leq 0.10$ (RMSEA < 0.05)	0.053	Excellent fit
NFI	$0.95 \leq \text{NFI} \leq 1.00$	$0.90 \leq \text{NFI} < 0.95$	0.907	Excellent fit
CFI	$0.97 \leq \text{CFI} \leq 1.00$	$0.90 \leq \text{CFI} < 0.95$	0.953	Excellent fit
FMIN		FMIN closer to 0	0.814	Good fit

Source: Author's own.

and 5.094 ($p < 0.01$), 4.396 ($p < 0.01$), and 3.828 ($p < 0.01$) for OP. The results showed that items measuring PE, CE, EE, IP, and OP were significant, with CR values exceeding 1.96 ($p < 0.05$). This indicates that PE, EE, and CE positively impact both IP and OP, supporting conclusion that IoT implementation significantly enhances employee performance and organizational outcomes.

Table 2.7. Hypothesis Testing.

Hypothesis		**Coefficient**
Hypothesis 1	IoT for teamwork improves healthy communication positively associated with organizational productivity	0.128*
Hypothesis 2	IoT positively associated with decision-making effectiveness	0.489**
Hypothesis 3	IoT-enabled awareness positively associated with performance appraisal for employee retention	0.339**
Hypothesis 4	The technology-oriented training positively associated with success in performance tracking	0.192**
Hypothesis 5	IoT-enabled data security positively associated with organizational transparency	0.682**
Hypothesis 6	IoT-based feedback positively associated with problem-solving	0.566**

Source: Author's own.

$^{*}p < 0.05$; $^{**}p < 0.01$.

Research emphasizes enhancing employee engagement to boost satisfaction and promote OP. The SEM technique helps identify precise relationships among variables in a specific context. Research shows that integrating IoT into HR practices fosters innovative initiatives that empower and enhance employee engagement.

Conclusion

The analysis concluded that IoT-based productivity is influenced by physical, cognitive, and emotional engagement. The three "entities" demonstrate the ability to exert both physical and mental effort, gain knowledge, engage in cognitive processes, interpret information, and form emotional attachments with their work or organization. The researchers have recognized the incorporation of IoT as highly important in facilitating problem-solving and decision-making.

Furthermore, this study concluded that integration of IoT in the health care would encourage employees to actively engage in their work and enhance their overall perspective, moving beyond mere job descriptions. Implementing IoT fosters coordination and teamwork to gather feedback on individuals' thoughts and contributions to organizational performance can improve the fair treatment of employees, internalize fairness perspectives, and increase transparency. In summary, an approach that strikes compromise between fairness and transparency is necessary to integrate IoT into personnel management effectively. This research study suggested that by employing IoT systems, the healthcare industry can enhance worker flexibility and transmission in communication, as well as

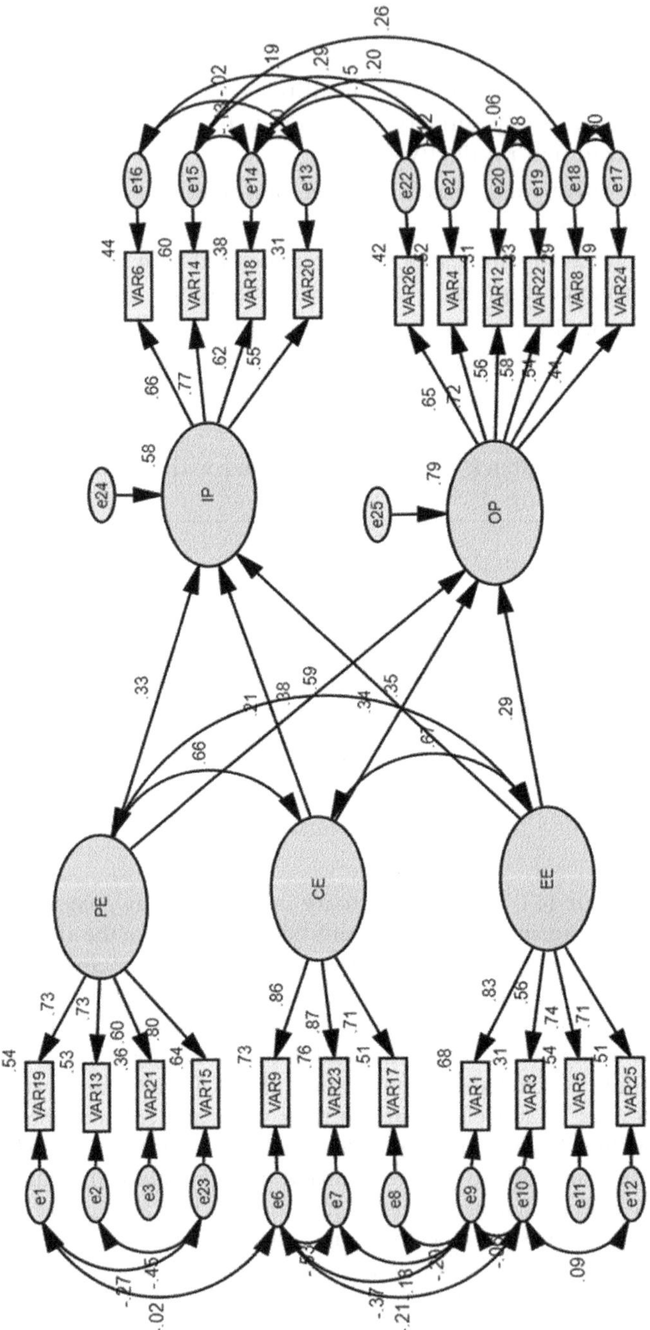

Fig. 2.2. Path Analysis. *Source:* Author's own.

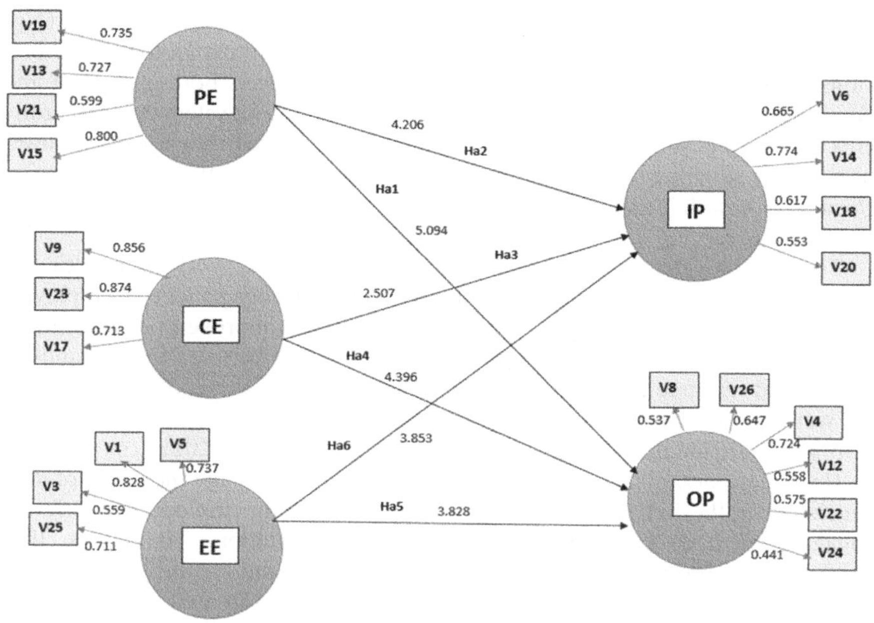

Fig. 2.3. Structural Model of Employee Engagement Between IP and OP in the Healthcare Sector. *Source:* Author's own.

team cohesion, collective efficacy, and favorable work relations. Implementing IoT in hospital administration greatly enhanced interpersonal knowledge, decreased stress, and improved comprehension and communication abilities. The application of IoT has positive impact on employees' cognitive functions (Agarwal & Dixit, 2020). The authors clarified that IoT-based systems aim to reduce human error, enhance data measurement, and store large amounts of data. Employee engagement is enhanced by organizational and personal elements that can impact it because of psychological empowerment. It had a favorable correlation with physical, cognitive, and emotional engagement. The adoption of IoT demonstrated an improvement in data-based decision-making, and it is associated with employee retention. Training encompasses the understanding of data analytics, physical devices involved in IoT network correlates with success in performance tracking, and finally, IoT-based feedback was positively associated with problem-solving.

Theoretical and Practical Implications

Employee engagement can be assessed through the utilization of various models. The research utilized a model that includes physical, cognitive, and emotional factors of engagement. To achieve a state of engagement, it is necessary to channel personal energies toward physical, cognitive, and emotional tasks (Nor et al., 2018). The primary contribution of this study is an expansion of the previously postulated framework showing how the IoT affects both individual and organizational output. It is fundamentally an object-centric system that can firmly affect employees' day-to-day tasks. These findings showed that it can empower workers by aligning with organizational goals. Consequently, this conclusion elucidated how IoT can empower workers systemically as a considerable and pervasive force.

The IoT has greatly enhanced the efficiency of skilled workers, resulting in significant improvements. The flexibility and level of engagement of employees also affect OP. By illustrating how IoT applications improve communication, teamwork, capacity building, etc. There is a connection between the demands of the job and resource costs as well as the social and organizational components of the work. All of these facets of work contribute to less stressful environment and help both individuals and organizations grow (Rabiul et al., 2021).

Healthcare organizations are required to effectively manage the influx of data generated by the IoT while also attracting and retaining employees by offering engaging methods for timely access to this information. To achieve this, employees need to be equipped with appropriate tools and for technology-driven organizational culture to be fostered. Implementing an IoT-based knowledge and learning system for documentation purposes can significantly assist new employees. IoT-centric knowledge management system provides employees with relevant content for on-the-job learning. For instance, augmented or virtual reality devices can be integrated with IoT elements or colleagues to facilitate task completion. Concurrently, organizations can leverage these technologies as educational resources by granting employees access to a knowledge management system (Sievers et al., 2021). The implementation of an IoT framework that delivers pertinent information to employees promptly can enhance access to opportunities and minimize information inaccuracies. By monitoring objects and processes, organizations can empower employees to leverage data for innovative purposes. Research has been conducted to explore the correlation between IoT and organizational effectiveness, revealing that increased employee engagement enhances the job resources associated with IoT, ultimately leading to improved profitability.

Novelty of Work

This study focused on the potential benefits of IoT in healthcare administration for better employee engagement. Streamlining processes, cutting down on paperwork, and lowering manual errors eventually increase operational efficiency. Along with employee engagement, the study also includes how IoT increased efficiency and improved productivity and security. The existing studies were mainly focused on the leadership role, work environment (Canavesi & Minelli, 2022), HRM (Sultana et al., 2020), training, and performance (Sendawula et al., 2018). Still, no study focused on the physical, cognitive, and emotional engagement constructs that influence employee engagement using the IoT, specifically in the healthcare industry. Therefore, the present study explores the various drivers and sub-factors like decision-making, problem-solving, technology-oriented training, the effectiveness of IoT for individual and OP, transparency, communication, performance tracking, etc. are impact employee engagement. Utilizing IoT has been shown to have a strong correlation with increased employee engagement, including physical, emotional, and cognitive participation.

Limitations of Study

Initially, this approach focuses on demonstrating the implementation of IoT in two distinct ways employee engagement and IoT integration. However, researchers are confident that the problems and solutions we have identified are significant for the healthcare industry. Subsequent surveys should aim to verify this information and encompass supplementary industries. Nevertheless, the reliability of IoT devices may be compromised due to network outages, signal interference, or bandwidth limitations, thereby hindering communication. It may be challenging to implement IoT systems successfully in isolated or rural locations with inadequate connectivity. Data privacy is a concern, particularly when private health information is exchanged in the healthcare industry. It presents a drawback in terms of data security concerns.

Future Work

To deal with the issues, more study needs to be done on a more gradual method of implementation in these areas. Besides that, it should investigate how to use information like biometrics and locations in a way that does not invade employees' privacy. Finally, need to do more quantitative empirical research to understand what these findings mean for the way people work in IoT and operations management. Researchers can also investigate work engagement in other fields, such as fashion, tourism, sports, education, and IT, by looking into the other important factors that affect employees in India or nearby countries.

Ethical Approval

The information was collected from various healthcare institutions following authorization from the appropriate governing bodies. Additionally, we assured each participant that their data would remain confidential unless they provided explicit consent. The institutions are well-informed about our research, and there are no ethical concerns present.

Acknowledgment

Special thanks to the UGC, Government of India, for extending financial support for this study as Ph.D. Research Fellow under the scheme of UGC SJSGC fellowship. The authors are also acknowledged to all the administrative staff for allowing data collection from different healthcare organizations.

References

Agarwal, H., & Dixit, G. (2020). Information technology usage and cognitive engagement: Understanding effects on users' cognitive processes. In S. K. Sharma, Y. K. Dwivedi, B. Metri, & N. P. Rana (Eds.), *IFIP advances in information and communication technology* (pp. 70–81). https://doi.org/10.1007/978-3-030-64861-9_7

Albdour, A. A., & Altarawneh, I. I. (2014). Employee engagement and organizational commitment: Evidence from Jordan. *International Journal of Business*, *19*(2), 192–212.

Aragón, M. I. B., Jiménez, D. J., & Valle, R. S. (2014). Training and performance: The mediating role of organizational learning. *Business Research Quarterly*, *17*(3), 161–173. https://doi.org/10.1016/j.cede.2013.05.003

Bailey, C., Madden, A., Alfes, K., & Fletcher, L. (2017). The meaning, antecedents and outcomes of employee engagement: A narrative synthesis. *International Journal of Management Reviews*, *19*(1), 31–53. https://doi.org/10.1111/ijmr.12077

Bakker, A. B., Demerouti, E., & Sanz-Vergel, A. I. (2014). Burnout and work engagement: The JD–R approach. *Annual Review of Organizational Psychology and Organizational Behavior*, *1*(1), 389–411. https://doi.org/10.1146/annurev-orgpsych-031413-091235

Canavesi, A., & Minelli, E. (2022). Servant leadership and employee engagement: A qualitative study. *Employee Responsibilities and Rights Journal*, *34*(4), 413–435. https://doi.org/10.1007/s10672-021-09389-9

Ceipek, R., Hautz, J., Petruzzelli, A. M., De Massis, A., & Matzler, K. (2021). A motivation and ability perspective on engagement in emerging digital technologies: The case of Internet of Things solutions. *Long Range Planning*, *54*(5), 101991. https://doi.org/10.1016/j.lrp.2020.101991

Christensen Hughes, J., & Rog, E. (2008). Talent management: A strategy for improving employee recruitment, retention and engagement within hospitality organizations. *International Journal of Contemporary Hospitality Management*, *20*, 743–757. https://doi.org/10.1108/09596110810899086

Chughtai, T. A. (2013). Role of HR practices in turnover intentions with the mediating effect of employee engagement. *WSEAS Transactions on Business and Economics*, *2*(10), 97–103. https://www.wseas.com/journals/bae/2013/5707-121.pdf

Dwivedi, A. D., Srivastava, G., Dhar, S., & Singh, R. (2019). A decentralized privacy-preserving healthcare blockchain for IoT. *Sensors*, *19*(2), 1–17. https://doi.org/10.3390/s19020326

Gibbons, J., & Schutt, R. (2010). *A global barometer for measuring employee engagement*. Conference Board. https://www.conference-board.org/publications/publicationdetail.cfm?publicationid=1738

Gryncewicz, W., Zygała, R., & Pilch, A. (2023). AI in HRM: Case study analysis. Preliminary research. *Procedia Computer Science*, *225*, 2351–2360. https://doi.org/10.1016/j.procs.2023.10.226

Haitaamar, Z. N., Sulaiman, A., Bendoukha, S. A., & Rodrigues, D. F. B. (2023). Lower inclination orbit concept for Direct-Communication-To-Satellite Internet-Of-Things using lean satellite standard in Near-Equatorial regions. *Applied Sciences*, *13*(9), 5654. https://doi.org/10.3390/app13095654

Holm, K., Jönsson, S., & Muhonen, T. (2023). How are witnessed workplace bullying and bystander roles related to perceived care quality, work engagement, and turnover intentions in the healthcare sector? A longitudinal study. *International Journal of Nursing Studies*, *138*, 104429. https://doi.org/10.1016/j.ijnurstu.2022.104429

Huang, S. Y. B., Huang, C., & Chang, T. (2022). A new concept of work engagement theory in cognitive engagement, emotional engagement, and physical engagement. *Frontiers in Psychology*, *12*. https://doi.org/10.3389/fpsyg.2021.663440

Javed, I., Niazi, A., Nawaz, S., Ali, M., & Hussain, M. (2023). Impact of workplace bullying on work engagement among early career employees. *PLoS One*, *18*(10), e0285345. https://doi.org/10.1371/journal.pone.0285345

Kahn, W. A. (1990). Psychological conditions of personal engagement and disengagement at work. *Academy of Management Journal*, *33*(4), 692–724.

Kossyva, D., Theriou, G., Aggelidis, V., & Sarigiannidis, L. (2023). Outcomes of engagement: A systematic literature review and future research directions. *Heliyon*, *9*(6), e17565. https://doi.org/10.1016/j.heliyon.2023.e17565

Kothari, C. (2017). *Research methodology*. Google Books. https://books.google.co.in/books?id=4aOrswEACAAJ

Li, C., Wang, J., Wang, S., & Zhang, Y. (2024). A review of IoT applications in healthcare. *Neurocomputing*, *565*, 127017. https://doi.org/10.1016/j.neucom.2023.127017

Li, Q., Kumar, P. M., & Alazab, M. (2022). IoT-assisted physical education training network virtualization and resource management using a deep reinforcement learning system. *Complex and Intelligent Systems*, *8*(2), 1229–1242. https://doi.org/10.1007/s40747-021-00584-7

Luu, T. T., Rowley, C., & Vo, T. T. (2019). Addressing employee diversity to foster their work engagement. *Journal of Business Research*, *95*, 303–315. https://doi.org/10.1016/j.jbusres.2018.08.017

Maassen, S. M., Van Oostveen, C., Vermeulen, H., & Weggelaar, A. M. (2021). Defining a positive work environment for hospital healthcare professionals: A Delphi study. *PLoS One*, *16*(2), e0247530. https://doi.org/10.1371/journal.pone.0247530

Mageswari, S. U. (2023). A conceptual study on employee engagement in healthcare industry during Covid-19. *Alochana Chakra Journal*, *9*(10), 159–165. https://www.researchgate.net/publication/373237523

Manonmani, P., Mark, J., Karthikeyan, R., & Uma, V. (2013). A study on employee engagement with special reference to steel casting manufacturing company, Coimbatore, Tamilnadu. *International Journal of Business and Management Invention*, *2*(1), 59–61.

Mikuletič, S., Vrhovec, S., Skela-Savič, B., & Žvanut, B. (2024). Security and privacy oriented information security culture (ISC): Explaining unauthorized access to healthcare data by nursing employees. *Computers & Security*, *136*, 103489. https://doi.org/10.1016/j.cose.2023.103489

Mohammed, B. G., & Hasan, D. S. (2023). Smart healthcare monitoring system using IoT. *International Journal of Interactive Mobile Technologies*, *17*(01), 141–152. https://doi.org/10.3991/ijim.v17i01.34675

Moyeenudin, H. M., & Anandan, R. (2021). IoT implementation at global enterprises for progressive human resource practices. In S. L. Peng, R. X. Hao, S. Pal (Eds.), *Proceedings of first international conference on mathematical modeling and computational science: ICMMCS 2020* (pp. 109–117). Springer. https://doi.org/10.1007/978-981-33-4389-4_12

Nissar, G., Khan, R. A., Mushtaq, S., Lone, S. A., & Moon, A. H. (2024). IoT in healthcare: A review of services, applications, key technologies, security concerns, and emerging trends. *Multimedia Tools and Applications*. https://doi.org/10.1007/s11042-024-18580-7

Nor, N. I. M., Arokiasamy, L., & Balaraman, R. A. (2018). The influence of Internet of Things on employee's engagement among generation Y at the workplace. *SHS Web of Conferences*, *56*, 03003. https://doi.org/10.1051/shsconf/20185603003

Onoue, T., Goto, M., Kobayashi, T., Tominaga, T., Ando, M., Honda, H., Yoshida, Y., Tosaki, T., Yokoi, H., Kato, S., Maruyama, S., & Arima, H. (2017). Randomized controlled trial for assessment of Internet of Things system to guide intensive glucose control in diabetes outpatients: Nagoya Health Navigator Study protocol. *Nagoya Journal of Medical Science*, *79*(3), 323–329. https://doi.org/10.18999/nagjms.79.3.323

Paul, P., & Singh, B. (2023). Healthcare employee engagement using the Internet of Things: A systematic overview. In P. Tyagi, N. Chilamkurti, S. Grima, K. Sood, & B. Balusamy (Eds.), *The adoption and effect of artificial intelligence on human resources management, part A* (pp. 71–97). *Emerald studies in finance, insurance, and risk management*. Emerald Publishing Limited. https://doi.org/10.1108/978-1-80382-027-920231004

Pincus, J. D. (2022). Employee engagement as human motivation: Implications for theory, methods, and practice. *Integrative Psychological and Behavioral Science/Integrative Psychological & Behavioral Science*, *57*(4), 1223–1255. https://doi.org/10.1007/s12124-022-09737-w

Priyashantha, K. G., De Alwis, A. C., & Welmilla, I. (2022). Promoting employee engagement: Concept paper for the development of a conceptual framework. *Wayamba Journal of Management*, *13*(2), 100. https://doi.org/10.4038/wjm.v13i2.7569

Rabiul, M. K., Mohamed, A. E., Patwary, A. K., Yean, T. F., & Osman, S. Z. (2021). Linking human resources practices to employee engagement in the hospitality industry: The mediating influences of psychological safety, availability and meaningfulness. *European Journal of Management and Business Economics*, *32*(2), 223–240. https://doi.org/10.1108/ejmbe-12-2020-0347

Ratta, P., Kaur, A., Sharma, S., Shabaz, M., & Dhiman, G. (2021). Application of blockchain and Internet of Things in healthcare and medical sector: Applications, challenges, and future perspectives. *Journal of Food Quality*, 1–20. https://doi.org/10.1155/2021/7608296

Rose, K., Eldridge, S., & Chapin, L. (2015). *The Internet of Things (IoT): An overview - Internet society*. https://www.internetsociety.org/resources/doc/2015/iot-overview/

Saks, A. M. (2022). Caring human resources management and employee engagement. *Human Resource Management Review*, *32*(3), 100835. https://doi.org/10.1016/j.hrmr.2021.100835

Saovapakhiran, B., Naruephiphat, W., Charnsripinyo, C., Baydere, S., & Ozdemir, S. (2022). QoE-Driven IoT architecture: A comprehensive review on system and resource management. *IEEE Access, 10*, 84579–84621. https://doi.org/10.1109/access.2022.3197585

Schaufeli, W. B., & Bakker, A. B. (2004). Job demands, job resources, and their relationship with burnout and engagement: A multi-sample study. *Journal of Organizational Behavior*, *25*(3), 293–315. https://doi.org/10.1002/job.248

Sendawula, K., Nakyejwe Kimuli, S., Bananuka, J., & Najjemba Muganga, G. (2018). Training, employee engagement and employee performance: Evidence from Uganda's health sector. *Cogent Business and Management*, *5*(1), 1–12. https://doi.org/10.1080/23311975.2018.1470891

Sievers, F., Reil, H., Rimbeck, M., Stumpf-Wollersheim, J., & Leyer, M. (2021). Empowering employees in industrial organizations with IoT in their daily operations. *Computers in Industry*, *129*, 103445. https://doi.org/10.1016/j.compind.2021.103445

Statistia. (2023a). *Expected shortages of healthcare staff in the U.S. in 2021, by occupation*. https://www.statista.com/statistics/1251107/predicted-shortages-of-healthcare-staff-in-the-us/

Statistia. (2023b). *Health professionals & hospitals*. https://www.statista.com/markets/412/topic/452/health-professionals-hospitals/#overview

Statistia. (2024). *Engagement of employees globally 2011-2023*. https://www.statista.com/statistics/699977/global-employee-engagement/

Subrahmanya, S. V. G., Shetty, D. K., Patil, V., Hameed, B. M. Z., Paul, R., Smriti, K., Naik, N., & Somani, B. K. (2022). The role of data science in healthcare advancements: Applications, benefits, and future prospects. *Irish Journal of Medical Science*, *191*(4), 1473–1483. https://doi.org/10.1007/s11845-021-02730-z

Sultana, S., Salman, Y., & Irfan, S. (2020). Exploring the relationship of HRM practices on employee motivation in public organizations: A systematic literature review. *Global Management Journal for Academic & Corporate Studies, 10*(1), 143–163.

Tripathi, P. M., Srivastava, S., Singh, L. B., Kapoor, V., & Solanki, U. (2021). A JD-R perspective for enhancing engagement through empowerment: A study on Indian hotel industry. *Journal of Hospitality and Tourism Management*, *46*, 12–25. https://doi.org/10.1016/j.jhtm.2020.11.007

Veleva, V., Bodkin, G., & Todorova, S. (2017). The need for better measurement and employee engagement to advance a circular economy: Lessons from Biogen's "zero waste" journey. *Journal of Cleaner Production*, *154*, 517–529. https://doi.org/10.1016/j.jclepro.2017.03.177

Wan Ahmad, W. N., Hisham Mohd Adib, M. A., & Sut Txi, M. R. (2022). Enhanced the anxiety monitoring system among athletes with IoT for sports performance: A review. *Journal of Physical Education and Sport*, *22*(11), 2700–2707. https://doi.org/10.7752/jpes.2022.11344

Chapter 3

Industry 4.0 Adoption in Telemedicine Industry of India: Present Evidence, Barriers and Future Recommendations

Nishtha Agarwal, Anand Jaiswal and Pushpa Negi

New Delhi Institute of Management, India

Abstract

The present chapter identifies and models the structural linkages between the barriers hindering Industry 4.0 adoption in telemedicine industry for a developing country like India. Ten barriers to the Industry 4.0 adoption in telemedicine industry are identified after a review of literature and discussion with health experts. The structural linkages between the barriers are modelled using the Interpretive Structural Modelling (ISM) method. The resulting digraph explains the relation between the barriers conveying that the improper allocation of resources is the most significant barrier followed by high cost of implementation, data inaccuracy and patient privacy. The outcomes of these barriers are possible fraud and abuse of the technology, digital divide among demographics and fear of technology among the healthcare givers. Leveraging analytics and predictive tools can optimize the distribution of funds, technology and training, avoiding wasteful spending to ensure that the telemedicine infrastructure is both efficient and effective.

Keywords: Industry 4.0; e-health; telemedicine; Interpretive Structural Modelling; barriers

Introduction

Healthcare is a critical sector for any country and holds profound importance for India as well. The healthcare industry, comprising of hospitals, medical devices, clinical trials, outsourcing, telemedicine, medical tourism, health insurance and medical equipment, ensures the well-being of its large and diverse population

Digital Transformation and Artificial Intelligence for Operational Excellence in Healthcare, 45–64

doi:10.1108/978-1-83662-314-420251010

(Healthcare System in India, Healthcare India – IBEF, 2024). Driven by investments from both private sector and the government, the Indian Healthcare Industry is valued at US$ 372 billion and caters to a geographically, socially and culturally diverse population (Healthcare System in India, Healthcare India – IBEF, 2024). The COVID-19 pandemic highlighted the need for a well prepared and adequately staffed healthcare system to handle public health emergencies. The rising population, economic growth and rising health awareness and prevalence of chronic and lifestyle diseases driven by education and information dissemination have also led to more individuals seeking healthcare services for both preventive and curative purposes (Zobair et al., 2020). Furthermore, healthcare schemes by the Government of India (GoI) aims at improving healthcare access and delivery to all, driving the need for more healthcare providers to meet the program's objectives (Ministry of Electronics and Information Technology, 2024). As the demand for healthcare professionals grows and the need to deliver healthcare services to even the remotest areas increase, e-Health offers a solution to these challenges.

E-health services, which include mobile health, medical knowledge management and telemedicine services, use electronic tools coupled with information and communication technology (ICT) platforms to deliver the required healthcare support and services (Bailo et al., 2021). With the use of ICT platforms, it reduces the requirement of non-essential visits by patients, thereby reducing the effort by patients, doctors, healthcare staff and reduces pressure at hospital resources (Nittari et al., 2022). Telemedicine, particularly, refer to the use of devices along with technological resources to gain access to a patient and their health information to assess, evaluate and diagnose them, as well as to decide if a visit to a healthcare centre is required. Earlier, in India, telemedicine was viewed as cutting edge and experimental with only few companies providing the services. However, today it is presently developing as a revolutionary tool for convenient and specialized healthcare in areas of specializations, including Pneumonology, Cardiology, Diabetic Outpatient Clinic, Urology, Rheumatology, to name a few (Nittari et al., 2022).

Telemedicine can be broadly categorized into five types, namely, video-conference-based patient consultations using the Picture Archiving Communications System in large hospitals, multimedia transmission to provide remote services such as first-aid directions, remote home care, remote training of patients or health professionals, and online medical counselling and health information sharing (Kim et al., 2020). It enabled continuity of care to patients keeping the doctor–patient interaction alive, which would often break owing to lack of funds, lack of availability of doctors, lack of resources at the hospital, etc. (Verma et al., 2021). Telemedicine has enormous potential in meeting the challenges of healthcare delivery to rural and remote areas besides several other applications in education, training and management in health sector. As a fast-emerging sector in India, telemedicine is getting adopted by likes of Apollo, AIIMS, Narayana Hrudayalaya, to name a few (Healthcare System in India, Healthcare India – IBEF, 2024). Virtual care, constituting tele-consult, tele-pathology, tele-radiology and e-pharmacy, is experiencing a stimulus in India with major hospitals adopting telemedicine services and fostering several Public–Private Partnerships (PPPs) (Healthcare System in India,

Healthcare India – IBEF, 2024). This growth is fuelled by the growth in domestic telemedicine market, which is expected to reach USD 5.5 billion by 2025 (Healthcare System in India, Healthcare India – IBEF, 2024). In a quest to further improve and ensure the penetration of healthcare services, the Ministry of Health and Family Welfare launched the e-Sanjeevani telemedicine service (MoHFW, GoI). e-Sanjeevani telemedicine services provide teleconsultations to walk-in patients at Health and Wellness Centres. It also empowers citizens to access health services in the confines of their homes through smartphones, laptops, etc. Progress in telemedicine, virtual assistants and data analytics is expected to create 2.7–3.5 million new tech jobs (MoHFW, GoI). To further enhance the functionalities of the existing telemedicine services in India, the GoI has taken several initiatives to integrate Industry 4.0 technologies. As of August 1, 2023, a total of 24.33 crore Ayushman cards have been created. The COVID-19 pandemic further fuelled the resilience of patients and professional healthcare to explore telemedicine as a way forward to achieve quality patient-centric and value-based healthcare (Verma et al., 2021). During the pandemic, the systemic use of ICT, technological infrastructure, data storage systems standardization of protocols by the GoI proved to be a boon for Indian telemedicine industry. The GoI also developed policies to prevent, detect and deter healthcare fraud and to ensure that eligible beneficiaries receive adequate treatment, through the use of Artificial Intelligence (AI) and machine learning (ML) (Rajendran & Chandrashekar, 2025). In a push to develop digital health ecosystem in India, Prime Minister Mr. Narendra Modi launched the Ayushman Bharat Digital Mission (GoI, Minister of Health and Family Welfare, 2021). The mission will connect the digital health solutions of hospitals across the country. Under this, every citizen will now get a digital health ID, and their health records are digitally protected using Blockchain technology, AI and ML. Also, the use of virtual assistants and data analytics in tele-medicine is expected to create 2.7–3.5 million new tech jobs. NITI Aayog in its report has also suggested that AI, wearables and mobile technologies along with Internet of Things (IoT) offer several avenues for investment (Ministry of Electronics and Information Technology, 2024). These devices have found applications in diagnosing and detecting possible lung abnormalities in Pneumatology, detect atrial fibrillation and early diagnosis of heart failure in Cardiology and provide e-prescriptions, e-consultation, diagnosis and home therapy instructions (Nittari et al., 2022). These technologies provide immense advantages to the healthcare industry in terms of remote monitoring, predictive analytics, data integration, population health management, collaboration and round the clock telepresence, thereby reducing burden on the healthcare resources. Despite immense advantages, their application is hindered by several barriers that are present in their implementation. The present study analyses these barriers which stall the implementation of Industry 4.0 technologies in telemedicine in context of Indian sub-continent. The rest of the study is organized as follows: Section "Industry 4.0 Adoption in Telemedicine in India" describes the Industry 4.0 adoption level in telemedicine in India which is followed by section "Barriers Hindering Implementation of Industry 4.0 in Telemedicine" that identifies the barriers hindering the Industry 4.0 adoption in telemedicine, especially in context of Indian sub-continent. These barriers are further analyzed in Section "Interpretive Structural Modelling" (ISM) considering the organizational, technological, regulatory, cultural, privacy, educational and economic issues. The Section "Result and Discussions" elaborates upon the results followed by Section "Implications, Conclusions and Future Recommendations" that concludes the chapter with theoretical and policy implications, limitations and future recommendations.

Industry 4.0 Adoption in Telemedicine in India

The Industry 4.0 concept has attracted global interest across several industries as it provides businesses with the ability to create smart industrial environments where systems, smart devices and products communicate and share information in real time. The introduction of Industry 4.0 yields the convergence of fragmented business systems and partners to form a value chain that self-adjusts, generates and shares information resulting in seamless integration and communication in delivering premium operations. Industry 4.0 framework is made of vertical, end-to-end and horizontal integration layers (Akhtar et al., 2024). The vertical integration connects the organization's decision-making with the shop floor level whereas the horizontal integration creates a value chain of business partners. This integration layers create foundation for implementing such technologies as Big Data and AI. Combined, these integration layers and technologies create Cyber Physical Systems (CPS), which is the heart of Industry 4.0. The Industry 4.0 finds applications in Laboratory Management Systems (LMS), Plant Information Management System (PIMS), Logistics, Safe Health Environment, sales and distribution planning, material management, production planning, quality management, plant maintenance, human resource management and financial accounting to name a few (Telukdarie & Sishi, 2018). Among these, Industry 4.0 has been influential in changing patterns of human work characterized by the emergence of remote medicine (telemedicine), biotechnology, data automation and AI (Ajmera & Jain, 2019). Telemedicine is remote monitoring and treatment of patients through sensors connected to the internet. The sensor can be placed in a device that is connected to a telecommunications device. Telemedicine is a long-distance health service using communication and information technology that can provide healthcare solutions for remote areas where health facilities are inadequate. The Industry 4.0 provides numerous applications for improving access, efficiency and quality of care of healthcare industry in general and telemedicine in particular as tabulated in Table 3.1.

Integration of Industry 4.0 technologies (Table 3.1) can further benefit the patients and enhance the services provided by the healthcare professionals, for example, improved access through the use of VR and AR that can provide medical training to professionals in remote areas. Drones and robots can deliver supplies and provide consultations in regions with limited healthcare infrastructure. Digital twins and AI can optimize treatment plans and predict health issues before they become critical. Surgical robots and AR, on the other hand, can enhance the precision of medical procedures, reducing errors and improving patient outcomes. Despite posing many advantages, its implementation has been

Table 3.1. Industry 4.0 Technologies and Their Applications in Telemedicine.

Industry 4.0 Technology	Definition	Author (Year)	Application in Telemedicine
Internet of Things (IoT devices)	Network of interconnected physical devices using sensors and other technologies to collect and exchange data over internet, enabling interaction with each other and their environments.	Thakur et al. (2023)	• Enable real-time monitoring of vital signs, remote health assessments. • Provide healthcare professionals with immediate insights into a patient's condition, allowing accurate responses.
Artificial intelligence (AI)	Simulation of human intelligence by machines. These processes include learning (acquiring information and rules), reasoning (using rules to reach approximate or definite conclusions) and self-correction.	Russell and Norvig (2016); Ajmera and Jain (2019); Khanuja et al. (2024)	• Analyze vast amounts of medical data, offering doctors valuable insights and predictions that aid in diagnosis and treatment planning.
Big data analytics	Process of examining large and varied datasets to uncover hidden patterns, unknown correlations, market trends, customer preferences and other business information.	Chen et al. (2014); Ajmera and Jain (2019); Khanuja et al. (2024)	• Identifying trends and patterns within patient data for more personalized and preventive healthcare approaches. • Detect early warning signs of diseases through analysis of large amount of varied data, track the effectiveness of treatments and predict outcomes.
Cyber physical systems (CPS)	Integrations of computation, networking and physical processes. Embedded computers and networks monitor and control	Rajkumar et al. (2010); Ajmera and Jain (2019); Khanuja et al. (2024)	• Enhance the security and privacy of telemedicine platforms, ensuring that sensitive patient

(Continued)

Table 3.1. *(Continued)*

Industry 4.0 Technology	Definition	Author (Year)	Application in Telemedicine
	the physical processes, usually with feedback loops where physical processes affect computations and vice versa.		information is safeguarded against cyber threats.
Virtual reality (VR)	VR is a three-dimensional computer-generated simulated environment, which attempts to replicate real world or imaginary environments and interactions, thereby supporting work, education, recreation and health.	Abbas et al. (2023); Khanuja et al. (2024)	• Create immersive training environments for medical professionals. • Used in physical therapy and rehabilitation, providing virtual environments where patients can perform exercises to recover motor skills. • Provide medical health treatment for creating controlled environments for exposure therapy, helping patients with PTSD, anxiety and phobias.
Augmented reality (AR)	Superimposition of digital imagery onto a real-world view, most commonly used currently in the form of mobile gaming and social medial applications.	Abbas et al. (2023); Khanuja et al. (2024)	• Real-time guidance to healthcare providers in remote locations, overlaying instructions or anatomical information during surgeries or medical procedures. • Help explain medical conditions and treatments to patients by visualizing complex medical information in an understandable format.

			• Provide assistance in diagnostic assistance for enhancing imaging techniques.
Mixed reality	Mixed reality (MR) is considered a more advanced development of AR technology whereby the digital content is anchored in the 3D space and can be physically manipulated in three dimensions by the user.	Abbas et al. (2023)	
Digital twins	Virtual representation of a physical object or system across its lifecycle, using real-time data to enable understanding, learning and reasoning.	Grieves and Vickers (2017); Khanuja et al. (2024)	• Create and simulate to predict health outcomes based on individual data. • It can continuously monitor patient health, providing real-time data and predictive insights to healthcare providers. • Furthermore, surgeons can continuously monitor patient health, providing real-time data and predictive insights to healthcare providers.
Drones	Drones, or unmanned aerial vehicles (UAVs), are aircraft without a human pilot on board. They are used for various purposes, including aerial photography, agriculture, delivery services and surveillance.	Floreano and Wood (2015); Khanuja et al. (2024)	• Transport medical supplies, medications and samples to and from remote or hard-to-reach areas, ensuring timely delivery. • Provide rapid delivery of life-saving medical equipment during emergencies.

(Continued)

Table 3.1. *(Continued)*

Industry 4.0 Technology	Definition	Author (Year)	Application in Telemedicine
			• Equipped with cameras and communication tools, drones facilitate remote consultations and inspections in inaccessible regions.
Robots	Programmable machines capable of carrying out a series of actions autonomously or semi-autonomously.	Siciliano et al. (2008); Ajmera and Jain (2019); Khanuja et al. (2024)	• Robotic systems can assist in minimally invasive surgeries, offering high precision and reduced recovery times for patients. • Equipped with telepresence capabilities, robots can facilitate consultations between doctors and patients, particularly in remote or underserved areas. • Physical therapy, assisting patients with exercises and movements and providing companionship and monitoring for elderly or disabled individuals.

Source: Compiled by authors from various sources.

identified to be difficult and has received limited success which points toward several barriers in its implementation. The following section discusses and analyses these barriers in detail.

Barriers Hindering Implementation of Industry 4.0 in Telemedicine

The rising population, economic growth and rising health awareness and prevalence of chronic and lifestyle diseases driven by education and information dissemination have also led to more individuals seeking healthcare services for both preventive and curative purposes (Zobair et al., 2020). Telemedicine has helped in the healthcare benefits to reach every corner of the Indian sub-continent, which can be further enhanced with Industry 4.0. Industry 4.0 makes telemedicine efficient, cost-effective and user friendly and brings greater applications. Despite the advantages, the usage of Industry 4.0 in telemedicine is hindered by several barriers (Akhtar et al., 2024). The barriers are identified from the literature and refined after discussions with the healthcare professionals from India. Eleven barriers are identified after these discussions which are listed as follows:

(1) *Improper Allocation of Resources (AR):* Small healthcare providers often face financial constraints, making it challenging to invest in advanced technologies like AI, IoT and data analytics. These technologies, though crucial, require substantial investment in infrastructure, training and ongoing support. The providers struggle to scale and optimize telemedicine solutions, limiting their reach and effectiveness. Additionally, scarcity of skilled human resources exacerbates the problem, hindering the sustainable integration of these technologies into healthcare systems (Akhtar et al., 2024).

(2) *Fear of Health Staff Toward Emerging Technology (FH):* Fear and low motivation among healthcare staff to embrace emerging technologies represent a significant barrier to Industry 4.0 implementation in telemedicine. The shift toward advanced technologies, like AI, IoT and big data analytics, requires new skills and a willingness to adapt. However, without adequate training, support, and incentives, healthcare workers may feel overwhelmed or threatened by these changes, leading to resistance (Venkataraman et al., 2024).

(3) *Lack of Government Support (LG):* Successful deployment of advanced technologies, like AI, IoT and big data analytics, requires strong governmental leadership and policy backing. This includes financial investment, regulatory frameworks and infrastructure development. The absence of supportive policies and incentives results in misdirection, lack of funding and coordination, which can lead to fragmented efforts and stalled progress. This can discourage private sector investment and innovation, further slowing down their integration and limiting their potential to improve healthcare outcomes, especially in underserved areas (Akhtar et al., 2024).

(4) *High Cost of Industry 4.0 Implementation (HC):* The advanced technologies require substantial financial investments in infrastructure, hardware, software and ongoing maintenance. Many healthcare providers, particularly in resource-poor settings, struggle to afford these costs, limiting the scalability and reach of telemedicine services. Additionally, the initial investment is often seen as risky, with uncertain returns, which further deters adoption, restricting access to cutting-edge healthcare solutions and widening the gap between well-funded and under-resourced healthcare providers (Mishra & Singh, 2022; Venkataraman et al., 2024).

(5) *Digital Divide Among Demographics (DD):* Many regions lack access to reliable internet, modern devices and digital literacy, which are essential for utilizing advanced technologies like AI, IoT, and data analytics. This disparity in digital infrastructure exacerbates healthcare inequalities, limits the reach of these solutions and hampers the uniform application of telemedicine, leading to a wider gap between urban and rural healthcare (Venkataraman et al., 2024).

(6) *Legislation Differences Across States (LD):* Each state may have its own set of regulations governing telemedicine practices, data privacy and technology use, leading to inconsistencies in how these services are deployed. This lack of uniformity creates challenges in standardizing telemedicine practices across the country, making it difficult to scale solutions nationwide. Providers navigate complex regulatory landscape, which slows implementation, increase costs and lead to fragmented services ultimately limiting the potential of telemedicine to deliver consistent, high-quality care across India (Ajmera & Jain, 2019).

(7) *Fraud and Abuse (FA):* Issues such as billing fraud, where providers might overcharge or falsely claim for services, undermine trust and financial integrity. Additionally, unauthorized access to patient data increases the risk of identity theft and privacy violations. These concerns necessitate robust security measures and compliance with stringent regulations to safeguard sensitive information. Ensuring proper authentication, monitoring for suspicious activities and implementing comprehensive fraud prevention strategies are crucial to mitigating these risks and maintaining the credibility and safety of telemedicine platforms (Mishra & Singh, 2022; Venkataraman et al., 2024).

(8) *Concerns About Patient Privacy (CP):* Protecting patient data and personal information is essential for maintaining trust and meeting legal and ethical standards. Telemedicine involves transmitting sensitive health information over digital networks, raising risks of data breaches and unauthorized access. Ensuring robust encryption, secure access controls and compliance with privacy regulations is crucial. These measures help prevent data misuse and reassure patients that their information is handled with the utmost confidentiality (Ajmera & Jain, 2019).

(9) *Data Inaccuracy (DI):* Data inaccuracy is a critical concern in telemedicine, as it can lead to misdiagnosis or inappropriate treatment. The risk arises from various factors, including errors in data entry, transmission issues or

limitations in the technology used. Inaccurate or incomplete data can impair diagnostic accuracy and treatment decisions, potentially compromising patient safety. Ensuring the integrity of data involves implementing rigorous validation processes, regular system checks and training for healthcare providers on accurate data handling (Ajmera & Jain, 2019).

(10) *Cultural Beliefs (CB):* Many cultures have a strong preference for face-to-face interactions with healthcare providers, valuing personal connection and trust in medical consultations. This deep-rooted preference can create resistance to remote consultations and AI-driven diagnostics, which may be perceived as impersonal or less reliable. Such cultural resistance can slow the integration of telemedicine innovations into mainstream healthcare, as patients and providers may be reluctant to embrace technologies that deviate from traditional practices.

Interpretive Structural Modelling

ISM identifies and helps understand the interrelationships among various variables of the system (here, barriers) (Sushil, 2012; Warfield, 1992). Not all barriers operate independently; some may be dependent on others or act as enablers. ISM allows for a structured exploration of how barriers influence one another, providing deeper insights into their underlying dynamics. Through ISM, barriers can be organized into a hierarchical structure, revealing which barriers are foundational and which are resultant. This hierarchy helps in identifying root barriers that, if addressed, could mitigate or even eliminate other dependent barriers, making the problem-solving process more efficient. By modelling barriers using ISM, it becomes clearer which barriers should be prioritized. Barriers that are more central or have greater influence on the system can be identified as key points of intervention. This enables organizations to focus their efforts on the most impactful areas, ensuring that their resources are utilized effectively. The ISM model can serve as a communication tool, helping stakeholders understand the complexity and interconnections of barriers. This shared understanding can foster collaboration and consensus on the most effective strategies to overcome the challenges. The steps involved in developing an ISM model are depicted in Fig. 3.1.

Post the identification of the variables for the study, the next step is to develop a structural self-interaction matrix (SSIM) (Fig. 3.1). It allows for pair-wise comparison between the variables. The pair-wise comparisons are performed using the terms used in Table 3.2, and SSIM is tabulated in Table 3.3.

At the third step of ISM, the SSIM is converted to initial reachability matrix (IRM) which is a binary matrix. For this purpose, the symbols used in the SSIM are substituted by 0 and 1 based on the relation between the variables depicted by the pair-wise comparisons in SSIM. The rules for conversion are discussed below. The IRM is depicted in Table 3.4.

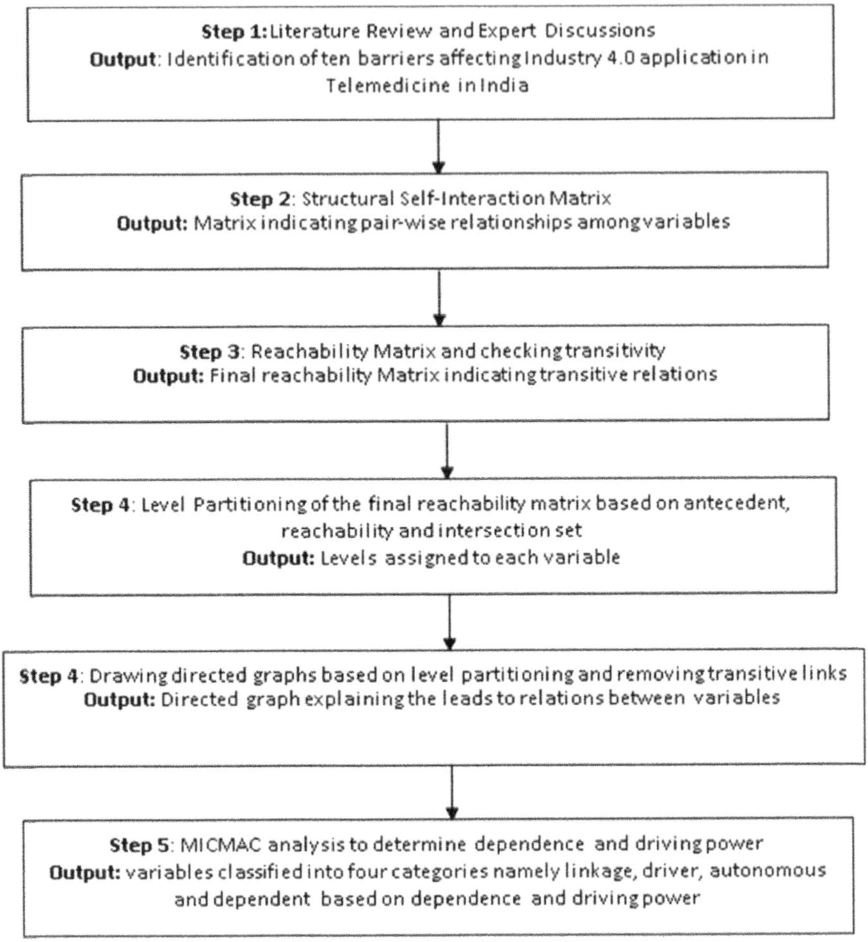

Fig. 3.1. Methodology Adopted in the Present Study. *Source:* Author's own work, adapted from Sushil (2012).

- If the (i, j) entry in the SSIM is a V, the (i, j) entry in the reachability matrix becomes 1 and the (j, i) entry becomes 0.
- If the (i, j) entry in the SSIM is an A, the (i, j) entry in the reachability matrix becomes 0 and the (j, i) entry becomes 1.
- If the (i, j) entry in the SSIM is an X, both the (i, j) entry and the (j, i) entry of the reachability matrix become 1.
- If the (i, j) entry of the SSIM is a 0, then both the (i, j) and (j, i) entries of the reachability matrix become 0.

Table 3.2. Terms Used in ISM Pair-wise Comparison.

Term Used to Denote Pair-wise Comparison	Significance
V	Variable 'i' influences variable 'j'
A	Variable 'j' influences variable 'i'
X	Variable 'i' and 'j' both influence each other
O	Variable 'i' and 'j' are unrelated

Source: Author's own work, adapted from Sushil (2012).

Table 3.3. Structural Self-Interaction Matrix.

	CP	DI	LG	AR	DD	HC	LD	CB	FH	FA
FA	A	A	A	A	X	A	O	O	V	
FH	O	O	A	A	X	A	O	O		
CB	O	O	A	A	V	A	V			
LD	O	O	A	A	V	A				
HC	V	V	V	A	V					
DD	A	A	A	A						
AR	V	V	V							
LG	A	A								
DI	X									
CP										

Source: Compiled after discussion from experts.

The gaps in the opinions provided by experts are filled by incorporating transitivity in the IRM. Transitive links are identified by checking how one variable leads to another. For example, if A leads to B and B leads to C, then A must lead to C, and if the relation between A and C is 0, it must be replaced by 1. The final reachability matrix is tabulated in the table. The transitive links are depicted with *. The Table 3.5 of FRM also tabulates the driving power and dependence of each variable. The driving power is the ability of an element to affect or influence other elements whereas the dependence reflects the degree to which the element is influenced or affected by other elements in the system. The driving power of a variable is obtained by adding all the row '1' whereas the dependence of the variable is obtained by adding all the column '1'.

The final reachability matrix is then used to obtain the reachability set, the antecedent set and the intersection set. The antecedent set for an element consists of itself and other elements that may affect it, while the reachability set for the element

Table 3.4. Initial Reachability Matrix.

	FA	FH	CB	LD	HC	DD	AR	LG	DI	CP
FA	1	1	0	0	0	1	0	0	0	0
FH	0	1	0	0	0	1	0	0	0	0
CB	0	0	1	1	0	1	0	0	0	0
LD	0	0	0	1	0	1	0	0	0	0
HC	1	1	1	1	1	1	0	1	1	1
DD	1	1	0	0	0	1	0	0	0	0
AR	1	1	1	1	1	1	1	1	1	1
LG	1	1	1	1	0	1	0	1	0	0
DI	1	0	0	0	0	1	0	1	1	1
CP	1	0	0	0	0	1	0	1	1	1

Source: Compiled after discussion from experts.

consists of itself and the other elements that it may affect them. The intersection set for the element then comprises of all elements which are common to its reachability and the intersection set. The elements at the top of the hierarchy are the ones for which the reachability and the intersection sets are same. These factors would not

Table 3.5. Final Reachability Matrix.

	FA	FH	CB	LD	HC	DD	AR	LG	DI	CP	Driving Power
FA	1	1	0	0	0	1	0	0	0	0	3
FH	1*	1	0	0	0	1	0	0	0	0	3
CB	1*	1*	1	1	0	1	0	0	0	0	5
LD	1*	1*	0	1	0	1	0	0	0	0	4
HC	1	1	1	1	1	1	0	1	1	1	9
DD	1	1	0	0	0	1	0	0	0	0	3
AR	1	1	1	1	1	1	1	1	1	1	10
LG	1	1	1	1	0	1	0	1	0	0	6
DI	1	1*	1*	1*	0	1	0	1	1	1	8
CP	1	1*	1*	1*	0	1	0	1	1	1	8
Dependence Power	10	10	6	7	2	10	1	5	4	4	

Source: Obtained after incorporating transitivity.

Note: The transitive links are depicted with *.

Table 3.6. Level Partitioning of the Variables

Element	Reachability Set	Antecedent Set	Intersection Set	Level
FA	1,2,6	1,2,3,4,5,6,7,8,9,10	1,2,6	I
FH	1,2,6	1,2,3,4,5,6,7,8,9,10	1,2,6	I
CB	1,2,3,4,6	3,5,7,8,9,10	3	III
LD	1,2,4,5	3,4,5,7,8,9,10	4,5	II
HC	1,2,3,4,5,6,8,9,10	5,7	5	VI
DD	1,2,6	1,2,3,4,5,6,7,8,9,10	1,2,6	I
AR	1,2,3,4,5,6,7,8,9,10	7	7	VII
LG	1,2,3,4,6,8	5,7,8,9,10	8	IV
DI	1,2,3,4,6,8,9,10	5,7,9,10	9,10	V
CP	1,2,3,4,6,8,9,10	5,7,9,10	9,10	V

Source: From Final reachability matrix.

lead to other factors above their own level in the ISM hierarchy. After determining the top-level factors, they were removed from the level partitioning process. This process was repeated until the level of all factors was identified (Table 3.6).

Result and Discussions

The present study sets out to identify the barriers that hinder the implementation of Industry 4.0 in telemedicine sector of India and assess the structural linkages between them. The present study sets out to achieve this objective using ISM. In its first phase, the study identified 10 barriers with the help of review of existing study and interviews with experts. These 10 barriers are improper allocation of resources, fear of health staff toward emerging technology, lack of government support, high cost of industry 4.0 implementation, digital divide among demographics, legislation differences across states, fraud and abuse, concerns about patient privacy, data inaccuracy and cultural beliefs (Ajmera & Jain, 2019; Akhtar et al., 2024; Khanuja et al., 2024; Venkataraman et al., 2024).

In the second phase, each expert contacted in the first phase performed a pair-wise comparison to assess the influence of one variable over the another resulting in SSIM depicted in Table 3.3. The SSIM is converted into binary form using the IRM (Table 3.4), and the transitive links between the variables is depicted in final reachability matrix (Table 3.5) along with the driving power and dependence for each variable. Based on the driving power and the dependence, the level partitioning for each variable is performed (Table 3.6), which gives seven levels as depicted in Fig. 3.2.

The hierarchical model in figure tells that improper allocation of resources (AR) (Variable 7) is a significant barrier for Industry 4.0 implementation in

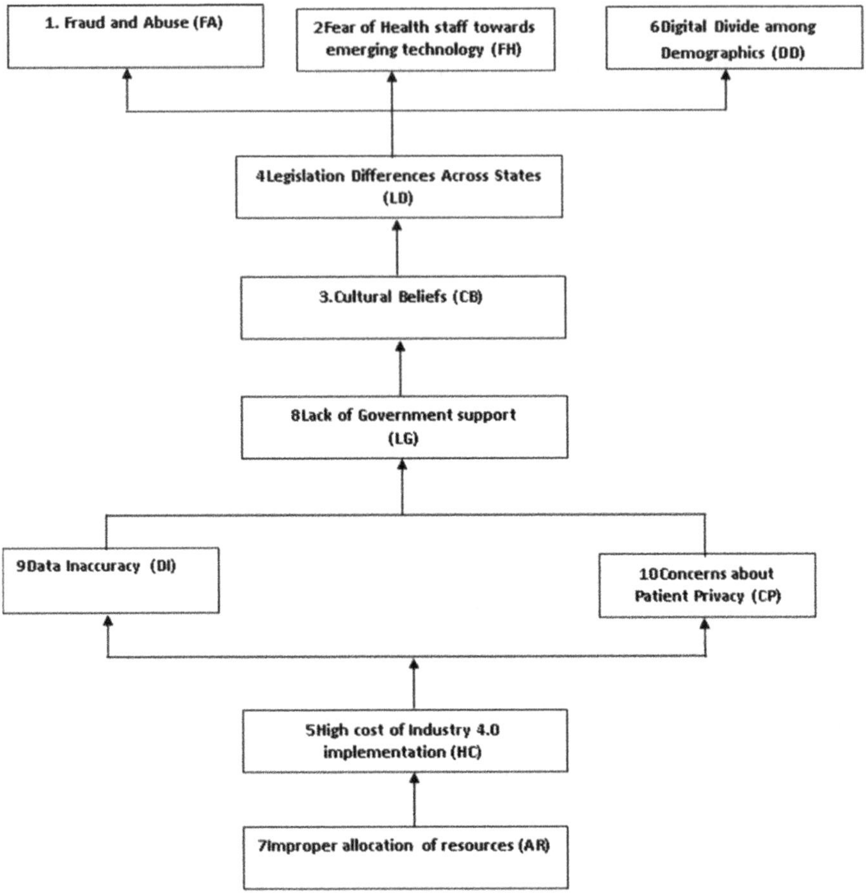

Fig. 3.2. ISM Digraph Depicting Leads to Relations Between Barriers of Industry 4.0 Adoption in Telemedicine. *Source:* From Table 3.6.

Indian telemedicine industry as it comes at the base of the hierarchy (Charan et al., 2008; Sushil, 2012). The unsuccessful implementation of Industry 4.0 results in fraud and abuse of the technology when implemented (Variable 1), fear among healthcare workers toward emerging technologies (Variable 2) and digital divide (Variable 6). These are the ultimate causes of unsuccessful implementation of Industry 4.0 technologies in telemedicine, as they appear at the top of the ISM hierarchy.

The improper allocation of resources (Variable 7) leads to high cost of Industry 4.0 technology implementation in telemedicine (Variable 5). Improper allocation of resources can lead to financial inefficiencies, making it harder for healthcare organizations to afford the high costs of Industry 4.0 technologies. The higher costs of may deter healthcare organizations in investing in Industry 4.0 technologies and have greater reliance on outdated systems resulting in data inaccuracy (Variable 9) and chances of compromise on consumer privacy (Variable 10).

Higher costs of technology and possible negative repercussions of data inaccuracy (Variable 9) and compromise on consumer privacy (Variable 10) often results in government perceiving a high financial burden on public healthcare systems (Variable 8). Often in developing countries like India, the governments may view these technologies to have a significant financial burden given the limited advantages from their implementation. Without adequate government support, telemedicine services may only be available to those who can afford them, leaving rural or economically disadvantaged citizens with limited access. This can create a perception that Industry 4.0 technologies like telemedicine exacerbate inequality, fostering resentment and negative beliefs that these advancements are designed for the elite rather than for the broader population (Variable 3). With negative beliefs from the citizens regarding Industry 4.0 technologies, local governments may face pressures from citizens to impose restrictive legislation on telemedicine. These states might pass laws that slow down or limit the adoption of telemedicine technologies, driven by the cultural resistance of their populations (Variable 4). The legislation difference across states (Variable 4) in Industry 4.0 implementation may lead to inconsistent regulatory oversight causing fraud and abuse of technology (Variable 1), create perception of risk and uncertainty causing fear of health staff toward emerging technology (Variable 2) and digital divide causing unequal access to digital infrastructure (Variable 6).

Implications, Conclusion and Future Recommendations

The present study focuses on identification and modelling of barriers that hinder the implementation of Industry 4.0 technologies in telemedicine industry in India. Such a study is important in the present context as the rising population, economic growth and rising health awareness puts pressures on existing medical infrastructure motivating the Government to reach a wider population. E-Health in this context provides a solution to these challenges with Industry 4.0 providing an added advantage of efficiency, accessibility and quality of healthcare services, leading to a transformative impact on how telemedicine and e-health are delivered. However, in the context of developing nations like India, there are several barriers which hinder its implementation. It is important to identify these barriers, understand their structural linkages and analyze how they lead to each other. The interaction between barriers and their structural linkages shall help managers in prioritization and supports better decision-making. The present study identifies these barriers with the help of literature review and discussions with experts from health industry. The discussion resulted in identification of 10 barriers, namely improper allocation of resources, fear of health staff toward emerging technology, lack of government support, high cost of Industry 4.0 implementation, digital divide among demographics, legislation differences across states, fraud and abuse, concerns about patient privacy, data inaccuracy and cultural beliefs.

The ISM models the structural linkages between the barriers and explains the leads to relations between them. The ISM model generates a digraph explaining how each variable explains the other variable. We find that improper allocation of resources (Barrier 7) is a significant barrier in context of Industry 4.0 implementation in telemedicine in context of developing nation like India. This barrier is significant since it is at the bottom of the hierarchical model and leads to other barriers. To address improper allocation of resources in the implementation of Industry 4.0 in telemedicine, a data-driven, needs-based approach should be adopted (Akhtar et al., 2024). Comprehensive need assessments can help identify areas that require the most attention, ensuring resources are directed toward high-priority regions, facilities or populations.

The improper allocation results in higher costs of implementation thereby hindering Industry 4.0 technologies implementation (Barrier 5). Industry 4.0 implementation in telemedicine for Indian sub-continent, hence, requires extensive IT infrastructure that requires regular maintenance and serviced regularly as any disruption in the integrated process will disrupt the entire system thereby reducing data inaccuracy and concerns about patient privacy (Barrier 9 and 10). Leveraging analytics and predictive tools can optimize the distribution of funds, technology and training, avoiding wasteful spending (Barrier 3) (Khanuja et al., 2024). Additionally, regular audits and performance tracking can help reassess resource use and adjust allocation strategies in real time to ensure that the telemedicine infrastructure is both efficient and effective. The fear of job disruption among health employees, special training can enhance their skills. Given that the fear of job disruption arises from uneven regulations across the nation, a uniform training policy must be developed for the health professionals (Barrier 1, 2 and 6).

The present study is a preliminary study into the identification and modelling of barriers hindering Industry 4.0 adoption in telemedicine industry in India. The rigour of the present study can be further enhanced by incorporating fuzziness into ISM. Additionally, Cross-Impact Matrix Multiplication Applied to Classification or MICMAC analysis can help managers in obtaining the autonomous, driving, dependent and linkage variables, which can help managers in prioritizing the actions taken on the barriers. The present study being a preliminary one, the sample of healthcare experts was small and limited to northern region only. The pair-wise comparison is also subjective in nature and may differ with change in panel. Future studies may utilize variance based studies to make the model more robust and may be performed in other developing nations, like Brazil, South Africa and Sri Lanka, to name a few ((Tortorella et al., 2023).

References

Abbas, J. R., O'Connor, A., Ganapathy, E., Isba, R., Payton, A., McGrath, B., Tolly, N., & Bruce, I. A. (2023). What is virtual reality? A healthcare-focused systematic review of definitions. *Health Policy and Technology*, *12*(2), 100741.

Ajmera, P., & Jain, V. (2019). Modelling the barriers of Health 4.0–The fourth healthcare industrial revolution in India by TISM. *Operations Management Research*, *12*(3–4), 129–145. https://doi.org/10.1007/s12063-019-00143-x

Akhtar, M. N., Haleem, A., Javaid, M., & Vasif, M. (2024). Understanding Medical 4.0 implementation through enablers: An integrated multi-criteria decision-making approach. *Informatics and Health*, *1*(1), 29–39. https://doi.org/10.1016/j.infoh.2023.11.001

Bailo, P., Gibelli, F., Blandino, A., Piccinini, A., Ricci, G., Sirignano, A., & Zoja, R. (2021). Telemedicine applications in the era of COVID-19: Telesurgery issues. *International Journal of Environmental Research and Public Health*, *19*(1), 323.

Charan, P., Shankar, R., & Baisya, R. K. (2008). Analysis of interactions among the variables of supply chain performance measurement system implementation. *Business Process Management Journal*, *14*(4), 512–529.

Chen, M., Mao, S., & Liu, Y. (2014). Big data: A survey. *Mobile Networks and Applications*, *19*, 171–209.

Floreano, D., & Wood, R. J. (2015). Science, technology and the future of small autonomous drones. *Nature*, *521*(7553), 460–466.

Grieves, M., & Vickers, J. (2017). Digital twin: Mitigating unpredictable, undesirable emergent behavior in complex systems. In *Transdisciplinary perspectives on complex systems: New findings and approaches* (pp. 85–113). Springer.

Healthcare System in India, Healthcare India – IBEF. (2024). *India brand equity foundation*. https://www.ibef.org/industry/healthcare-india

Khanuja, A., Sreedharan, R., & Sharma, N. (2024). Bibliometric analysis on usage of Industry 4.0 technologies in healthcare. *The TQM Journal*. https://doi.org/10.1108/TQM-08-2023-0252

Kim, D. W., Choi, J. Y., & Han, K. H. (2020). Risk management-based security evaluation model for telemedicine systems. *BMC Medical Informatics and Decision Making*, *20*, 1–14.

Ministry of Electronics and Information Technology. (2024). *Annual report (2024–25)*. Pib.gov. https://www.meity.gov.in/static/uploads/2024/12/10fcadec462c330211502fed3d24ea83.pdf

Minister of Health and Family Welfare (2021). Prime Minister of India launches countrywide Ayushman Bharat Digital Mission. *Press Information Bureau*. https://www.pib.gov.in/PressReleaseIframePage.aspx?PRID=1758511

Mishra, V., & Singh, J. (2022). Health technology assessment of telemedicine interventions in diabetes management: Evidence from UAE. *FIIB Business Review*. https://doi.org/10.1177/23197145221130651

Nittari, G., Savva, D., Tomassoni, D., Tayebati, S. K., & Amenta, F. (2022). Telemedicine in the COVID-19 era: A narrative review based on current evidence. *International Journal of Environmental Research and Public Health*, *19*(9), 5101.

Rajendran, S. R., & Chandrashekar, B. S. (2025). The essence of telemedicine in Health 4.0: A futuristic approach. In *Digitalization and the transformation of the healthcare sector* (pp. 331–358). IGI Global Scientific Publishing.

Rajkumar, R., Lee, I., Sha, L., & Stankovic, J. (2010, June). Cyber-physical systems: The next computing revolution. In *Proceedings of the 47th design automation conference* (pp. 731–736). https://doi.org/10.1145/1837274.1837461

Russell, S. J., & Norvig, P. (2016). *Artificial intelligence: A modern approach*. Pearson.

Siciliano, B., Khatib, O., & Kröger, T. (Eds.). (2008). *Springer handbook of robotics* (Vol. 200). Springer.

Sushil. (2012). Interpreting the interpretive structural model. *Global Journal of Flexible Systems Management*, *13*(2), 87–106. https://doi.org/10.1007/s40171-012-0008-3

Telukdarie, A., & Sishi, M. N. (2018, December). Enterprise definition for Industry 4.0. In *2018 IEEE international conference on industrial engineering and engineering management (IEEM)* (pp. 849–853). IEEE.

Thakur, K., Pathan, A. S. K., & Ismat, S. (2023). Internet of things (IoT). In *Emerging ICT technologies and cybersecurity: From AI and ML to other futuristic technologies* (pp. 165–183). Springer Nature.

Tortorella, G. L., Prashar, A., Antony, J., Fogliatto, F. S., Gonzalez, V., & Godinho Filho, M. (2023). Industry 4.0 adoption for healthcare supply chain performance during COVID-19 pandemic in Brazil and India: The mediating role of resilience abilities development. *Operations Management Research*, *17*(2), 389–405. https://doi.org/10.1007/s12063-023-00366-z

Venkataraman, A., Fatma, N., Edirippulige, S., & Ramamohan, V. (2024). Facilitators and barriers for telemedicine systems in India from multiple stakeholder perspectives and settings: A systematic review. *Telemedicine and e-Health*, *30*(5), 1341–1356.

Verma, V., Krishnan, V., & Verma, C. (2021). Telemedicine in India - An investment of technology for a digitized healthcare industry: A systematic review. *Revista Română de Informatică Şi Automatică*, *31*(4), 33–44. https://doi.org/10.33436/v31i4y202103

Warfield, J. N. (1992). Mathematical bibliography for interpretive structural modelling. https://citeseerx.ist.psu.edu/document?repid=rep1&type=pdf&doi=ac935b2d668e56a0a82d3ef49fee9c363b74f0f5

Zobair, K. M., Sanzogni, L., & Sandhu, K. (2020). Telemedicine healthcare service adoption barriers in rural Bangladesh. *Australasian Journal of Information Systems, 24*.

Chapter 4

Precision Medicine: Market and Its Potential in the Healthcare Industry

Meenal Kulkarni[a] *and Moumita Sharma*[b]

[a]Symbiosis Institute of Health Sciences, Symbiosis International (Deemed University), Pune, India
[b]MIT-World Peace University, India

Abstract

Customized treatment plans based on environmental, lifestyle, and genetic principles are presently revolutionizing health care. This chapter traces the evolution of precision medicine (PM), emphasizing some of the basic principles and ever-expanding impact that the PM field exerts on modern-day medical practice. PM aims at maximizing therapeutic response while minimizing side effects and improving diagnostic accuracy, which can potentially yield benefits for the individual patient and the healthcare systems in general. With a global push for commercialization, technological advancement, and innovation funding from major industries, PM has been growing at an accelerated rate. The insights on market segmentation and regional analyses show the differences in growth patterns and investment opportunities among diverse healthcare systems. Advanced technologies, such as Artificial Intelligence (AI), omics sciences, implantable biosensors, big data analytics, and Internet of Things (IoT), contribute substantially to PM. Enabled by these advancements, precision health care now has new possibilities with data-driven decision-making, predictive analytics, and customized therapeutics. The journey into the future of PM will witness the formulation of novel treatments based on advances in personalized drug development, aided diagnostics, and genetic discoveries; the flipside of the PM story will be the data security, ethical issues, and regulatory compliance that must be looked into to ensure its long-standing acceptance. This chapter studies the commercial dynamics, technological advancements, and possible future directions in PM, and these elements are vital for every stakeholder willing to expedite improvements in patient outcomes and individualized health care.

Digital Transformation and Artificial Intelligence for Operational Excellence in Healthcare, 65–83

doi:10.1108/978-1-83662-314-420251013

Keywords: Precision medicine; personalized treatment; Artificial Intelligence in medicine; big data and IoT in health care; healthcare market trends; future of healthcare innovation

Introduction

Precision medicine (PM) denotes the use of a medical model that tailors healthcare treatments based on the individual's genetic makeup, environment, and lifestyle, offering more targeted, effective, personalized and thus a precise treatment. Additionally, PM leverages Artificial Intelligence (AI) for studying large volumes of genetic, clinical, and lifestyle data that offer more personalized treatment plans. The integration of Electronic Health Records (EHR), wearables, and genomic databases contributes to the massive volume of data that AI and machine learning (ML) algorithms can process, making PM more feasible and scalable.

Evolution of PM

Two staff reporters named Robert Langreth and Michael Waldholz published an article named "NEW ERA OF PERSONALIZED MEDICINE: Each Unique Genetic Profile by targeting drugs" in 1999, which came in *The Wall Street Journal* that introduced PM to the public for the first time. In the same article, single nucleotide consortium (SNP) also finds the mention of an alliance between research institutions and pharma organizations in the United States and United Kingdom with Wellcome Trust Foundation. Later, the article reappeared in "*The Oncologist.*" The article explains about poor treatment plan of existing therapy (pharmacotherapy), variability in genes, and heterogeneity in diseases and denies the "One-size-fits-all" approach. This article argues that best best-known drug for disease treatment only works for 50–60% of people. The term was again explained by "Spear et al. (2001)" based on trends in molecular medicine, which shows the connection between PM and pharmacotherapy, then it was discovered that this relation can provide treatment for every single patient (König et al., 2017). There are a number of terms exist like stratified medicine, PM, and personalized medicine, but the basic concept remains the same. In 1960s and 1970s, the principle came into existence that said "the right drug for the right patient at the right time." And now, PM uses the same concept to cure the patient (Gameiro et al., 2018), but times have changed now and we have a better understanding of the molecular understanding of physiotherapy and the mechanism of action of drugs, which is important for PM (Jørgensen, 2019).

As depicted in Fig. 4.1, medicine has evolved a lot over the period of time; in the past, medicine was practiced as per symptoms intimated/seen in patients and on physician's knowledge, but currently, the use of medicine is based on evidence using clinical trials and research. The future of medicine lies in working through

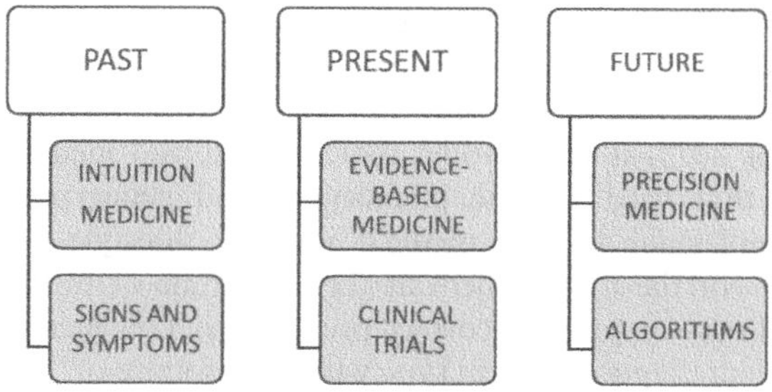

Fig. 4.1. The Precision Medicine Evolution. *Source:* Author's own source.

algorithms, connecting to the genome, epigenetics, lifestyle, and environment relating to PM (Gameiro et al., 2018).

Due to the expense and complexity of treating each patient individually, treatments are typically created for the average person. This one-size-fits-all strategy, however, is not always effective. Inappropriate medicine accounts for 30% of annual hospital admissions. Most of the time, researchers have attempted to create a precise diagnosis by including, if possible, the signs and symptoms of a particular disease or, if that is not possible, at least something that is like the disease. PM guarantees precise diagnostics by tying together accurate prognostic data with accurate therapies.

Over time, new terms have evolved describing the evolution and rise of accuracy in the field of medicine as described below (König et al., 2017):

- Individualized medicine – Unique treatment for every individual.
- Personalized medicine – Treatment prioritized to patient needs and preference.
- Precision medicine – Treatment optimized for genetics, lifestyle, and environment.
- Stratified medicine – Grouping of patients by biological features into narrow strata.

The terms personalized medicine and PM have been used interchangeably by the European Society for Medical Oncology for some time now. PM has become the favored word over customized medicine over the past eight to 10 years. Prawase Wasi proposed the phrase "precision medicine." Following that, in January 2015, former US president Barack Obama introduced the PM program, making the term of absolute preference (Jørgensen, 2019).

To prevent, detect, and cure disease, personalized medicine makes use of data about a person's genes, proteins, lifestyle, and surroundings. For instance, PM can use relevant data about a patient's tumor to help in diagnosis, treatment planning, and evaluation of the effectiveness of the treatment or prognosis. According to the US FDA website, personalized medicine, also known as PM, is a cutting-edge method of customizing illness prevention and treatment that considers individual differences in genetics, environment, and habits (Gray et al., 2018).

By the end of 2015, it was known that personalized medicine referred to a medical model that used specific phenotypes and genotypes to characterize patients (e.g., molecular testing, medical imaging, lifestyle data) for creating effective therapy for the right patient at the right time or to identify a person's propensity for illness or provide correct prevention. This means that the development of pertinent diagnostics is in sync with the promise of "omics" technology in the treatment of patients and the development and implementation of individualized therapy. Additionally, genetics, molecular medicine, pharmacology, bioinformatics, statistics, and epidemiology are all included in PM (Gómez-López et al., 2019).

Even though precision has probably always been a goal of medicine, treatment of very precise biologic abnormalities, such as specific aberrations in gene structure or regulation, transcription, or post-transcriptional molecular pathways, is referred to as PM. Therefore, patients with comparable indications and symptoms, such as a similar type of tumor, could be divided into subsets with distinctive yet very precise molecular flaws necessitating separate therapies (Jarow, 2018).

The medical field is looking for much more accurate treatment strategies. The PM approach divides people into three subpopulations according to how susceptible they are to a particular disease, develops treatments taking into account one's lifestyle, environment, and genetic variability and examines trends that can help increase the effectiveness of the treatments (Jørgensen, 2019).

Overview of PM

With age being a common factor in all of these ailments, the healthcare sector currently spends 50% of its budget on fatal illnesses like cancer, cardiovascular disease, and degenerative disorders (König et al., 2017). For targeting in a better way, the sector must focus on prediction, prevention, personalization, and participation (Jørgensen, 2019). And here "precision" is better term to refer categorization of people into subpopulations using their genetic patterns, drug response, lifestyles, and environmental and cultural factors. This does not mean unique treatment for every patient as that will be financially and technically difficult (Gameiro et al., 2018).

Recently, there has been a lot of emphasis placed on PM, which is currently popular in mainstream medicine. The focus is shifting from treating diseases to helping each patient individually using a tailored data-driven strategy, big data, and the omics revolution (Lin et al., 2017). PM is a revolution in technologies and science that also meets needs in public health services due to next-generation sequencing (NGS)'s rapid technological advances and the intense competition in molecular targeted medication exploitation. PM is therefore crucial for the healthcare system (Duffy, 2016).

This approach of PM will allow healthcare professionals to make more accurate diagnoses and create professional treatment plans (Kosorok & Laber, 2019). Anciently, drug development practices were passive, and patients had to wait for symptoms to show for getting cured or treated as environmental and genetic factors are responsible mostly for serious diseases such as Alzheimer's disease and cancer (Jørgensen, 2019). For these kinds of diseases, the leading cause of death is not fully discovered which then led to imprecise and unsuccessful treatment. The PM approach is crucial for moving away from "one-size-fits-all" approaches as it will offer a direction to reduce side effects, treatment cost and ineffective treatment regimens (Gameiro et al., 2018).

Numerous potentially targetable proteins and pathways that are activated by gene mutations, methylation alterations, and dysregulated gene expression have been discovered by cancer genome research. By quickly analyzing each patient's disease for its unique genetic landscape, PM will be able to identify effective treatments for that specific malignancy (Putignani et al., 2019). Through extensive research, scientists have understood more about the genetics behind disease progress and disease behavior. It has become clear that many diseases are associated with genetic changes (König et al., 2017). Based on the availability of human genome reference sequences, now it is possible to understand the role of genomic variation among different individuals and populations and an increased understanding of how genomic mutations affect disease has permitted us to find the impact of these mutations on health on a larger scale (Putignani et al., 2019). Furthermore, this comprehension lets us understand how specific genetic changes cause disease and how diseases like cardiovascular diseases, diabetes, and cancer in single person behave differently than in another (Subramanian et al., 2020). In this case, professionals can change the therapy to make it more efficiently (Putignani et al., 2019).

Health care has altered considering the reduced mortality brought on by chronic illnesses, noncontagious ailments, and infectious diseases, which has a significant effect on the price of public health. Now that diseases can be prevented or treated in a tailored manner, health care should move away from reactive medicine that relies on symptoms, assessment, and therapy (Álvarez-Machancoses et al., 2020).

The foundation PM has been the development of a massive data network that combines clinical information from specific individuals, their genomic history, and already conducted studies on the molecular basis of disease (Álvarez-Machancoses et al., 2020). This innovative approach to patient assessment can make use of omics, clinical, and fundamental laboratory data. Additionally, its clinical uses go beyond just personalized genetic sequencing and molecular targeted medicine. Molecular pathology, omics analysis, molecular detection, molecular imaging, and other terms with larger meanings are also associated with PM (Borovska, 2018). The likelihood of finding novel treatments and using medications more effectively is higher with a high success rate and less waste in the system if we mix and connect all emerging technologies, including omics, data based on genetic information, predictive modelling, and AI (Johnson et al., 2021).

The most popular method for PM applications is NGS, but proteomics and metabolomics assays are becoming more accurate and user-friendly. Yet, to advance treatment development, medical practice, and patient care, a wide range of disruptive technologies must be adopted (Álvarez-Machancoses et al., 2020).

The value of PM may not extend to everyone. Certain populations are not expected to benefit from this revolutionary technology. This is because some precision treatments do not work or are not affordable for these populations. For everyone to benefit from PM, the industry is working on eliminating inequalities in the system (Duffy, 2016).

But the limitation with PM is the generation of "big data" and its utilization. Its different forms, its storage which is crucial to consider if potential of PM has to be utilized at its maximum.

On the other hand, an in-depth analysis of this big data when done appropriately is likely to provide an unprecedented opportunity for integrative approaches and evolving into all-inclusive system of medicine (Borovska, 2018).

Precision Medicine

PM can identify the most accurate and effective treatment plan, speed up the recovery process, potentially extend life expectancy for the patients, and reduce the time cost and failure rate of pharmaceutical trials.

As evident from Fig. 4.2, healthcare providers, pharmaceutical firms, the government, patients, regulators, digital technology businesses, academics, diagnostics, and payers are among the stakeholders in the PM. Research, application, and collaboration-based momentum are required for PM. Academic, social, economic, and policy players should all work together to advance PM (König et al., 2017).

Understanding people's genetics, molecular profiles, and clinical characteristics will enable PM to treat patients more effectively in the future. To accurately diagnose and treat a particular disease, PM examines the genes and proteins that are already found in the body. Development will also be aided by significant discoveries like single nucleotide polymorphism and microarray/biochips. Additionally, millions of cases of cancer are diagnosed each year, which will benefit from precision treatment (Johnson et al., 2021).

PM Market

PM market is very competitive and growing very fast. It is competitive because of its market players. Players are mostly focusing on finding solutions, product improvement, and development to maintain and expand their market position. The advent in PM has brought a major paradigm shift in drug delivery and disease diagnosis. The proliferation of sequencing methods, especially NGS, is expected to drive the market due to rising cost of sequencing and the development in the area of genomics as described through Fig. 4.3.

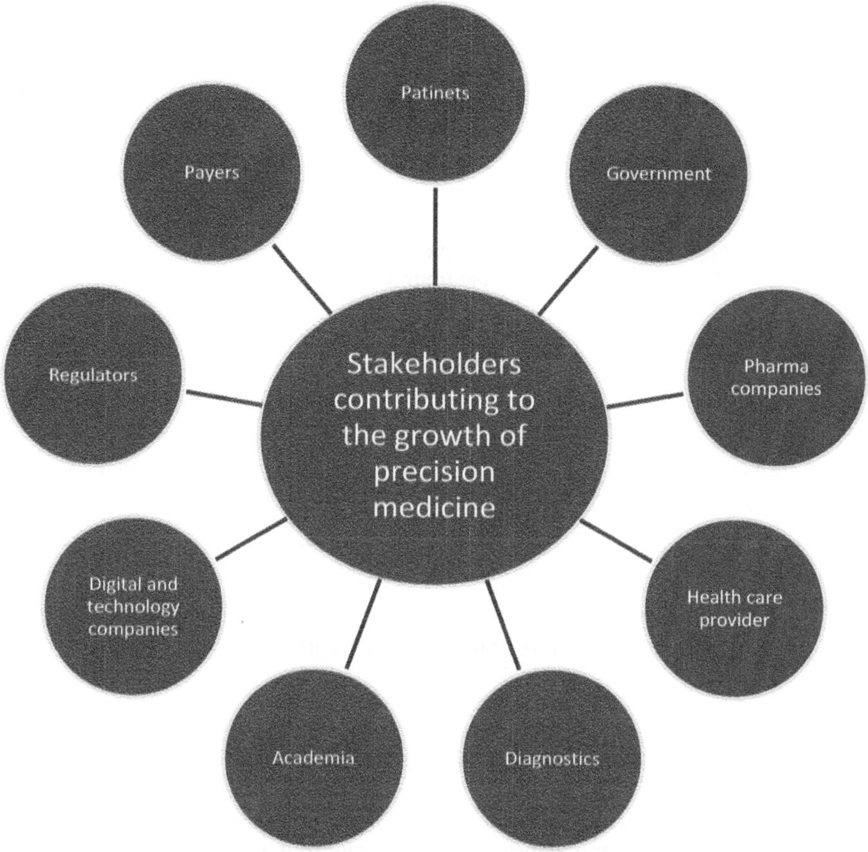

Fig. 4.2. Stakeholders Contributing to the Growth of Precision Medicine. *Source:* Author's own source.

Benefits of PM for Patients and the Healthcare System

- Targeted treatment and trial-and-error during prescribing.
- Reduction in adverse drug reactions (ADR).
- Emphasis on prevention than reaction.
- Revealing other targeted uses for drugs.
- Use of gene therapy to replace molecular pathways.
- Reduction in patient adherence.
- Shift to patient-centric care.
- Control in overall cost of health care (PM insights).

Fig. 4.3. Beneficiaries: Community, Patients, Clinicians, Researchers. *Source:* Author's own source.

The market is mainly directed by increasing approval of drugs, diagnostic assays, inexpensive DNA profiling, increasing cancer incidence and the rise of data-driven health care. Additionally, the increasing use of "multi-omics" in research and the high prevalence of high throughput sequencing platforms are driving the PM market (Lin et al., 2017). Demand for customized products is rising drug discovery cost, and increasing regulatory requirements and development in the diagnostics area appears to provide different tools and relevant clinical and biological information to appeal to different pharmaceutical companies.

The number of oncology medications approved with expanded sets beyond the initial drug label has significantly increased. Knowledge relating to significant genetic changes and the expression of pertinent biomarkers has also grown. If personalized therapies show more promising results with fewer side effects, patients will show compliance toward them and chronic disease treatments will show good impact (Álvarez-Machancoses et al., 2020).

Due to newly created diagnostic products and low-cost clinical trials for PM, Asia-Pacific is expected to increase favorably during the projected period. Additionally, it is anticipated that growing economies and disposable money in developing nations, like India, will increase the need for PM in the area. Due to continuing research and significant investment in healthcare infrastructure and technology, the region provides a variety of growth opportunities in the healthcare sector. PM is currently highly appreciated and has received financial support through national policy changes and industry sponsorship, particularly in the United States and China, but the support has been disorganized (Pregelj et al., 2018).

The assessed size of the worldwide market for PM is 66.1 billion USD dollars (2021) and is anticipated to increase to 175.64 billion USD dollars by 2030 and will be having 11.5% compound annual growth rate between 2020 and 2030 (CAGR) (Horii, 2016). AI and ML is going to play a vital role in driving the market growth. For instance, foundation One CDx's Advanced Diagnostic Laboratory Test (ADLT), which predominantly treats solid tumors and incorporates a number of companion diagnostics, was approved by Foundation Medicine in May 2018 (Pfizer Pipeline, 2025). The market for drug discovery technology has recently grown significantly, and in 2020, it is anticipated to generate the most income. Advances in pharmacogenomics are predicted to open the door to a considerable expansion of PM medication discovery. With the global incidence of cancer expected to rise, so will the demand for PM. The demand for PM is also predicted to grow with the increasing prevalence of cancer worldwide. With PM growth, pharmaceutical companies are also working on customizing treatments (Álvarez-Machancoses et al., 2020). In addition, major players are establishing manufacturing and research facilities in developing countries.

Regional Insights

Several nations, including the United States, China, Australia, Qatar, South Korea, and in Europe, England, France, Denmark, Germany, Finland, and the Netherlands, are incorporating various PM initiatives. The USA-based program "All of us" is changing the way modern medicine is practiced by boosting population-based genome sequencing and connecting it to clinical data to better understand disease prevention. Another strategy is the United Kingdom's "100,000 Genomes Project," which is producing a sizable amount of data from cancer and uncommon disorders to guide therapeutic decision-making (Personalized Medicine Coalition, 2020). Favorable government initiatives and greater funding for the creation of innovative new treatments for efficient illness management are the main drivers of the demand for PM (Horii, 2016).

Market Segmentation

The segmentation of the market is based on different factors/categories identified, for instance, market segmented by technology includes bioinformatics, gene sequencing, companion diagnostics, drug discovery, big data analytics and others.

Market segmented by application includes oncology, immunology, CNS, respiratory, and others.

The market is also segmented based on end users such as diagnostic companies, healthcare IT, pharmaceutical companies, and some others.

There is another way of segregating the market based on sequencing technology which covers ion semiconductor sequencing, pyrosequencing, synthesis sequencing, ligation sequencing, nanopore sequencing, single molecule real-time sequencing, and chain termination sequencing.

Market segmentation by product includes consumables, instruments, and services.

The route of administration involves oral and injectables.

Regional market gets segmented as Asia-Pacific, North America, Europe and other which further get divided into countries (Personalized Medicine Coalition, 2020).

Some Key Players in the PM Market

- Pfizer.
- Infosys.
- Roche.
- Novates.
- GSK.
- Biocrates life sciences.
- Qiagen.
- Eagle Genomics.
- Intomics.
- Tepnel Pharma Services.
- Teva Pharmaceuticals.
- AstraZeneca.
- Eli Lilly & Company.
- Bristol-Myers Squibb.
- Thermos Fisher Scientific Inc.
- Quest Diagnostics.
- Nano String Technologies.
- Menarini Silicon Biosystems.

Only few companies such as Roche, Pfizer, GSK, Abbott, and Novartis have significant commercial market capability and presence. PM is driving the growth in every healthcare stream, which will offer opportunities for mutual benefit to all in the chain (Horii, 2016).

Pfizer

Pfizer sees increased focus and scientific opportunities in precision therapies. They believe that there will be continued role for broad based medicine.

Few Pfizer's PMs:

- IBRANCE (Palbociclib) – cell cycle inhibitor for ER+ breast cancer.
- BRAFTOVI (Encorafenib) – melanoma and colorectal cancer.
- LORBRENA (Lorlatinib) – anaplastic lymphoma kinase inhibitor.

Five core therapeutic areas of Pfizer:

(1) Oncology.
(2) Inflammation and immunology.
(3) Vaccine.
(4) Rare disease.
(5) Internal medicine (Pfizer Pipeline, 2025).

Roche

It has acquired flatiron company (healthcare technology) at $ 1.9 billion to accelerate the focus on medicine (Álvarez-Machancoses et al., 2020).

Other

In order to construct the "All-in-one Health Cloud" in 2015, the top three medical imaging businesses, Siemens Healthcare, Philip Healthcare, and GE Healthcare, have come up with a plan together. Through the purchases of Phytel (population Health), Explorys (cloud), Merge (imaging), as well as Truven (analytics), IBM Watson increased its value by more than $4 billion (Borovska, 2018).

Opportunities

As science advances, health care is rapidly moving toward PM. PM uses genetic knowledge and other advances in medical technology to provide a deeper understanding of disease. Overall, PM has tremendous and irreplaceable potential for improving patient outcomes and challenging the future of health care (Personalized Medicine Coalition, 2020).

PM offers the chance to concentrate on early detection and intervention rather than response at end-stage disease. PM can assist reduce costs associated with numerous entrenched inefficiencies, such as trial-and-error dosage, ADR, late-stage diagnosis, and reactive medicine. For improved patient care and lower costs, value-based payment and delivery models can be implemented with the help of PM.

Genetic testing may occasionally be able to save lives. For instance, the risk of breast or ovarian cancer for women with BRCA1 or BRCA2 gene variants is up to 85%. Preventive interventions like illness surveillance, chemoprevention, or risk-reducing surgery can be provided by the BRCA1 and BRCA2 genetic tests. In addition to PM, a new strategy called precision nutrition similarly tailors diets to a person's genetics, lifestyle, and environmental circumstances (Berciano et al., 2022).

Countries like China, India, Australia, the Middle East, and African countries have large populations with high-risk diseases. The gene sequencing treatment offers great opportunities for the expansion of the PM market. Gene therapy is also the most profitable market as gene sequencing is an inevitable step in gene therapy, with a heavy investment this area will drive growth for the PM industry. Globally increasing prevalence of cancer is likely to increase demand for gene therapy (Álvarez-Machancoses et al., 2020).

PM technology advancement is anticipated to continue, led by initiatives like the PM Initiative and the 100,000 Genomes Project (Love-Koh et al., 2018). Other than technology, healthcare stakeholders should work together to develop business models to make PM affordable. At this point, PM is an expensive method but working toward this problem can bring a major change in the healthcare system (Jørgensen, 2019). PM now accounts for one-quarter of approvals of novel drugs by a policy given by FDASIA & FDA reauthorization act which can be done with less clinical trials and less development and review time (Pregelj et al., 2018).

PM and Technology

AI

PM's objective of personalizing care for each patient necessitates access to vast amounts of data, which AI can combine to develop tailored strategies for. AI can spot complex patterns and improve human talents. Numerous data collecting and analytics tools support PM's ability to personalize care. AI and PM are combining to assist with challenging issues in personalized health care (Johnson et al., 2021).

PM and AI have synergies that have an impact on the healthcare system and are in line with the goal of preventing and early diagnosing diseases that affect an individual. This could gradually lessen the burden of sickness on the general population, which would subsequently lower the expense of preventable health care for everyone (Johnson et al., 2021).

Fig. 4.4 shows the expanse of utilization of AI in PM, where AI and PM are required for treatment plans using clinical, genomic, social, and behavioral health determinants and risk prediction. AI can analyze data, help professionals, improve patient interaction, discovery of new genes, and accelerate the acceptance of PM. Healthcare professionals should have digital tools that help them to understand complex data coming from precision engineering (Álvarez-Machancoses et al., 2020).

AI facilitates the development of insights, enables the system to reason and learn, and improves clinical decision-making through complicated computation and inference. The three guiding principles for a successful application of AI in the healthcare industry are data and security, analytics and insights, and shared expertise. With the use of AI and PM, the most challenging problems in

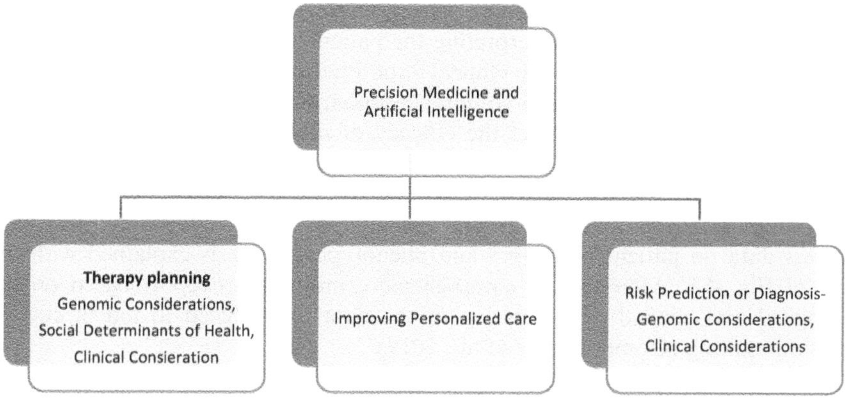

Fig. 4.4. Utilization of Artificial Intelligence in Precision Medicine. *Source:* Author's own source.

individualized care are being resolved. (1) One of the main challenges when using AI in PM is that the environment and workflows where the AI model would be deployed may have an impact on model performance and clinical efficacy. (2) It is essential to create a secure and controlled environment for data management, sharing, and storage, and this necessitates new technology developments, collaboration, as well as the creation of new rules, regulations, and economic models (Álvarez-Machancoses et al., 2020).

Recent advancement in technology indicates that there is no personalized medicine without AI and continue as it demands significant computing power, algorithms that can learn on its own by deep learning which also needs cognitive capacities as physicians, and we need to put emphasis on combining these algorithms with physician's knowledge (Álvarez-Machancoses et al., 2020).

The Omics Technology

This information enables researchers and clinicians to offer a wide range of clinical, genetic, and immunological information on the patient and his lifestyle, including habits, personal relationships, feeding, stress elements, sports activities, etc., as well as interaction with the environment, such as exposure to pathogens, drugs, pollution, nutrients, and other factors that make up the exposomes. These "omics data" are multidimensional, utilizing patient counts, genomic and metagenomic sequences, metabolites, immunological profiles, and other significant patient metrics. Once the data are catalogued, they are arranged in architectural systems that allow for the reading of usable data (Putignani et al., 2019).

The incorporation of genomics into standard clinical procedures necessitates the development of systems and workforces that can manage the volume and complexity of genetic data. To get a mechanistic knowledge of a patient's disease and to enable more individualized treatment, bioinformatics plays a crucial role in processing, visualizing, and interpreting the patient's multi-omics profiles as well as integrating those profiles with clinical data. Pharmacogenomics makes use of a person's genetic information to comprehend pharmacokinetic and pharmacodynamic variations and to predict the efficacy of medications. Additionally, biopharmaceutical companies are concentrating more on creating PM (Gómez-López et al., 2019).

Computational infrastructures are needed for PM to effectively store and process data on patient genotypes and phenotypes, which is explained with the help of Fig. 4.5. After that, a comprehensive multi-omics report based on the biological and clinical interpretation of the data is produced to aid in clinical decision-making (Gómez-López et al., 2019).

Implantable Biosensor

Biosensors are analytical tools with a biological sensing component that can convert a biological reaction into electrical signals and can continuously report information on the concentration of the target analyte. The use of implantable biosensors in PM is becoming more and more popular as a result of microfabrication processes. Devices are designed to enable continuous patient monitoring, minimizing the number of invasive interventions needed and facilitating the administration of medication therapies at predetermined intervals. In order to improve patient care, engineering, chemistry, science, and medicine have come together to produce implanted biosensors. This invention can promote new efforts and aid in disease detection and treatment. Biosensor drug delivery systems can lower the possibility of a patient receiving an excessive or insufficient dosage while

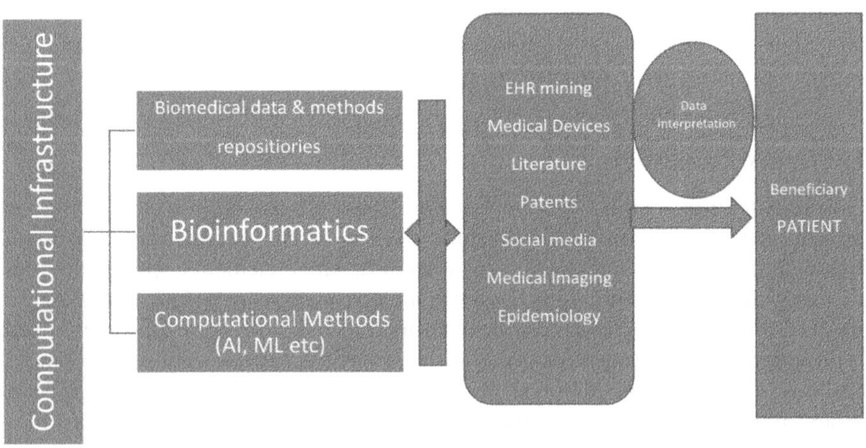

Fig. 4.5. Precision Medicine Workflows With Computational Infrastructure. *Source:* Author's own source.

yet enabling the patient to receive the medication at a precise time (Gray et al., 2018).

Big Data Analytics and the Internet of Medical Things

PM and big data analytics come together in "in silico" knowledge data discovery (in silico KDD), which enables the creation and use of intelligent digital consultants that support clinicians and researchers in accurately diagnosing disease and recommending the best course of treatment for each patient. Big genomic data ecosystems collecting and consolidating molecular omics data, medical wearables data, and data from in silico technological experiments are where big data analytics and PM meet. The steps of a typical computational pipeline for data, data from medical wearables, and data from in silico technological testing are all included in the computational workflow. Data gathering and modeling, the prepossessing stage (filtering, Problem dimensionality, reduction, multiple sequence alignment), the data analytics stage comprising result visualization and interpretation, and the expert's estimation of interest are all included in the computational workflow (Borovska, 2018).

IomT

Mobile applications for remote health monitoring systems, or digital health advisers, which enable conversations between patients and doctors over a protected connection, are examples of IomT-enabled infrastructure. An interconnected network of mobile devices "integrated with electronics, software, sensors, and network connectivity, which enables these items to collect and exchange data," is known as the "Internet of Medical Things" (Borovska, 2018).

Future Potential

Fig. 4.6 gives a comprehensive idea about collection, processing, sharing, and monitoring of health data shown by PM life cycle, used by various healthcare providers and pharma companies, which is then utilized to build better models.

Technological Developments

"Omics"-Based Biomarkers

Pfizer is integrating a variety of biotechnology tools and data sets such as genomics, epigenomics, proteomics, and transcriptomics which will enhance and accelerate drug discoveries. Biobanks and biomarkers are essential for human genetics and omics analysis to discover and develop brand new PM. According to Pfizer, this will help in the understanding of responses to medicines and vaccines to generate novel insights and will link to patients and researchers by AI intersection (Pfizer Pipeline, 2025).

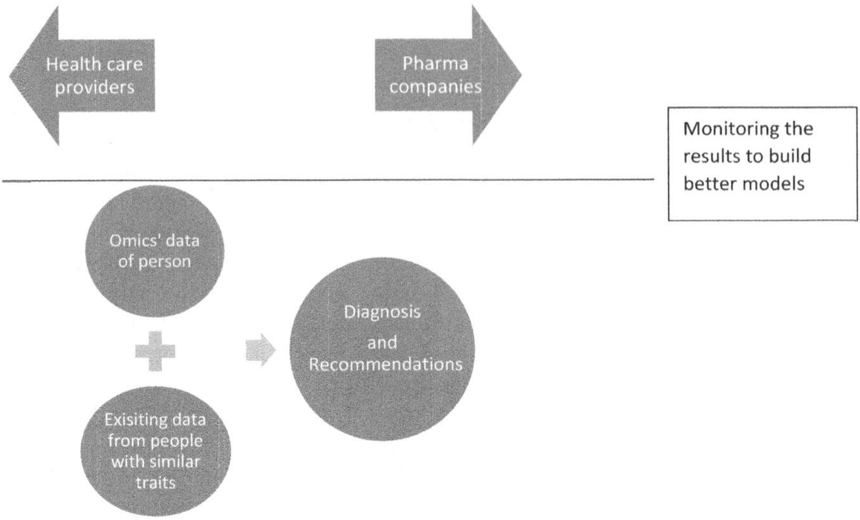

Fig. 4.6. Collection, Processing, Sharing, and Monitoring of Health Data Shown by Precision Medicine Life Cycle. *Source:* Author's own source.

As predicted that the use of these concepts such as proteomics and metabolomics will become popular in the next decade partially replacing genomics. These tests especially individual tests will provide information on multiple disease treatment pathways, treatment options or disease risks which is called "multiparametric tests." Whole genome sequencing is the widest end of this scale, potentially providing information on risk and treatment decisions for hundreds of diseases (Love-Koh et al., 2018).

Complex Algorithms

Over the next 10 years, experts predict that the usage of AI-based algorithms to enhance clinical decision-making will increase. These algorithms need a larger data collection or knowledge base, which includes many different variables like genetic data, EHR, and sociodemographic traits. Utilizing the information gathered, these data will aid in making accurate treatment plans for the patient and prognosis predictions for the patient. The process of updating the algorithms on a regular basis when fresh data are introduced to the knowledge base will be known as evolutionary testing. Initial methods for this kind of clinical usage have already been developed. We also combine AI-based technology with advances in imaging to integrate scan results into our knowledge base and develop algorithms to provide more accurate information (Love-Koh et al., 2018).

Health Apps

Numerous capabilities are available in health apps that can help with disease management, accept, and process patient-entered data and record physiological data like heart rate. The most sophisticated applications will also incorporate AI-based technology, and some of them are probably classified as PM apps. In the ensuing 10 years, this will dramatically increase. Digital experts predict that apps that analyze social and lifestyle health variables like physical exercise will help stratify patients (Love-Koh et al., 2018).

Areas to Discover in the Future

One area is cancer where several mutations have led to different types of cancer; therefore, such patients can receive mutated gene-targeted therapy and variables considered in cancer determination, which includes genes involved in DNA repair, cell division, and apoptosis. The detection of neoantigens using data sources has met with great success when identifying tumor and tumor cells can be detected in plasma, and neoantigen-based vaccines can be used for personalized treatment. Another area to discover is pharmacogenomics, the focus on making genotype information available during drug prescribing. Another initiative is there called IGNITE – Implementing Genomics in practices which focuses on solving problems of translating genomic research into clinic.

3D tissue engineering platforms with microfluidic network systems are what is meant by the term "organ-on-a-chip," and they can be used to examine a substance's effects realistically. Instead of doing direct trials, pharmacological interventions can now be tested in vitro thanks to the development of patient-specific organs on chips. It would be able to develop a patient-specific organ-on-a-chip using induced pluripotent stem cells (iPSCs) from adult tissue, such as liver cells or neurons, to evaluate the effects of various medications on a patient's tissue. A better method might then be suggested based on this screening. The possibility of regenerative therapy with PM can be connected to personalized stem cell therapies. Before being sent into a patient's body, gene editing technology can improve stem cells or treat genetic diseases (Gameiro et al., 2018).

Conclusion

PM is based on the unique concept that two patients infected with the same disease need not have the same physical response to the disorder. However, it depends on the environment and the patient's genes and symptoms. PM is a step toward understanding diverse patient groups and providing care that is uniquely focused on their needs. Many regions around the globe have started investing in PM and have initiated projects to support PM. Strong market players like Pfizer, Infosys, Roche, and Novartis are also working on clinical trials in PM.

Changes in the environment and lifestyle is responsible for increasing diseases which can be addressed by PM. AI and big data will provide support for easing the process, solving data-related issues, and accelerating the process. Technologies such as AI, omics, implantable biosensors, big data, and internet of medical things are helping to clear the obstruction in the way of PM.

PM bears the potential to transform the future of the healthcare sector with its proliferation in the next decades by changing service delivery way. The healthcare sector is likely to adopt new evaluation methods and processes that will reflect the changes for ensuring continuity to ensure the cost-effectiveness of new treatments and services.

References

Álvarez-Machancoses, Ó., DeAndrés Galiana, E. J., Cernea, A., Fernández de la Viña, J., & Fernández-Martínez, J. L. (2020). On the role of artificial intelligence in genomics to enhance precision medicine. *Pharmacogenomics and Personalized Medicine*, *13*, 105–119. https://doi.org/10.2147/PGPM.S205082

Berciano, S., Figueiredo, J., Brisbois, T. D., Alford, S., Koecher, K., Eckhouse, S., Ciati, R., Kussmann, M., Ordovas, J. M., Stebbins, K., & Blumberg, J. B. (2022). Precision nutrition: Maintaining scientific integrity while realizing market potential. *Frontiers in Nutrition*, *9*. https://www.frontiersin.org/articles/10.3389/fnut.2022.979665

Borovska, P. (2018). Big data analytics and internet of medical things make precision medicine a reality. *International Journal of Internet of Things and Web Services*, *3*, 24–31. http://www.iaras.org/iaras/journals/ijitws

Duffy, D. J. (2016, May 1). Problems, challenges and promises: Perspectives on precision medicine. *Briefings in Bioinformatics*, *17*(3), 494–504. https://doi.org/10.1093/bib/bbv060

Gameiro, G. R., Sinkunas, V., Liguori, G. R., & Auler-Júnior, J. O. C. (2018, December). Precision medicine: Changing the way we think about healthcare. *Clinics*, *73*, e723.

Gómez-López, G., Dopazo, J., Cigudosa, J. C., Valencia, A., & Al-Shahrour, F. (2019, May 21). Precision medicine needs pioneering clinical bioinformaticians. *Briefings in Bioinformatics*, *20*(3), 752–766. https://doi.org/10.1093/bib/bbx144

Gray, M., Meehan, J., Ward, C., Langdon, S. P., Kunkler, I. H., Murray, A., & Argyle, D. (2018). Implantable biosensors and their contribution to the future of precision medicine. *The Veterinary Journal*, *239*, 21–29. https://www.sciencedirect.com/science/article/pii/S1090023318304180

Horii, I. (2016). 創薬に向けたヒト細胞　組織の利用: Precision medicine への展開. *RSMP*, *6*, 71–79. https://www.jstage.jst.go.jp/article/rsmp/6/1/6_71/_pdf/-char/ja

Jarow, J. P. (2018). Personalized reproductive medicine: Regulatory considerations. *Fertility and Sterility*, *109*(6), 964–967. https://www.sciencedirect.com/science/article/pii/S0015028218302826

Johnson, K. B., Wei, W.-Q., Weeraratne, D., Frisse, M. E., Misulis, K., Rhee, K., Zhao, J., & Snowdon, J. L. (2021, January). Precision medicine, AI, and the future of personalized health care. *Clinical and Translational Science*, *14*(1), 86–93.

Jørgensen, J. T. (2019, July). Twenty years with personalized medicine: Past, present, and future of individualized pharmacotherapy. *The Oncologist*, *24*(7), e432–e440.

König, I. R., Fuchs, O., Hansen, G., von Mutius, E., & Kopp, M. V. (2017, October 1). What is precision medicine? *European Respiratory Journal, 50*(4), 1700391. http://erj.ersjournals.com/content/50/4/1700391.abstract

Kosorok, M. R., & Laber, E. B. (2019). Precision medicine. *Annual Review of Statistics and Its Application, 6*, 263–286.

Lin, J.-Z., Long, J.-Y., Wang, A.-Q., Zheng, Y., & Zhao, H.-T. (2017). Precision medicine: In need of guidance and surveillance. *World Journal of Gastroenterology, 23*, 5045–5050.

Love-Koh, J., Peel, A., Rejon-Parrilla, J. C., Ennis, K., Lovett, R., Manca, A., Chalkidou, A., Wood, H., & Taylor, M. (2018). The future of precision medicine: Potential impacts for health technology assessment. *PharmacoEconomics, 36*(12), 1439–1451. https://doi.org/10.1007/s40273-018-0686-6

Personalized Medicine Coalition. (2020, November 17). *The Personalized Medicine Report: Opportunity, challenges, and the future* (6th ed). Personalized Medicine Coalition.

Pfizer Pipeline update: Q1 2025. (April 29, 2025). Pfizer Inc. https://cdn.pfizer.com/pfizercom/product-pipeline/Q1_2025_Pipeline_Update_29APR2025.pdf

Pregelj, L., Hwang, T. J., Hine, D. C., Siegel, E. B., Barnard, R. T., Darrow, J. J., & Kesselheim, A. S. (2018, May 1). Precision medicines have faster approvals based on fewer and smaller trials than other medicines. *Health Affairs, 37*(5), 724–731. https://doi.org/10.1377/hlthaff.2017.1580

Putignani, L., Gasbarrini, A., & Dallapiccola, B. (2019, November). Potential of multiomics technology in precision medicine. *Current Opinion in Gastroenterology, 35*(6), 491–498.

Subramanian, M., Wojtusciszyn, A., Favre, L., Boughorbel, S., Shan, J., Letaief, K. B., Pitteloud, N., & Chouchane, L. (2020). Precision medicine in the era of artificial intelligence: Implications in chronic disease management. *Journal of Translational Medicine, 18*, 472. https://doi.org/10.1186/s12967-020-02658-5

Chapter 5

Impact of Online Health Information (OHI) on Patient Behavior and Doctor–Patient Relationship: A Review and Analysis

Nidhi Gupta and Pooja Sharma

Geeta University, India

Abstract

The ubiquity of Web 2.0 and the general availability of the internet have revolutionized the way people look for health information and put the conventional doctor–patient relationship to the test. With an emphasis on the Indian setting, this study investigates how online health information (OHI) affects patient attitudes, behavior, and the doctor–patient interaction. In the past, patients only relied to their physicians for medical advice. However, the internet has emerged as a major source of health-related information, greatly impacting decisions and ideas about health. People are empowered by OHI's accessibility, but its reliability and credibility is questionable. The findings highlight the necessity for healthcare practitioners to interact with patients' online information-seeking behavior and point them in the direction of reliable sources. Further, it is recommended that healthcare practitioners should also continuously monitor the information source's credibility and report the same to the concerned authorities if they find any false information.

Keywords: Online health information (OHI); doctor–patient relationship; internet health information; patient attitude; healthcare communication; information technology

Digital Transformation and Artificial Intelligence for Operational Excellence in Healthcare, 85–101

doi:10.1108/978-1-83662-314-420251016

Introduction

Online Health Information (OHI) refers to health-related content like disease symptoms, treatment options, preventive care, and patient experiences etc. available on digital platforms such as websites, social media, and mobile applications. While OHI has empowered individuals with accessible health insights, concerns regarding misinformation and the reliability of sources remain critical. Since the inception of healthcare services, doctors have been the primary source of information for patients (Ong et al., 1995; Vanderminden & Potter, 2010). Apart from consulting doctors, people had limited exposure to health information through traditional media such as newspapers, magazines, radio, and television. With the advent of Web 2.0, internet has emerged as transformational shock to everyone (Chiu, 2011; Chung, 2013). Internet has permeated every aspect of daily life, profoundly influencing how people manage their health concerns globally (Nazir & Soroya, 2021; Rains & Karmikel, 2009; Soroya et al., 2021). It has become a primary source of health-related information, with a growing number of users turning to online resources (Daraz et al., 2019; Zhang & Kim, 2022). Many patients now use search engines and OHI both before consulting a healthcare professional and in some cases as a substitute to the doctor (Hesse et al., 2005; Popovac & Roomaney, 2022). The information patients obtain from online sources significantly shapes and influences their health beliefs, behaviors, and healthcare decisions (Hesse et al., 2005; Kealey & Berkman, 2010; McKinley & Wright, 2014).

Healthcare services are inherently professional, intangible, and heterogeneous in nature which centered on the service provider (doctor) and a service taker (patient) (Yang & Zhang, 2019). Communication and the relationship between patients and physicians are the nerves to the healthcare system (Haluza et al., 2017; Vanderminden & Potter, 2010), emphasizing on a strong bond between patient and doctor (Goodman, 2010). The widespread use of the internet, particularly for readily accessible healthcare services, has altered attitudes toward the medical profession and the doctor–patient relationship (Kim & Kim, 2009). From a consumer perspective, technology has enabled patients' self-management (Calthorpe et al., 2020). The easy availability of OHI has significantly impacted consumer perception (Chen et al., 2018; Zhao et al., 2021) and greatly influenced the relationship and communication between patients and doctors (Tan & Goonawardene, 2017; Van Riel et al., 2017).

Looking for health information online has become a daily activity (Kivits, 2006; Tan & Goonawardene, 2017; Van Riel et al., 2017). People extensively use the internet to obtain initial opinions on health issues and fill information gaps outside of clinics (Frosch et al., 2012; Lee et al., 2015). There are thousands of health-related websites available online, utilized by millions daily. According to a survey reported by Statista in 2023, over 70% of consumers who used the internet for medical research started their search on search engines like Google or Bing. Medical information websites, such as WebMD and Healthline, were the second most common starting point, cited by approximately half of the respondents. The routine use of the internet as a source of health information directly impacts the health-related knowledge, attitudes, and practices of the general population, as well as the doctor–patient relationship (Eysenbach, 2003; Eysenbach & Köhler, 2002). The majority of patients search Google for specific medical conditions, before consulting a doctor. The statistic about over 1.3 billion people using digital health in 2024 highlights the tremendous growth of the digital health sector especially after COVID-19. Fitness trackers, smartwatches, and online doctor consultations are becoming mainstream as people prioritize convenience and preventive health care. Platforms like telemedicine not only reduce the burden on physical healthcare infrastructure but also increase access to care, especially in remote or underserved areas, as per Statista 2024 report. The purpose of these Google searches is to manage their own healthcare independently and to decide whether they need any professional help. Sometimes, dissatisfaction during medical consultations prompts these searches (Eysenbach, 2003).

When patients visit a doctor, their interactions involve exchanging information about diagnoses, remedies, and its side effects (Ong et al., 1995). Traditionally, patients rely on doctors for objective and reliable information (Haluza et al., 2017). This reliance creates an information asymmetry and imbalance, with authoritative, decision-making medical experts on one side and passive patients on the other side with little or no knowledge (Ong et al., 1995; Vanderminden & Potter, 2010). However, with the broader availability of online healthcare information, this imbalance has shifted toward increased patient involvement, collaboration, and informed or shared medical decision-making through online communities (McMullan, 2006; Ong et al., 1995; Tan & Goonawardene, 2017).

In business-to-consumer (B2C) e-commerce platforms, sharing patient experiences about doctors on online forums and medical websites has become widespread internationally (Duggan et al., 2011; Kordzadeh, 2020; Vijay et al., 2017). These reviews help patients gather relevant information about a doctor's service quality, influencing their choices (Grabner-Kräuter & Waiguny, 2015; Isautier et al., 2020). Many online health communities (OHCs), also known as doctor-rating websites, serve as strong marketing tools and also act as word-of-mouth platforms in various countries. For instance, in Britain, doctors can be evaluated on the National Health Service website (Isautier et al., 2020). Similarly, in the United States, popular doctor-rating websites like RateMDs.com, HealthGrades.com, and Vitals.com facilitate this process. Globally, Google My Business, Vitals, HealthGrades, WebMD, RateMDs, Yelp, ZocDoc, RealSelf, CareDash, and Facebook are among the popular platforms users generally access for healthcare information and doctors evaluation (DigitalisAdmin, 2022).

Online health platforms offer a wide range of services, including written consultations, telephone consultations, video consultations, and outpatient registration services. But, it is also observed that OHI is incomplete, inaccurate, outdated, or even misleading in some cases (Haluza et al., 2017). However, in Health technology assessment, care through hybrid method is still preferred over pure form of telecare due to several factors like clinical effectiveness followed by safety, cost effectiveness, and ease of use (Sun et al., 2022). Internet users often interpret OHI in their own and determine its reliability and relevance (Zhang & Kim, 2022; Zhao et al., 2021). But, those who lack the necessary skills and literacy in media, internet, and e-health might misinterpret or misuse OHI (Finney Rutten et al., 2019; Liu et al., 2023; Soroya et al., 2021). Failure to properly select and appraise OHI can lead to anxiety, confusion, escalating health concerns (Eysenbach & Köhler, 2002; Liu et al., 2023), and undesirable health behaviors such as self-diagnosis and self-treatment (Tan & Goonawardene, 2017).

Need of Study

The internet has made health information conveniently and freely accessible, leading to a shift toward health consumerism (Vanderminden & Potter, 2010). Nowadays, individuals can educate themselves online about medical conditions and health-related issues independently or in conjunction with consulting a physician (Tan & Goonawardene, 2017; Vanderminden & Potter, 2010). Many people access these websites without considering the credibility, accuracy, and reliability of the information provided (Chen et al., 2018; Finney Rutten et al., 2019). The use of the internet by patients as a source of health and disease information is expanding rapidly, potentially leading to significant changes in health behavior and affecting the doctor–patient relationship both positively and negatively (Roter et al., 2011).

Given the rising trend in the use of online healthcare information, it is crucial to study its impact on patient attitudes and behavior. Several studies have examined whether online information can empower patients and enhance the patient–doctor relationship (Roter et al., 2011; Sinclair, 2007). However, there is a lack of literature to study the impact of OHI availability on patient attitudes in the Indian environment. This study aims to bridge this gap and contribute to understanding the impact of OHI, its positive and negative effects, and how it can be used as a marketing tool. A better understanding of the mechanisms behind health-related internet use and health outcomes can help health communicators and practitioners design more effective health promotion initiatives using interactive media. This can contribute to improved health outcomes in the digital age (Macgregor et al., 2010). Furthermore, it will enhance our understanding of the doctor–patient relationship in the era of Artificial Intelligence (AI).

Review of Literature

Research indicated that using the internet for health-related activities has led to improved health and self-care management among individuals. This trend has grown globally due to its associated benefits (Finney Rutten et al., 2019). However, there are concerns about the reliability and quality of OHI (Tan & Goonawardene, 2017). The credibility of this information is crucial for consumers, especially when it pertains to health. Health information is deemed more beneficial by consumers if they find it reliable (Shang et al., 2021).

The dynamics of the doctor–patient relationship have been influenced by internet health searches. There has been an increase in complaints against doctors and a rise in health expenses in various countries (Iverson et al., 2008). In some countries, doctors' services are even included in consumer protection acts. With the advent of information technology, patients have been influenced by the digital revolution (Chen et al., 2018). This has led to a shift from confidence in doctors to suspicion and doubt (Iverson et al., 2008). The traditional reliance on family doctors as the first point of medical contact is replaced by internet searches (Hornik & Niederdeppe, 2008; Kim & Kim, 2009).

Two Types of Behavior

People's behavior in acquiring OHI can be categorized into two major groups. The first is information seeking and the second is information scanning (Bigsby & Hovick, 2018; Waters et al., 2016). The first group of users included an active, purposive, and systematic search to address specific health-related queries (McKenzie, 2003; Niederdeppe et al., 2007; Ruppel, 2016). While the second group consisted users with less purposeful engagement and routine information which requires noncritical actions (Bigsby & Hovick, 2018; DigitalisAdmin, 2022; Shang et al., 2021). The distinction between the two is based on the orientation of the person seeking health information. Health information seeking behavior is considered to be more active as compared to scanning, which is closer to routine behavior and not any specific goal-oriented search (Liu et al., 2023; McKenzie, 2003). Contrary to this, McKenzie (2003) described this mode of information acquisition as active scanning involving attending to a source as potentially valuable without any specific expectations (McKenzie, 2003). Some scholars also supported this view that the need for effortful attention and retention means information scanning goes beyond mere exposure (Hornik & Niederdeppe, 2008; Shim et al., 2006). The present study has attempted to incorporate both the aspects for a better understanding of impact of OHI on patient's behavior.

Positive and Negative Aspects of OHI

The widespread OHI has both positive and negative effects on the doctor–patient relationship (Van Riel et al., 2017). Patients who search the internet for health information find it helpful for asking questions or seeking second opinions. Studies have shown that internet searches can positively impact patients' knowledge about diseases (Oliveira, 2014). This can assist clinicians in explaining diseases and treatments. Despite the rise of OHI, mostly patients still consider doctors their favorite source of health information, maintaining trust in their physicians even when online information differs (Roter et al., 2011). Clinicians' insights, experience, and encouragement are essential for helping patients accurately interpret and apply online information (Van Riel et al., 2017). Patients should recognize that doctors possess the knowledge, training, and ability to apply this information appropriately. Positive aspects of OHI include greater patient involvement in understanding long-term conditions, better adherence to preventive measures, and following clinicians' guidelines (Li, Song, et al., 2019).

The internet and OHI have not only contributed to changes in health care and the emergence of health consumerism (Chiu, 2011; Haluza et al., 2017; Iverson et al., 2008) but also posed new challenges for physicians. Patients want doctors to refer them to reliable health websites and critically appraise OHI in the context of their health (Lee et al., 2015; Li, Song, et al., 2019). Some scholars argue that discussing and interpreting OHI might become a crucial task for doctors, with physicians acting as the ultimate referent (Li, Song, et al., 2019). However, literature suggests that most patients do not discuss their internet searches during doctor visits, finding it difficult to ask questions or disagree with doctors (Chung, 2013; Frosch et al., 2012; Galarce et al., 2011; Imes et al., 2008). This is due to that patients usually avoid appearing confrontational or disrespectful and not wanted to challenge doctors' expertise (Gualtieri, 2009; Imes et al., 2008; Sommerhalder et al., 2009), which could negatively impact the relationship (Chiu, 2011; Frosch et al., 2012; Lee et al., 2015). Research highlights the positive aspects of OHI, such as better-informed patients, more appropriate and efficient use of healthcare services (Broom, 2005; Tan & Goonawardene, 2017), and improved patient–physician communication and decision-making, leading to better health outcomes (Fauzi, 2023; Sommerhalder et al., 2009).

OHI can also undermine individual and public health. Concerns about the quality and reliability of OHI persist globally ranging from evidence-based work to personal opinions and anecdotes (Fauzi, 2023). Most people who search for medical information on Google do so to gain knowledge before visiting a doctor (Li et al., 2020). Although internet searches provide easy access to information, concerns about content quality and its effects on the doctor–patient relationship still remain (Kim & Kim, 2009). Unreliable information may lead to misguided self-treatment, incorrect diagnoses, longer clinic visits, and doubt about doctors' diagnoses and treatments (Chung, 2013; Li et al., 2020). Unnecessary tests and treatments mentioned online may increase financial burdens on patients. It is the clinician's responsibility to provide unbiased, scientific guidelines about medical conditions (Sommerhalder et al., 2009; Thapa et al., 2021). There were instances which have shown that medical information online can be scientifically inaccurate, incomplete, and biased, with controversial treatment information often influenced by commercial interests (Li, Ma, et al., 2019; Lu & Zhang, 2021).

From doctor's perspective, this type of information can lead to problematic perceptions of doctors also (Roter et al., 2011; Sinclair, 2007). Clinicians often find it challenging to treat patients who self-medicate based on internet searches. Such patients may develop complications due to incorrect self-treatment, and it can be difficult for clinicians to convince them that the information and treatments found online are inappropriate (Roter et al., 2011). Some doctors report feeling irritated by patients' questions based on online information. Physicians are often not receptive to discussing internet information brought by patients, feeling dominated by them, which can lead to a poor doctor–patient relationship (Li, Ma, et al., 2019). Additionally, many doctors have critically evaluated online medical information and found it scientifically inaccurate (Lu & Zhang, 2021; Liu et al., 2022). But Ai in health care plays a crucial role in shaping patient outcomes within the healthcare sector. AI-driven medical systems are designed to assist patients at every stage of their healthcare journey. Additionally, clinical intelligence utilizes patient medical data to generate insights that contribute to improving their quality of life. Several notable clinical intelligence systems have been developed to enhance patient care and overall healthcare delivery (Shaheen, 2021).

Material and Methods

Research Objectives: The study aims to investigate the impact of OHI on patients' emotions, health intentions, self-reported decisions, and the doctor–patient relationship.

Sample Size: This study employed a sample of 363 respondents who have access to the internet and use it for health-related information.

Data Collection: A structured questionnaire using Likert scale was developed and distributed online to gather data on participants' emotions, health intentions, and self-reported decisions related to the availability of OHI.

Data Analysis: Descriptive statistics like frequencies and percentages were used to analyze the data. The chi-square test was employed to assess the association between different variables and participants' responses regarding the impact of OHI on their emotions, health intentions, and self-reported decisions.

Data Analysis and Interpretations

Table 5.1 provides insights into the impact of OHI on patients' emotions, health intentions, and self-reported decisions. It shows the percentage of respondents who experienced various emotions and intentions, as well as their reported decisions based on the availability of OHI. 30.02% of respondents felt anxious or fearful, while 23.97% felt a sense of support or relief. Additionally, 49.03% expressed a desire to change their diet, and 20.11% expressed a desire to change other habits such as quitting smoking or limiting alcohol intake. Furthermore, 44.08% reported an intention to increase their healthy physical activity. The table also indicated self-reported decisions such as asking the doctor for suggestions or questions about diagnosis or treatment (39.94%), asking for referrals for additional screening tests (34.99%), and making appointments with a doctor (42.96%). Notably, a smaller percentage of respondents reported taking drugs or changing medication without consulting a doctor (9.92%), and even fewer reported resigning from planned tests or medications (6.06%). The Chi-square and p-values provide statistical significance for these findings, indicating the relationship between OHI and patients' emotions, intentions, and decisions.

Table 5.2 presents the topics most commonly read online by respondents searching health information either for general or any specific purpose. The majority of respondents (42.3%) sought information regarding treatments and their associated side effects, indicating a significant interest in understanding the potential outcomes and risks of medical interventions. Dietary advice is also a popular topic among the users, with 23.1% of respondents seeking guidance on

Table 5.1. Emotions, Health Intentions, and Self-Reported Decisions Regarding Availability of Online Health Information.

Emotions/Health Intsention/ Self-Reported Decisions	Yes		No		Chi-Square	p value
	N	%	N	%		
Feeling anxious or fear	109	30.02	254	69.97	139.85	0
Feeling of support or relief	87	23.97	276	76.03	210.32	0
Desire to change diet	178	49.03	185	50.96	0.468	0.480
Desire to change other habits, ex. quitting smoking, limiting alcohol	73	20.11	290	79.89	219.85	0
Increasing healthy physical activity	160	44.08	203	55.92	5.850	0.023
Asking the doctor for suggestions or questions about the diagnosis or treatment of diseases	145	39.94	218	60.06	32.36	0
Asking the doctor for referral/ additional screening tests	127	34.99	236	65.01	72.98	0
Taking the drug or changing the medication without consulting a doctor	36	9.92	327	90.08	493.26	0
Resignation from planned tests or medicines used	22	6.06	341	93.94	568.16	0
Making an appointment with a doctor	156	42.96	207	57.02	8.231	0

Source: Compiled from primary survey.

nutrition and dietary habits. Additionally, a substantial portion of respondents (29.9%) searched for information related to symptoms, indicating a desire to understand and address health concerns that they may be experiencing. A smaller proportion of respondents (4.7%) accessed information on ways to live with their

Table 5.2. Topics Most Commonly Read Online.

Topics	N	%
Dietary advice	84	23.1%
Way to live with my diseases	17	4.7%
Treatment and its side effects	99	42.3%
Symptoms	70	29.9%
Total	363	100%

Source: Compiled from primary survey.

Table 5.3. Impact of Increasing Availability of Online Health Information on Doctor–Patient Relationship.

Impact	*N*	%
Detoriated	73	20.1%
No change Occurred	82	22.6%
Improved	208	57.3%
Total	363	100%

Source: Compiled from primary survey.

diseases, suggesting a lesser focus on long-term management strategies. Overall, the table highlights the diverse range of health-related topics that individuals are interested in exploring online, with treatment-related information being the most sought topic among the respondents.

Table 5.3 illustrates the impact of the increasing availability of OHI on the doctor–patient relationship. It represents the number (*N*) and percentage (%) of respondents who reported different impacts. The majority of respondents (57.3%) indicated that the availability of OHI had improved their relationship with their doctors. This suggests that access to health information online may empower patients with enhanced communication and foster collaboration with healthcare providers. Conversely, a smaller proportion of respondents (20.1%) reported a deterioration in the doctor–patient relationship due to OHI, indicating potential challenges or conflicts arising from differing perspectives or information sources. Additionally, 22.6% of respondents reported that there was no change in their relationship with their doctors despite the increased availability of OHI. Overall, the table highlights the varied impacts of OHI on the doctor–patient relationship, with a majority of respondents perceiving positive changes.

Table 5.4 presents the dilemma between doctor's advice and the availability of OHI. It shows the number (*N*) and percentage (%) of respondents who reported different approaches to handling this dilemma. The results indicate that nearly half of the respondents (49.6%) preferred to equally consider both doctor's advice and online information. This suggests that a significant portion of patients value both traditional medical expertise and the wealth of information available online, seeking to integrate both sources in their decision-making process. On the other hand, a quarter of the respondents (25.6%) reported trusting online information only, indicating a growing reliance on digital sources for health-related guidance. Conversely, 24.8% of respondents preferred to solely rely on their doctor's advice, underscoring the continued importance of the physician–patient relationship and professional medical guidance. Overall, the table reflects the complex dynamics between traditional healthcare providers and the expanding influence of OHI, highlighting varying preferences among patients in navigating this dilemma. The large majority of the respondents are still relying on the doctor's advice either as a

Table 5.4. Dilemma Between Doctor's Advice and Online Health Information Availability.

Dilemma	*N*	%
Solely rely on Doctor's advice	90	24.8%
Equally consider both Doctor's advice and online information.	180	49.6%
Trust online information only	93	25.6%
Total	363	100%

Source: Compiled from primary survey.

sole source of information or in conjunction with the online information availability.

These findings reveal the complex interplay between OHI, patient emotions, doctor–patient relationships, and decision-making processes. They emphasize the need for healthcare providers to acknowledge and address patients' information-seeking behaviors while also fostering trust, open communication, and shared decision-making in clinical practice. Additionally, efforts to improve the quality and accessibility of OHI are crucial to empower patients and enhance their healthcare experiences.

AI in Healthcare

AI in healthcare encompasses various techniques for gathering online data in the field of health care. In recent years, AI has been increasingly utilized to enhance healthcare delivery, offering personalized health information, facilitating virtual consultations, and enabling remote monitoring, among other applications. By analyzing patient data, such as prescription histories and vital signs, AI algorithms can assist healthcare providers in enhancing medication management and reducing the risk of adverse drug events. This can lead to improved patient safety and better health outcomes. Furthermore, AI has the potential to increase transparency in health care by offering patients more detailed information about their health and treatments. This empowers patients to make informed decisions regarding their care, fostering trust between them and healthcare providers. The integration of AI in medical radiology, in particular, holds great promise for enhancing diagnostic accuracy and improving patient outcomes.

Discussion

In recent years, a technological revolution has transformed internet access and, consequently, the availability of OHI. The internet has become a swift and easily accessible source of information that patients increasingly rely on (Eysenbach, 2003). This information sparks emotions, motivations, and influences decisions related to health, including the selection of healthcare providers like doctors. Just as consumers have long turned to online platforms to assess service providers before making choices, this trend has also extended to healthcare services (Chang et al., 2021). Online platforms now play a pivotal role in providing information that guides decisions about choosing the right doctor, with their impact which is expected to grow in the future. The impact of e-health facilities may vary across countries due to differing healthcare systems. In private health care, which operates under free market rules, patients freely choose their healthcare providers (Chou et al., 2018). Building on previous findings, additional studies indicate that OHI significantly shapes consumer behavior and attitudes (Chang et al., 2021). However, consumers often fail to evaluate the reliability of the information they receive, putting them at risk of health misinformation. Health misinformation, characterized by unsupported health-related claims, poses a serious threat to public health (Deng et al., 2019; Lee et al., 2017). To counter these risks, it is crucial to develop reliable sources of health information. The present study has assessed the impact of online healthcare information and its impact on patient's emotions, intentions, and decisions. Notably, the majority of respondents exhibited a positive attitude toward OHI, frequently integrating it with professional medical advice rather than replacing physician consultations. This aligns with existing research indicating that informed patients tend to engage in more meaningful discussions with their doctors, ultimately improving the overall doctor–patient relationship. Additionally, mobile health applications and wearable health devices have introduced new avenues for self-monitoring and personalized health care, further shaping consumer engagement with OHI.

The findings of the study revealed that people are prone to access the OHI in today's world. People are using OHI chiefly to understand the treatment and its probable side effects, for dietary related advice and to diagnose the disease for the symptoms they are feeling. Further, majority of people have a favorable attitude toward the online information and are using it in conjunction with the doctor's advice. People are also agreed that OHI have helped in improving the overall doctor–patient relationship. By incorporating a stronger theoretical foundation and aligning with existing research, this study underscores the dual nature of OHI – its potential to empower patients and enhance healthcare engagement while simultaneously posing risks due to misinformation. Future research should explore strategies to optimize OHI utility while ensuring that patients have access to reliable, evidence-based medical information.

Conclusion

In conclusion, the spread of internet health information signifies a dramatic change in the way people obtain and use knowledge about health care (Sun et al., 2022). Patients may now choose their healthcare providers more wisely and participate more actively in their health management thanks to this digital revolution. But it also presents difficulties, especially when it comes to guaranteeing the authenticity and dependability of the data shared online. There is a strong need to verify the reliability of internet sources, as consumers are increasingly relying on digital platforms for health-related information (Wu & Lu, 2017). Healthcare providers also need to adjust themselves to this evolving environment by bringing up the topic of OHI during patient consultations and offering advice on how to assess online sources critically. One can leverage OHI to enhance healthcare outcomes while reducing the hazards associated with disinformation by encouraging cooperation among patients, healthcare providers, and technology developers (Mishra & Singh, 2022; Wu et al., 2021).

The study will greatly help in improving the doctor–patient relationship which is at the center of healthcare services. The doctor should be more vigilant toward the sources the patients are using for additional help. It is also an urgent need of the time that doctors should evaluate the reliability and credibility of these sources. Further, the study has unlocked the complex mechanism of doctor–patient relationship which brings insights for marketers to use the online platforms for the marketing and brand building of their product or services. Online platforms offer a wide options and interactive tools to increase the patient engagement and enhanced personalized care services which helps in boosting the business and brand building, if used in an effective manner. The further researches in this field can be conducted to explore the effect of demographic variables in the complex dynamics of doctor–patient relationship. However, AI in health care adds significant value through machine learning algorithms that help in accurate disease diagnosis, personalized treatment planning, and prediction of patient outcomes. By the use of AI, patient medical treatment can be managed properly that reduces risk of misinformation or loss of medical history data. Moving forward, healthcare providers and patients will benefit from AI tools that aid in both decision-making and the evaluation of online health resources.

References

Bigsby, E., & Hovick, S. R. (2018). Understanding associations between information seeking and scanning and health risk behaviors: An early test of the structural influence model. *Health Communication*, *33*(3), 315–325.

Broom, A. (2005). Virtually healthy: The impact of internet use on disease experience and the doctor-patient relationship. *Qualitative Health Research*, *15*(3), 325–345.

Calthorpe, R. J., Smith, S., Gathercole, K., & Smyth, A. R. (2020). Using digital technology for home monitoring, adherence and self-management in cystic fibrosis: A state-of-the-art review. *Thorax*, *75*(1), 72–77.

Chang, Y. S., Zhang, Y., & Gwizdka, J. (2021). The effects of information source and eHealth literacy on consumer health information credibility evaluation behavior. *Computers in Human Behavior*, *115*, 106629.

Chen, Y. Y., Li, C. M., Liang, J. C., & Tsai, C. C. (2018). Health information obtained from the internet and changes in medical decision making: Questionnaire development and cross-sectional survey. *Journal of Medical Internet Research*, *20*(2), e47.

Chiu, Y. C. (2011). Probing, impelling, but not offending doctors: The role of the internet as an information source for patients' interactions with doctors. *Qualitative Health Research, 21*(12), 1658–1666.

Chou, W. Y. S., Oh, A., & Klein, W. M. (2018). Addressing health-related misinformation on social media. *JAMA, 320*(23), 2417–2418.

Chung, J. E. (2013). Patient–provider discussion of online health information: Results from the 2007 health information national trends survey (HINTS). *Journal of Health Communication, 18*(6), 627–648.

Daraz, L., Morrow, A. S., Ponce, O. J., Beuschel, B., Farah, M. H., Katabi, A., & Murad, M. H. (2019). Can patients trust online health information? A meta-narrative systematic review addressing the quality of health information on the internet. *Journal of General Internal Medicine, 34*, 1884–1891.

Deng, Z., Hong, Z., Zhang, W., Evans, R., & Chen, Y. (2019). The effect of online effort and reputation of physicians on patients' choice: 3-wave data analysis of China's good doctor website. *Journal of Medical Internet Research, 21*(3), e10170.

DigitalisAdmin. (2022, September 9). *Top 10 doctor review sites you should be monitoring - digitalis medical.* Digitalis Medical. https://digitalismedical.com/blog/doctor-review-sites/

Duggan, A. P., & Thompson, T. L. (2011). Provider–patient interactions and related outcomes. In T. L. Thompson, R. Parrott, & J. F. Nussbaum (Eds.), *The routledge handbook of health communication* (pp. 439–452). Routledge.

Eysenbach, G. (2003). The impact of the Internet on cancer outcomes. *CA: A Cancer Journal for Clinicians, 53*(6), 356–371.

Eysenbach, G., & Köhler, C. (2002). How do consumers search for and appraise health information on the world wide web? Qualitative study using focus groups, usability tests, and in-depth interviews. *BMJ, 324*(7337), 573–577.

Fauzi, M. A. (2023). Knowledge sharing in health community of practice (CoP) and online health communities (OHCs): A bibliometric analysis. *Journal of Information and Knowledge Management, 22*(03), 2350006.

Finney Rutten, L. J., Blake, K. D., Greenberg-Worisek, A. J., Allen, S. V., Moser, R. P., & Hesse, B. W. (2019). Online health information seeking among US adults: Measuring progress toward a healthy people 2020 objective. *Public Health Reports, 134*(6), 617–625.

Frosch, D. L., May, S. G., Rendle, K. A., Tietbohl, C., & Elwyn, G. (2012). Authoritarian physicians and patients' fear of being labeled 'difficult'among key obstacles to shared decision making. *Health Affairs, 31*(5), 1030–1038.

Galarce, E. M., Ramanadhan, S., & Viswanath, K. (2011). Health information seeking. In T. L. Thompson, R. Parrott, & J.F. Nussbaum (Eds.), *The routledge handbook of health communication* (pp. 194–207). Routledge.

Goodman, K. W. (2010). Ethics, information technology, and public health: New challenges for the clinician-patient relationship. *Journal of Law Medicine & Ethics, 38*(1), 58–63.

Grabner-Kräuter, S., & Waiguny, M. K. (2015). Insights into the impact of online physician reviews on patients' decision making: Randomized experiment. *Journal of Medical Internet Research, 17*(4), e93.

Gualtieri, L. N. (2009). The doctor as the second opinion and the internet as the first. In *CHI'09 extended abstracts on human factors in computing systems* (pp. 2489–2498).

Haluza, D., Naszay, M., Stockinger, A., & Jungwirth, D. (2017). Digital natives versus digital immigrants: Influence of online health information seeking on the doctor–patient relationship. *Health Communication*, *32*(11), 1342–1349.

Hesse, B. W., Nelson, D. E., Kreps, G. L., Croyle, R. T., Arora, N. K., Rimer, B. K., & Viswanath, K. (2005). Trust and sources of health information: The impact of the internet and its implications for health care providers: Findings from the first health information national trends survey. *Archives of Internal Medicine*, *165*(22), 2618–2624.

Hornik, R., & Niederdeppe, J. (2008). Information scanning. In *The international encyclopedia of communication*. https://doi.org/10.1002/9781405186407.wbieci026

Imes, R. S., Bylund, C. L., Sabee, C. M., Routsong, T. R., & Sanford, A. A. (2008). Patients' reasons for refraining from discussing internet health information with their healthcare providers. *Health Communication*, *23*(6), 538–547.

Isautier, J. M., Copp, T., Ayre, J., Cvejic, E., Meyerowitz-Katz, G., Batcup, C., & McCaffery, K. J. (2020). People's experiences and satisfaction with telehealth during the COVID-19 pandemic in Australia: Cross-sectional survey study. *Journal of Medical Internet Research*, *22*(12), e24531.

Iverson, S. A., Howard, K. B., & Penney, B. K. (2008). Impact of internet use on health-related behaviors and the patient-physician relationship: A survey-based study and review. *Journal of Osteopathic Medicine*, *108*(12), 699–711.

Kealey, E., & Berkman, C. S. (2010). The relationship between health information sources and mental models of cancer: Findings from the 2005 health information national trends survey. *Journal of Health Communication*, *15*(Suppl. 3), 236–251.

Kim, J., & Kim, S. (2009). Physicians' perception of the effects of internet health information on the doctor–patient relationship. *Informatics for Health and Social Care*, *34*(3), 136–148.

Kivits, J. (2006). Informed patients and the internet: A mediated context for consultations with health professionals. *Journal of Health Psychology*, *11*(2), 269–282.

Kordzadeh, N. (2020). Toward quality transparency in healthcare: Exploring hospital-operated online physician review systems in northeastern United States. *Health Policy and Technology*, *9*(1), 56–61.

Lee, K., Hoti, K., Hughes, J. D., & Emmerton, L. M. (2015). Consumer use of "Dr Google": A survey on health information-seeking behaviors and navigational needs. *Journal of Medical Internet Research*, *17*(12), e288.

Lee, K., Hoti, K., Hughes, J. D., & Emmerton, L. (2017). Dr Google is here to stay but health care professionals are still valued: An analysis of health care consumers' internet navigation support preferences. *Journal of Medical Internet Research*, *19*(6), e7489.

Li, G., Fan, G., Chen, Y., & Deng, Z. (2020). What patients "see" doctors in online fever clinics during COVID-19 in Wuhan? *Journal of the American Medical Informatics Association*, *27*(7), 1067–1071.

Li, Y., Ma, X., Song, J., Yang, Y., & Ju, X. (2019). Exploring the effects of online rating and the activeness of physicians on the number of patients in an online health community. *Telemedicine and e-Health*, *25*(11), 1090–1098.

Li, Y., Song, Y., Zhao, W., Guo, X., Ju, X., & Vogel, D. (2019). Exploring the role of online health community information in patients' decisions to switch from online to offline medical services. *International Journal of Medical Informatics*, *130*, 103951.

Liu, J., & Niederdeppe, J. (2023). Health information scanning. In E. Ho (Ed.), *In the International Encyclopedia of health communication* (pp. 1–6). John Wiley & Sons, Inc.

Liu, Z., Zhang, C., Luo, C., Ou, J., Song, M., Yang, L., & Guo, T. (2022). Evaluation of online andrology medical services in central regions of China during the COVID-19 pandemic: A cross-sectional data analysis study. *Inquiry: The Journal of Health Care Organization, Provision, and Financing*, *59*. https://doi.org/10.1177/00469580221134431

Lu, X., & Zhang, R. (2021). Impact of patient information behaviours in online health communities on patient compliance and the mediating role of patients' perceived empathy. *Patient Education and Counseling*, *104*(1), 186–193.

Macgregor, R. C., Hyland, P. N., & Harvie, C. (2010). Associations between driving forces to adopt ICT and benefits derived from that adoption in medical practices in Australia. In *Handbook of research on developments in e-health and telemedicine: Technological and social perspectives* (pp. 652–668). IGI Global.

McKenzie, P. J. (2003). A model of information practices in accounts of everyday-life information seeking. *Journal of Documentation*, *59*(1), 19–40.

McKinley, C. J., & Wright, P. J. (2014). Informational social support and online health information seeking: Examining the association between factors contributing to healthy eating behavior. *Computers in Human Behavior*, *37*, 107–116.

McMullan, M. (2006). Patients using the internet to obtain health information: How this affects the patient–health professional relationship. *Patient Education and Counseling*, *63*(1–2), 24–28.

Mishra, V., & Singh, J. (2022). Health technology assessment of telemedicine interventions in diabetes management: Evidence from UAE. *FIIB Business Review*, *0*(0). https://doi.org/10.1177/23197145221130651

Nazir, M., & Soroya, S. H. (2021). Health informatics: Use of internet for health information seeking by Pakistani chronic patients. *Journal of Library Administration*, *61*(1), 134–146.

Niederdeppe, J., Hornik, R. C., Kelly, B. J., Frosch, D. L., Romantan, A., Stevens, R. S., & Schwartz, J. S. (2007). Examining the dimensions of cancer-related information seeking and scanning behavior. *Health Communication*, *22*(2), 153–167.

Oliveira, J. F. D. (2014). The effect of the internet on the patient-doctor relationship in a hospital in the city of São Paulo. *JISTEM-Journal of Information Systems and Technology Management*, *11*, 327–344.

Ong, L. M., De Haes, J. C., Hoos, A. M., & Lammes, F. B. (1995). Doctor-patient communication: A review of the literature. *Social Science & Medicine*, *40*(7), 903–918.

Popovac, M., & Roomaney, R. (2022). Measuring online health-seeking behaviour: Construction and initial validation of a new scale. *British Journal of Health Psychology*, *27*(3), 756–776.

Rains, S. A., & Karmikel, C. D. (2009). Health information-seeking and perceptions of website credibility: Examining Web-use orientation, message characteristics, and structural features of websites. *Computers in Human Behavior*, *25*(2), 544–553.

Roter, D. L., & Hall, J. A. (2011). How medical interaction shapes and reflects the physician–patient relationship. In T. L. Thompson, R. Parrott, & J.F. Nussbaum (Eds.), *The Routledge handbook of health communication* (pp. 83–96). Routledge.

Ruppel, E. K. (2016). Scanning health information sources: Applying and extending the comprehensive model of information seeking. *Journal of Health Communication, 21*(2), 208–216.

Shaheen, M. Y. (2021). Applications of artificial intelligence (AI) in healthcare: A review. *ScienceOpen Preprints*. https://doi.org/10.14293/S2199-1006.1.SOR-.PPVRY8K.v1

Shang, L., Zhou, J., & Zuo, M. (2021). Understanding older adults' intention to share health information on social media: The role of health belief and information processing. *Internet Research, 31*(1), 100–122.

Shim, M., Kelly, B., & Hornik, R. (2006). Cancer information scanning and seeking behavior is associated with knowledge, lifestyle choices, and screening. *Journal of Health Communication, 11*(S1), 157–172.

Sinclair, F. (2007). In need of TLC: A doctor-patient relationship fit for the future. *Scottish Foundation, 1*(7), 1–13.

Sommerhalder, K., Abraham, A., Zufferey, M. C., Barth, J., & Abel, T. (2009). Internet information and medical consultations: Experiences from patients' and physicians' perspectives. *Patient Education and Counseling, 77*(2), 266–271.

Soroya, S. H., Farooq, A., Mahmood, K., Isoaho, J., & Zara, S. E. (2021). From information seeking to information avoidance: Understanding the health information behavior during a global health crisis. *Information Processing & Management, 58*(2), 102440.

Sun, H., Li, J., Cheng, Y., Pan, X., Shen, L., & Hua, W. (2022). Developing a framework for understanding health information behavior change from avoidance to acquisition: A grounded theory exploration. *BMC Public Health, 22*(1), 1115.

Tan, S. S. L., & Goonawardene, N. (2017). Internet health information seeking and the patient-physician relationship: A systematic review. *Journal of Medical Internet Research, 19*(1), e9.

Thapa, D. K., Visentin, D. C., Kornhaber, R., West, S., & Cleary, M. (2021). The influence of online health information on health decisions: A systematic review. *Patient Education and Counseling, 104*(4), 770–784.

Van Riel, N., Auwerx, K., Debbaut, P., Van Hees, S., & Schoenmakers, B. (2017). The effect of Dr Google on doctor–patient encounters in primary care: A quantitative, observational, cross-sectional study. *BJGP open, 1*(2).

Vanderminden, J., & Potter, S. J. (2010). *Challenges to the doctor-patient relationship in the twenty-first century* (pp. 355–372). The new Blackwell companion to medical sociology.

Vijay, T. S., Prashar, S., Parsad, C., & Kumar, M. (2017). An empirical examination of the influence of information and source characteristics on consumers' adoption of online reviews. *Pacific Asia Journal of the Association for Information Systems, 9*(1), 5.

Waters, E. A., Wheeler, C., & Hamilton, J. G. (2016). How are information seeking, scanning, and processing related to beliefs about the roles of genetics and behavior in cancer causation?. *Journal of Health Communication, 21*(Suppl. 2), 6–15.

Wu, H., Deng, Z., Wang, B., & Gupta, S. (2021). How does service price influence patients' decisions? An examination of the free-market pricing mechanism in online health communities. *Electronic Markets*, 1–17.

Wu, H., & Lu, N. (2017). Online written consultation, telephone consultation and offline appointment: An examination of the channel effect in online health communities. *International Journal of Medical Informatics*, *107*, 107–119.

Yang, H., & Zhang, X. (2019). Investigating the effect of paid and free feedback about physicians' telemedicine services on patients' and physicians' behaviors: Panel data analysis. *Journal of Medical Internet Research*, *21*(3), e12156.

Zhang, Y., & Kim, Y. (2022). Consumers' evaluation of web-based health information quality: Meta-analysis. *Journal of Medical Internet Research*, *24*(4), e36463.

Zhao, Y., Da, J., & Yan, J. (2021). Detecting health misinformation in online health communities: Incorporating behavioral features into machine learning based approaches. *Information Processing & Management*, *58*(1), 102390.

Chapter 6

Understanding the Perception of Artificial Intelligence Use in Healthcare Among Educational Youth: A Grounded Theory Approach

Monica Verma and Monika Nijhawan

New Delhi Institute of Management, India

Abstract

Technology is essential to our day-to-day existence. Technology integration is advantageous in producing solutions that are more precise and quicker. The field of Artificial Intelligence (AI) is expanding quickly across several industries, including healthcare. Therefore, before incorporating AI into the system, it is important to understand people's perspectives and factors affecting the acceptance of AI in healthcare. This study investigates the views of youthful, educated individuals regarding the obstacles they perceive to be in the way of AI's adoption in the healthcare industry. Using the Grounded Theory approach, an exploratory qualitative study of 32 young PGDM students was carried out in Delhi. The findings of the study indicate that young people are ready to adopt and be treated by AI machines if rigorous testing is done and approved by relevant health authorities. Findings also revealed that the data privacy of patients was a major concern among young people before implementing AI in the modern healthcare sector.

Keywords: Healthcare; artificial intelligence; perception; attitude; awareness; role of AI

Introduction

Artificial Intelligence (AI) in general refers to the field of computer science to make machines so intelligent that they can do all tasks which require human

Digital Transformation and Artificial Intelligence for Operational Excellence in Healthcare, 103–117

doi:10.1108/978-1-83662-314-420251018

intelligence. The advantages of this technology's integration with the healthcare industry remain mostly unknown to many. It has always been controversial whether humans would empower AI or AI would empower humans. The Indian Government defines AI as a machine's capacity to carry out cognitive functions, including higher-order reasoning and 100% accurate and efficient problem-solving. The NASSCOM research states that the Indian healthcare market was estimated to be worth \$372 billion in 2022 and is projected to expand at a compound annual growth rate (CAGR) of around 20% between 2023 and 2030. India's healthcare industry is adopting more advanced technology because of the COVID-19 pandemic. According to Forbes (2023), the healthcare sector has been given INR 89,155 crore in the Union budget 2023–2024 to carry out all the cutting-edge, innovation-based healthcare activities on a large scale.

With the increase in technology and its usage, there comes a new theory and development for making computers intelligent in the field of AI. There is hardly any area where AI is not used today from speech recognition, image analysis, autonomous vehicles, fraud detection, customer services, the gaming industry and the healthcare sector (Abuzaid et al., 2022). AI has quickly changed several industries, most notably healthcare, where it improves treatment effectiveness and diagnostic precision. Despite its advantages, patients and healthcare professionals continue to worry about data privacy, ethical ramifications, and even job displacement (Fritsch et al., 2022; Hashiguchi et al., 2022). AI has greatly improved healthcare, especially for diagnostic jobs like radiology imaging. Nevertheless, most of the AI systems are created with clinicians in mind, paying little attention to patient-facing platforms that aid people in comprehending complicated medical information (Hashiguchi et al., 2022; Ogolodom et al., 2023).

The purpose of this study is to investigate how educated youth view and feel about the use of AI in healthcare. This exploratory study evaluates the factors driving the adoption of AI in the healthcare industry using the grounded theory approach. This study presents several of the major conclusions from the investigation. The format of the chapter is as follows: The literature on how young professionals perceive using AI in healthcare is reviewed in the next section. The research approach used to conduct this study comes next. Subsequent sections showcase the analysis and outcome, culminating in a discussion that encompasses limitations and prospects.

Literature Review

AI is the ability of machines to do complex work on their own without any human intervention. According to NASSCOM, the impact of AI in the healthcare sector is expected to grow to nearly 20% from 2023 to 2030. Union budget 2023–2024 has allotted \$372 billion in 2022. The post-pandemic COVID-19 importance of AI is on its brim. One of the most promising applications in which AI is getting lots of success is in the analysis of X-rays. There are chances that while examining some disease symptoms, some pattern gets missed by using trained machines

(Fritsch et al., 2022). Castagno and Khalifa (2020) laid emphasis on the potential to improve diagnostic accuracy and telehealth. As per Fritsch et al. (2022), biasness is one of the challenges as there are chances that biased data can lead to biased predictions. Although some acknowledge the potential benefits of AI, others worry about deskilling, moral conundrums and privacy dangers Hashiguchi et al., (2022). Moreover, the establishment of explicit legal frameworks will address ethical concerns and improve accountability. All things considered, improving education and establishing strong legal frameworks are crucial for removing obstacles to the adoption of AI, and further study is required to explore diverse attitudes across healthcare disciplines.

With the use of machine learning advancements and the growing availability of electronic health data, AI has the potential to revolutionize the healthcare industry. AI has many uses in the fields of clinical care, public health and biomedical research, but its incorporation into everyday practice is still relatively new, with most implementations still in the conceptual stage. Although the number of scholarly articles on AI in healthcare has increased from 88 in 1980 to over 15,000 by 2020, there are still worries about accuracy, efficacy and ethical issues (Fritsch et al., 2022). AI tool development has surged due to the COVID-19 pandemic, especially in the diagnostics area. However, according to conflicting reports from healthcare providers, these tools frequently interfere with clinical procedures rather than improving them. AI's potential applications include healthcare process auditing, health outcome prediction using a variety of data sources as well as expediting administrative work. But for integration to be successful, strong policy frameworks are needed to guarantee data security, quality and appropriate regulation. Additionally, ethical considerations must be addressed to optimize AI's advantages and minimize its risks in the healthcare industry. By improving patient care and operational efficiency, AI integration in telehealth is transforming the healthcare industry (Castagno & Khalifa, 2020). By maximizing resource allocation and facilitating remote consultations, AI tackles significant issues in the healthcare industry, including data overload and the growing demand for medical services. The swift expansion of data originating from medical devices and electronic health records presents prospects for AI to derive significant insights for clinical judgment and patient tracking. AI's major uses in telehealth include transdisciplinary information sharing, better healthcare IT, and intelligent diagnosis support. To fully realize AI's potential, however, issues with data quality, ethical considerations and patient privacy must be resolved. Additionally, AI plays a noteworthy role in advancing sustainability in healthcare by lowering the carbon footprint connected with in-person visits and improves access for underserved populations. This literature review employs a systematic approach to identify gaps and insights in the current understanding of AI's impact on telehealth, emphasizing the need for interdisciplinary collaboration to advance this field.

AI in healthcare, especially post-pandemic, has improved the healthcare sector in various ways, including patient care, diagnostic diseases, administrative processes and aiding in research purposes. Fritsch et al. (2022) have shown that the typical use cases of AI in medicine are image analysis tasks in radiology, ophthalmology, dermatology and pathology. However, AI is also aiding in clinical risk prediction, diagnostics and therapeutics. AI-driven X-rays tools have outperformed such as predicting COVID-19 likelihood based on symptoms. AI along with NLP helps in understanding, interpreting and generating human languages, which in turn helps healthcare workers to make faster and better decisions. On the other hand, rule-based expert systems where rules are predefined in the system help healthcare workers to make fast decisions on specific symptoms. AI is also aiding in gynaecology, prostate, neck, head and all kinds of surgical operations with the help of robots (Castagno & Khalifa, 2020). The researchers have categorized the role of AI as physical and virtual (Ogolodom et al., 2023). The virtual part helps in recording the healthcare system and the physical part like robots helps in surgeries, prostheses for handicapped people and elderly care. Medical practitioners have benefited from AI in the following areas: medical imaging, predictive modelling and decision assistance, epidemic and syndromic surveillance, geocoding health data and health information systems (Secinaro et al., 2021). This will help doctors in the diagnostic process. Finally, AI can enhance health services management in supporting doctors, nurses and administrative staff (Hossain et al., 2022). By facilitating communication between patients and their medical teams throughout hospital stays, these AI applications assist healthcare professionals in improving patient–provider relationships by providing instant access to patient data and increasing patient engagement and knowledge about their care. Many applications, including voice recognition, data mining and the ability to forecast physical deterioration, are currently utilized in nursing procedures Abuzaid et al. (2022). Even though AI seems promising, further study is needed to properly evaluate its effectiveness and investigate potential new uses in the medical field. Global medical services are changing due to the digitalization of healthcare, which is being driven by technologies like AI and Internet of Things (IoT), yet many healthcare personnel are still unprepared. Studies show that the adoption of digital health is hampered in nations including Finland, Saudi Arabia, Germany, Austria and Saudi Arabia by outmoded curricula, a lack of training and obstacles like cost and privacy concerns. Public opinion is still supportive in Bangladesh although healthcare digitization is moving slowly due to a lack of skilled labour and insufficient technical support, but little research has been done on the readiness of healthcare personnel (Hossain et al., 2022). By examining the perspectives, technical skills and difficulties faced by Bangladeshi healthcare workers in the context of digital transformation, this research aims to close this gap.

Castagno and Khalifa (2020) show that there were fewer positive results about usage of AI as some people were not much aware whereas there were a portion of people who had some knowledge about the matter. Overall, people believed AI can work wonders if used wisely. Abuzaid et al. (2022) analyzed that AI is now spreading its wings in each sector from hospitality and speech recognition to nursing. AI usage in the field of healthcare is increasing day by day.

In the study of Zhang et al. (2021), the authors have analyzed the perception and awareness among Youth in India to integrate AI in healthcare sector. The authors have revealed that integration of AI is very helpful and reduces the effort and time of healthcare workers in decision-making. Curiosity arises among users regarding usage and scope while using them. Another finding of his study talks about the limitations of AI. Over reliance, lack of creativity and zeal are some of the shortcomings of AI in its integration. In accordance with Secinaro et al. (2021), the study shows that it is very tough and challenging to learn something new and diverse at the older stage of life. Older people are at that stage where accepting and learning something new and diverse is not at all easy, and it is not possible for them to accept these challenges with open arms. They are trying to be in power with the present generation, but still there are some problems which are tough to mitigate completely. The studies of Fritsch et al. (2022) and Saxena et al. (2024) talked about the opinion of healthcare professionals to diagnose any disease or complication using AI. They feel that AI-driven tools give repeated but reliable data by extracting from various sources. AI is transforming healthcare by improving patient care and streamlining operations. The study by Kasula (2023) presents a theoretical framework for integrating AI into healthcare by synthesizing on AI applications, technology integration and operational strategies. It focuses on personalized care, clinical decision support, predictive analytics and efficiency. Further, the author addresses ethical considerations, regulatory compliance, interoperability and scalability and finally provides implementation strategies, stakeholder engagement models and iterative adoption plans. No human jobs and requirements will be needed with the progressive development of AI stated in Gupta & Mukherjee (2025). The study also discusses ethical issues like fairness and transparency, stressing that AI must be used responsibly. Businesses need to ensure AI is safe, transparent and user-friendly so that more people feel confident using it. The majority also think that patients and healthcare providers will communicate less because of digitization. In this context further in this study few potential challenges faced in adopting AI in the healthcare sector have been identified below. Based on the Literature Review, below is the summary of the challenges in using AI shown in Table 6.1 and potential of AI is shown in Table 6.2 in the healthcare industry.

Methodology

Grounded Theory Approach

As the objective of the study was to explore the perception of young people of Delhi/NCR in using AI in the healthcare sector and the challenges faced by them in acceptance of this technology, Grounded Theory was used to analyze the perceptions of young graduates in adopting AI in the healthcare sector.

Grounded Theory (Glaser & Strauss, 1967) is a systematic and inductive qualitative research method used to construct new theories and rationales hidden inside the data (Fassinger, 2005). The development of the theory helps the

Table 6.1. Challenges in Using AI in the Healthcare Sector.

Reference	Challenges Identified	Detail
Fritsch et al. (2022) and Hashiguchi et al. (2022)	Confidentiality	Risk of leakage of patient's data.
Fritsch et al. (2022) and Hashiguchi et al. (2022)	Insurance coverage	Insurance company has to decide the extent of coverage if the treatment is completely done by AI.
Fritsch et al. (2022)	Biasness	Biased data can lead to biased predictions.
Fritsch et al. (2022) and Saxena et al. (2024)	Implementation challenges	AI implementation can be very expensive and can have other operational challenges.
Castagno and Khalifa (2020)	Reliability	As there are chances that data can get stolen so there arises a dilemma whether we should rely on the AI or not.
Fritsch et al. (2022)	Ethical dilemma	Concerns about biasness, accountability and transparency arises.

Source: Created by authors.

researcher to understand the problems faced by a group of participants and how they deal with the problem (Glaser, 1992, 1998). In Grounded Theory, the researcher collects and discovers data in an unbiased and objective manner as a neutral observer. Grounded Theory consists of defining, developing and negotiating perspectives and social perceptions through interaction (Strauss & Corbin, 1998). It is a step-by-step process consisting of:

- data collection and analysis;
- open coding (identifying concepts and categories);
- axial coding (establishing relationships between categories;
- selective coding (developing the core category and theory).

Data Collection

In-depth open-ended interviews were conducted to explore the perception of young people toward the adoption and use of AI in the healthcare sector. A total of 32 youth pursuing PGDM course from reputed management institutions of

Table 6.2. Potential of AI in Healthcare Sector.

Study	Advantage	Detail
Fritsch et al. (2022) and (Secinaro et al., 2021)	Increase efficiency	By analyzing large datasets and helping in recognizing patterns in a more accurate way.
Fritsch et al. (2022) and Hashiguchi et al. (2022)	Improve risk prediction	AI can diagnose risks at an early stage hence the predictions are accurate, and prescriptions are followed likewise.
Amjad et al. (2023) and Castagno and Khalifa (2020)	Potential to improve diagnostic accuracy and telehealth	All the algorithms and data from multiple sources along with machine learning helps to improve accuracy.
Castagno and Khalifa (2020) and Secinaro et al. (2021)	Operational efficiency	With the use of automation, supply chain management, good decision making skill and resource optimization.
Zhang et al. (2021)	Seeking medical information	Work as a very reliable source to seek any type of information.
Abuzaid et al. (2022) and Amjad et al. (2023)	Helps in nursing practices	Wide and Complex tasks can be easily sorted out using AI.

Source: Created by authors.

Delhi/NCR were interviewed. To ensure consistency and dependability, the study protocol remained the same for each interview. To ensure the data's dependability, in-person interviews with each respondent were conducted using the same set of questions. Ten to 15 minutes were spent on each interview. The purpose of the research was explained at the beginning of each interview, and following the conversation, the facts were verified, and the interviewees' individual opinions were noted. To maintain accuracy, audios were shared with the respondents. The interview was considered appropriate for analysis once the accuracy was verified.

The authors wrote descriptions of each participant from the recorded interviews. The descriptions included demographic details and a summary of the most important theme addressed in the interview. These descriptions were used as a ready reckoner to validate the conceptual model developed at a later stage.

Open Coding

"The analytic process of identifying the concepts along with their perspectives and dimensions" is known as open coding (Corbin & Strauss, 1990, p. 101). Open coding starts with breaking down data (interviews in the present study) into distinct units called "Thought Units", which can range from a phrase to several sentences. In the current research, interviews were listened to and relistened, and the descriptions were read and reread to identify relevant parts of the interviews relating to the research questions. The next step was assigning codes which were done in the following manner: "S" was used for young graduates pursuing PGDM courses, 1, 2, 3, 4... was the respondent number, "Y" if they were aware of the application of AI in the healthcare sector, "N" if they were not aware of the use of AI in the healthcare sector and i, ii, iii, ...was the number of reasons given by that respondent. Thus, S5Yi meant that Respondent 5 is aware of the application of AI in the healthcare sector and gives the first reason for it. For identification of the categories, authors presented their logic, and when both reached a consensus after many deliberations with open coding acting as the base, that category was accepted.

Axial Coding

Axial coding can be defined as "the process of establishing relationships between categories and subcategories" (Corbin & Strauss, 1990, p. 123). It involves analyzing the conditions, content, interactions and consequences associated with a category, thus giving structure to the emerging theory. In the present study, axial coding was done through an elaborate brainstorming session in which various categories and subcategories were identified. Grounded Theory requires good articulation for categorization as the data are vast and open-ended. Each member provided their own logic to identify each category, and after the logic was approved by all members, the category was declared to exist.

Selective Coding

Selective Coding is the "process of integration and refining the theory" (Corbin & Strauss, 1990, p. 143). In this phase, a core category was created with other categories around it to build upon the theory. This process included questioning and re-questioning the rationale behind the extracted core category and the established relationships. To determine the causal relationships, the participant examined the connectors and searched for important terms such as influence on, results in, causes, follows, together with, etc. Thus, linkages were identified.

Result

In this study, we were able to make conclusions about the elements influencing people's thoughts about accepting AI in healthcare by looking at the patterns found in the interviews. The starting assumption was that young people were not fully aware of the usage of AI in healthcare, but contrary to this, the study reveals that out of 32 students, all were aware of using AI in healthcare. Another important thing was revealed that out of 32 respondents, 21 respondents showed major concerns about Data Privacy; they wanted to have government or relevant health authorities' assurance for the safety of all the patient data from cyber-attacks or any kind of leakages.

Factors Affecting Adoption of AI in the Healthcare Sector

Category I

The majority of the young, educated respondents revealed that patients' data are highly sensitive and requires high protection to ensure the privacy of the patients. Typical responses of this category are as follows:

> "According to me patients' data is highly sensitive and ensures its privacy by using AI".
> "I feel data privacy is the major challenge because protecting patient data is very crucial".
> "I guess there is a lack of medical data safety".
> "According to me, medical data is highly sensitive hence any kind of cyber-attack can lead to security risks".
> "From my perspective, data of patients suffering from critical ailments is in danger".
> Based on the above responses, Category I was named "**Lack of Data Privacy of Patients.**"

Category II

Many respondents talked about the errors generated by AI machines based on the historical data which was used to train those machines. AI machines predict the output based on the diverse samples that are fed into these machines.

> "I am really worried about the output generated by machines. If the data is collected from a specific geographic location or for a specific age group or gender, then the prediction may not be accurate for other geographic locations or different age groups or gender".
> "According to me if AI machines are trained with biased data like specific zip code, age, gender and income group then prediction will also be biased".
> "I feel that sample data on which machines are trained should be unbiased and large in quantity so that better health predictions are done from these machines"
> The responses helped to name category II as "**Biased Prediction".**

Category III

Many respondents were apprehensive about the affordability of AI-enabled treatments. Some of the responses include:

"I feel that developing and maintaining AI can be expensive and can act as a barrier".
"In my opinion, It is not accessible to every section of the society as it is very expensive".
"It is not easy to adopt this technology, especially by small hospitals because of high cost".
"I feel complete integration and automation will be too expensive to adopt this technology".
The responses helped to name Category III as "the **High Cost of using AI**".

Category IV

Few respondents had the view that someone should be accountable in case any untoward incident takes place when using AI. Some of the responses include:

"I feel accountability and transparency and prioritizing the needs and rights of patients should be there".
"There is no sense of accountability and ethics associated if anything wrong occurs".
"In my opinion, ethical issues can arise which may or may not comply with medical regulations".
"I feel that it is not easy to regulate all the measures ethically".
"Disruptions with AI can occur very easily hence there is not much safety associated with this".
The responses helped to name Category IV as "**Lack of Accountability.**"

Category V

Many of the respondents talked about the difficulty in new technology adoption. A few of the responses are shown below:

"I feel there can be resistance to adopt new technologies due to fear of job loss".
"I feel the people who are working with doctors in managing and handling data will lose their livelihood".
"I feel there will be no jobs if we go for a complete automation system".
"I have a fear of unemployment if we go for AI integration".
The responses helped to name the Category V as "**Lack of Job Security.**"

Category VI

Few respondents talked about rigorous testing before implementing AI clinically on patients with stringent Government guidelines. A few of the responses are shown below:

"I would accept it if the system is approved by relevant health authorities after well testing".
"According to me, the system should be rigorously tested to ensure the safety of the patients and approved by health regulatory bodies".
The responses helped to name Category VI as "**Lack of Government Regulations**".

Category VII

Many of the respondents talked about the availability of the right resources. A few of the responses are shown below:

"According to me sufficient resources, such as advanced hardware and software are unavailable for its integration".
"I feel that there is a gap in thinking between developers, doctors, and patients to design a successful model".
"I think there should be a proper collaboration between technology guy, doctors and other health care workers along with stakeholders to develop a successful framework before integrating AI".

"As per me in a country like India, we don't have such advanced technologies and enough resources which will completely transform the manual systems into automation in the health sector".

The responses helped to name the Category VII as "**Lack of Resources**".

Category VIII

Many of the respondents talked about the attitude of medical and para-medical staff. A few of the responses are shown below:

"I feel that there is a generation gap in the adoption of new technologies. Experienced doctors or older healthcare workers may not be easily ready to adopt new technologies".
"In my opinion, doctors should get proper and regular training to feel comfortable in adopting new technologies".
"In my view, doctors are not that capable when it comes to handling and managing AI with their traditional practice".
The responses helped to name Category VIII as "**Lack of Attitude.**"

Based on the respondents' responses, a model was developed consisting of the factors that acted as the main source of challenges to the acceptance of AI given in Fig. 6.1.

Discussions

The purpose of this study is to find out the main challenges influencing successful adoption of AI in the healthcare sector. The analysis shows that every young respondent is aware about use of AI in the modern healthcare sector, but only 56% of our total respondents agreed to be treated by AI provided its applications are tested rigorously and approved by health regulatory bodies.

Our study says that 100% of young graduates are aware of AI integration in the health sector, which is also aligned with the study done by Fritsch et al. (2022). Young professionals are ready to adopt the new technologies. The study also reveals that the majority (56.25%) of young people are ready to adopt and get treated by AI in the medical sector, which is consistent with previous research (Codari et al., 2019). They also feel that technology should be adopted for efficient and faster results provided the results remain unbiased. A total of 21 young professionals have raised their concerns about the data privacy or safety of patient data which is more dangerous than a nuclear bomb. Therefore, keeping the data safe for all patients is the most important factor leading to the adoption of AI in the healthcare sector. Our study is aligned with the findings done by Fritsch et al.

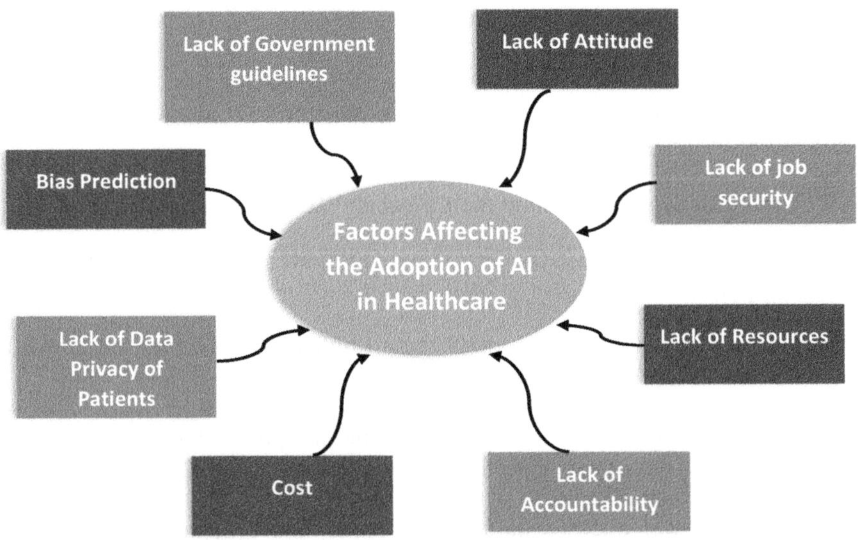

Fig. 6.1. Factors Affecting the Adoption of AI in the Healthcare Sector. *Source:* Created by authors.

(2022) and Hashiguchi et al. (2022), which focused on data privacy as a major hindrance in adopting AI in the medical sector. Another factor that was highlighted in this study is the implementation challenges and availability of resources. Respondents think there is a huge gap in communication between our doctors, patients and healthcare workers. Our respondents also believe there should be a proper framework designed before implementation in a clinical setting to ensure the satisfaction of all the stakeholders. Our study has also highlighted other important challenges, such as the attitude of healthcare workers, cost factors and biased predictions, in adapting new technologies in the modern healthcare sector. These factors are supported by earlier authors (Castagno & Khalifa, 2020; Fritsch et al., 2022; Hashiguchi et al., 2022; Saxena et al., 2024) in their findings.

Initially, respondents did not want to accept the treatment done completely by AI machine. However, when explained the potential and long-term benefits, they agreed that if the challenges currently faced by patients and healthcare workers are taken care of, they will be ready to be treated by AI-enabled machines. This is supported by many earlier researchers. In research done by earlier researchers (Amjad et al., 2023; Castagno & Khalifa, 2020) from year 2020 to 2023, they highlighted the strength of AI in the early prediction of any disease which results in early curing of patients with better accuracy rates. In general, if collaborative insights involving senior health professionals, government, patients and software developers are considered, it could pave a well-structured model for the health industry. This will improve the nation's healthcare system, making India a stronger nation.

Limitations and Future Direction

Future researchers can expand research on AI in the healthcare sector by using more diverse and inclusive samples from different geographical locations, socioeconomic backgrounds and different age groups to generalize the AI models with reduced bias.

Conclusion

The findings of this study highlight both the challenges and the huge potential associated with AI adoption in the healthcare sector. The educated young professionals are aware of the benefits and harms of the use of AI in the healthcare sector and demonstrate a willingness to embrace AI-driven treatments. But their adoption of AI-enabled treatment is contingent upon thorough testing, government guidelines and the assurance of unbiased results. Concerns about data privacy emerge as a crucial barrier, emphasizing the necessity of strong security measures to safeguard the patient information. In addition, the attitude and mindset of the health care professionals, cost associated, problems in implementation of AI technology and communication gaps among stakeholders are other significant factors impacting adoption of AI in healthcare sector.

Since AI has the potential to transform the Indian healthcare system to global standards, there is a need for all the stakeholders to come on a common platform to develop a well-structured AI implementation framework and effectively integrate it with the healthcare sector, thus ensuring better patient care.

References

Abuzaid, M. M., Elshami, W., & Fadden, S. M. (2022). Integration of artificial intelligence into nursing practice. *Health Technology*, *12*(6), 1109–1115.

Amjad, A., Kordel, P., & Fernandes, G. (2023). A review on innovation in healthcare sector (telehealth) through artificial intelligence. *Sustainability*, *15*(8), 6655.

Castagno, S., & Khalifa, M. (2020). Perceptions of artificial intelligence among healthcare staff: A qualitative survey study. *Frontiers in Artificial Intelligence*, *3*, 578983.

Codari, M., Melazzini, L., Morozov, S. P., van Kuijk, C. C., Sconfienza, L. M., & Sardanelli, F. (2019). Impact of artificial intelligence on radiology: A EuroAIM survey among members of the European society of radiology. *Insights Imaging*. *10*, 105. https://doi.org/10.1186/s13244-019-0798-3

Corbin, J., & Strauss, A. (1990). Grounded theory research: Procedures, canons and evaluative criteria. *Qualitative Sociaology*, *13*, 3–21.

Fassinger, R. E. (2005). Paradigms, praxis, problems, and promise: Grounded theory in counseling psychology research. *Journal of Counseling Psychology*, *52*, 156–166. https://doi.org/10.1037/0022-0167.52.2.156

Forbes. (2023). https://www.forbes.com/advisor/in/health-insurance/ai-in-healthcare/

Fritsch, S. J., Blankenheim, A., Wahl, A., Hetfeld, P., Maassen, O., Deffge, S., Kunze, J., Rossaint, R., Riedel, M., Marx, G., & Bickenbach, J. (2022). Attitudes and perception of artificial intelligence in healthcare: A cross-sectional survey among patients. *Digital Health*, *8*. https://doi.org/10.1177/20552076221116772

Glaser, B. G. (1992). Emergence vs forcing: Basics of grounded theory analysis: Strategies for qualitative research (Aldine, New York) in Bhal, K. T. and N. Debnath (2007), exploring cognitive moral logics using grounded theory: The case of software piracy. *Journal of Business Ethics*, *81*, 635–646.

Glaser, B. G. (1998). *Doing grounded theory: Issues and discussions*. Sociology Press.

Glaser, B. G., & Strauss, A. L. (1967). *The discovery of grounded theory: Strategies for qualitative research*. Sociology Press.

Gupta, A. S., & Mukherjee, J. (2025). Framework for adoption of generative AI for information search of retail products and services. *International Journal of Retail & Distribution Management*, *53*(2), 165–181.

Hashiguchi, T. C. O., Oderkirk, J., & Slawomirski, L. (2022). Fulfilling the promise of artificial intelligence in the health sector: Let's get real. *Value in Health*, *25*(3), 368–373.

Hossain, M. S., Syeed, M. M., Fatema, K., & Uddin, M. F. (2022). The perception of health professionals in Bangladesh toward the digitalization of the health sector. *International Journal of Environmental Research and Public Health*, *19*(20), 13695.

Ogolodom, M. P., Mbaba, A. N., Johnson, J., Chiegwu, H. U., Ordu, K. S., Okej, M. C., Daniel Ochong, A., Brownson Egop, E., Ugwem Jeremiah, C., Kenneth Madume, A., Nyenke, C. U., Dambele, M. Y., Joseph, D. Z., Bakre, A. F. K.,

Balogun, E. O., Alazigha, N., & Nwodo, V. K. (2023). Knowledge and perception of healthcare workers towards the adoption of artificial intelligence in healthcare service delivery in Nigeria. *AG Salud, 1*, 16.

Saxena, A. K., Ness, S., & Khinvasara, T. (2024). The influence of AI: The revolutionary effects of artificial intelligence in healthcare sector. *Journal of Engineering Research and Reports, 26*(3), 49–62.

Secinaro, S., Calandra, D., Secinaro, A., Muthurangu, V., & Biancone, P. (2021). The role of artificial intelligence in healthcare: A structured literature review. *BMC Medical Informatics and Decision Making, 21*, 1–23.

Strauss, A., & Corbin, J. (1998). *Basics of qualitative research techniques*. Sage Publications.

Zhang, Z., Genc, Y., Wang, D., Ahsen, M. E., & Fan, X. (2021). Effect of AI explanations on human perceptions of patient-facing AI-powered healthcare systems. *Journal of Medical Systems, 45*(6), 64.

Chapter 7

Adoption of AI-Driven Mental Health Apps Among the Younger Generation: An Extended Technology Acceptance Model (TAM) Approach

Sarita Nagvanshi, Mohd Junaid Akhtar, Vinod Kumar and Teena Singh

New Delhi Institute of Management, India

Abstract

This study investigates the factors influencing the adoption of Artificial Intelligence (AI)-driven mental health applications among younger generations, focusing on Gen Z and Millennials. By extending the Technology Acceptance Model (TAM) with additional constructs such as trust, social influence (SI), hedonic motivation (HM) and price value, the research provides a deeper understanding of the drivers behind attitudes and intentions toward using these apps. Primary data were gathered through a questionnaire targeting Gen Z and Millennials, and the analysis was conducted using structural equation modelling (SEM). The findings reveal that perceived ease of use, HM and trust significantly enhance attitudes toward using AI-based mental health apps, while perceived usefulness does not directly affect attitudes or intentions. Additionally, attitude serves as a mediator between factors like ease of use and HM and the intention to adopt these applications. The study underscores the critical role of trust and SI in increasing adoption rates. Developers are encouraged to prioritise data privacy and transparency to build user trust. These insights are valuable for app developers, healthcare providers and policymakers aiming to promote the acceptance of AI-based mental health solutions. Future research should expand the demographic scope and employ longitudinal studies to better understand changing user behaviours over time.

Digital Transformation and Artificial Intelligence for Operational Excellence in Healthcare, 119–143

doi:10.1108/978-1-83662-314-420251020

Keywords: Technology Acceptance Model (TAM); mental health; health care; Artificial Intelligence; Gen Z; structural equation modelling

Introduction

Mental disorders, which affect a significant portion of the world's population at any given time, are a major cause of disability globally (WHO, 2024). Unfortunately, many people do not receive the essential help because of a variety of barriers, including limited access to mental health care, societal stigma and financial restrictions (AIHW, 2024; Clement et al., 2015; Oexle et al., 2018). According to estimates from the World Health Organization (WHO, 2024), suicide claims the second-highest global death toll among those between the ages of 15 and 29 taking over 800,000 lives annually. Moreover, it suggests that a huge portion of the population in both developed and developing countries does not receive adequate mental health treatments (Jacinto Convit, 2021; WHO, 2022). The swift progression of Artificial Intelligence (AI) technologies has significantly influenced numerous domains, particularly healthcare, where AI-driven applications are increasingly deployed to support mental health services. These AI-based mental health apps provide a diverse array of services, encompassing personalised diagnosis, real-time monitoring, and immediate feedback, thus addressing the escalating demand for accessible and cost-effective mental health care. With smartphones and mobile health technologies becoming prevalent, these applications have found a strong following among younger individuals, especially Genn Z and Millennials, who tend to be more digitally savvy.

The emergence of Cyber Health Psychology has profoundly revolutionised the provision of mental health support (Casu et al., 2024). The incorporation of technological advancements in the realm of mental health has fundamentally transformed social interactions, modes of communication and even the construction of individual identities (Ancis, 2020). Virtual psychotherapeutic methods have revealed efficacy for prevalent mental health challenges, encompassing but not limited to depression, anxiety, substance use disorders and eating disorders (Taylor et al., 2021). The integration of technological and psychological dimensions, particularly through spatial computing and AI, has yielded promising outcomes (Spiegel et al., 2024). The global market for mental health applications, encompassing chatbots, was at USD 6.2 billion in 2023, with an expected annual growth rate of 15.2% from 2024 to 2030 (Grand View Research, 2022). As of 2022, mental health, meditation and sleep tracking applications constituted less than 15% of health-related applications, thereby highlighting significant potential for expansion in this domain (Statista, 2024). Digital mental health interventions specifically address the needs of young populations by leveraging technology for mental health evaluation, support, prevention and treatment purposes. For example, AI and machine learning (ML) frameworks are utilised in anticipating mental health problems (Iyortsuun et al., 2023), while chatbots powered by AI provide psychological support (Psychology Today, 2023; Wies et al., 2021). Chatbots like Woebot and Gabby, crafted for mental health therapy, have shown effectiveness in reducing depressive symptoms and automating certain aspects of therapeutic processes, which highlights a promising outlook for the development of AI-driven counselling systems (Fitzpatrick et al., 2017; Miner et al., 2017).

Despite the potential benefits, a continual divergence remains evident between the rapid progressions in digitally mediated mental health interventions and the successful integration of these tools (Fiske et al., 2019). Although the Technology Acceptance Model (TAM) has been extensively used to investigate the uptake of diverse technologies, its use concerning AI-based mental health apps remains inadequately studied, particularly in relation to the incorporation of constructs such as trust, social influence (SI), price value (PV) and hedonic motivation (HM). Existing research predominantly concentrates on general mHealth applications, frequently neglecting the distinctive challenges and barriers to adoption that are characteristic of AI-based mental health technologies. Furthermore, there exists an absence of comprehensive models that amalgamate cognitive, emotional and social dimensions to furnish a holistic comprehension of user adoption behaviour within this particular domain.

This study aims to advance the TAM by studying variables such as trust, SI, HM and PV to attain a more comprehensive insight into the acceptance of AI-based mental health apps among Gen Z and Millennials. It aims to (1) examine how perceived usefulness (PU), perceived ease of use (PEU), trust, SI, HM and PV impact the attitude towards and the intention to use (ITU) AI-driven mental health apps and (2) analyse how attitude serves mediates the relationship between these factors and the ITU AI-based mental health apps. The study aims to provide a novel understanding of the factors that affect the acceptance of such apps.

The chapter follows a systematic format. Initially, a comprehensive review of the existing literature is undertaken to establish a foundational understanding of the principal concepts, which will subsequently lead to formulation of a theoretical model and the development of hypotheses. Subsequently, the methodology for data collection, the characteristics of the sample and the instruments employed to evaluate the proposed model are presented. Thereafter, the results are articulated, followed by discussion of the findings and implications. The study concludes with the limitations and future scope.

Theoretical Framework and Hypothesis Development

Technology Acceptance Model

Davis (1989) offers a comprehensive model for understanding the adoption and utilisation of new technology by individuals. The TAM framework emphasises the cognitive and psychological determinants of technology acceptance (Marangunić & Granić, 2015). Its core constructs, PU and PEU, play a significant role in forming a person's attitude (ATT) towards technology (Hong et al., 2006). These perceptions establish a person's ATT, influencing their intent to accept or reject the technology (Davis, 1989). The effectiveness of TAM in understanding technology adoption is well-recognised, thanks to its solid theoretical basis, making it fit for research related to the adoption of mental health apps (Kim et al., 2022; Palos-Sanchez et al., 2021). Furthermore, its proven success in previous health care research demonstrates its relevance for studying the adoption of mental health apps (Kleine et al., 2023).

Recent studies have extended Davis's (1989) TAM to include a wider range of variables, addressing previous criticism and for wider range of acceptance (Leso & Cortimiglia, 2022). Therefore, to effectively capture the nuanced dynamics of adoption intentions for AI-based mental health apps, the original TAM constructs have been supplemented with variables such as trust in AI mechanism (TRS), HM, SI and PV. This extended framework deepens our understanding of technology adoption by presenting a complete picture of factors affecting behavioural intentions of adopting AI based mental health apps (Kelly et al., 2023; Liu et al., 2022). This approach demonstrates TAM's adaptability and relevance across various research areas, including the adoption intention of AI-based mental health apps (Palos-Sanchez et al., 2021). Further, this study has utilised TAM as it stands as the most frequently used framework for understanding e-health applications acceptance (Chauhan & Jaiswal, 2017).

Perceived Usefulness

PU means the extent to which someone believes that utilising a technology will lead to better job performance (Davis, 1989; Dwivedi et al., 2017). Therefore, within this framework, the construct can be described as the degree to which an individual thinks that using AI-based mental health apps will benefit them. Previous studies indicated that PU has an effect on the attitude and intention towards using mental health app (Ahmed et al., 2024; Chauhan & Jaiswal, 2017; Palos-Sanchez et al., 2021). Therefore, the following hypotheses have been proposed:

H1a: 'Perceived usefulness has a positive impact on attitude towards using AI-based mental health apps'.
H1b: 'Perceived usefulness has a positive impact on intention to use AI-based mental health apps'.

Perceived Ease of Use

PEU is a key factor in technology adoption (Almaiah et al., 2022). Individuals are more likely to adopt technology if they think it is easy to use and will make their tasks easier (Alsyouf et al., 2023; Luo et al., 2024). The same is true in adoption of AI-based mental health apps. Previous studies highlighted the effect of PEU on adopting healthcare apps (Jeon & Park, 2015; Cho, 2016). Jain et al. (2024) studied the effect and influence of PEU on attitude towards using mental health apps. Therefore, the following hypotheses have been postulated:

H2a: 'Perceived ease of use has a positive impact on attitude towards using AI-based mental health apps'.

H2b: 'Perceived ease of use has a positive impact on intention to use AI-based mental health apps'.

Hedonic Motivation

HM involves playfulness, fun, enjoyment and a sense of entertainment (Al-Azawei & Alowayr, 2020). The concept of HM is more likely associated with fun and playfulness than with the goal of completing tasks (Chang et al., 2011; Salimon et al., 2017). Motivation theory suggests that HM may play a pivotal role in determining users' acceptance of technology (Yang, 2013). Research has found that HM is an important factor in technology adoption, as it encourages a positive user attitude (Salimon et al., 2017; Sarker et al., 2023). This has also been confirmed in studies on the adoption of mental healthcare apps (Alam et al., 2021; Schmidt, 2022). Therefore, based on the evidences found in literature, following hypotheses have been proposed:

H3a: 'Hedonic motivation has a significant impact on attitude towards using AI-based mental health apps'.

H3b: 'Hedonic motivation has a significant impact on intention to use AI-based mental health apps'.

Price Value

The majority of mobile apps are free to download, with vendors trying to attract more consumers to use the app and ultimately make purchases (Al-Adwan & Sammour, 2020; Yu, 2012). The PV is deemed acceptable by the user when the advantages of using the technology surpass the associated costs (Venkatesh et al., 2012). PV builds on the concept of perceived value, where the evaluation involves comparing the perceived benefits with the sacrifices incurred (Teo et al., 2015; Khazaei, 2019). The technology usage might be influenced if the perceived benefits are greater than the monetary sacrifices made for IT applications (Natarajan et al., 2017; Vidal-Silva et al., 2024). Previous studies have demonstrated the significant influence of PV on the ITU mental healthcare apps (Chakraborty & Paul, 2023; Li et al., 2024). Similarly, Sarker et al. (2023) studied the effect of PV on consumer attitude and found the positive relationship between them. Therefore, based on the evidence found in previous research, following hypotheses have been postulated:

H4a: 'Price value has a significant impact on attitude towards using AI-based mental health apps'.

H4b: 'Price value has a significant impact on intention to use AI-based mental health apps'.

Social Influence

SIs can be understood as the processes through which individuals exert direct or indirect influence over the thoughts, feelings and actions of others (Vries et al., 1995). A person is often heavily influenced by their social circle, including relatives, friends and colleagues (Azhar et al., 2022; Han et al., 2010). In the context of using AI, Venkatesh et al. (2012) defines SI as 'the degree to which an individual perceives that important others believe he or she should use AI' (Cao et al., 2021). Earlier studies suggest that using AI is heavily influenced by social pressure (Hong, 2022; Nadella et al., 2023). Li et al. (2024) studied the use of AI chatbots for mental health and found that SI positively related to continuing use of mental health apps. Holtz et al. (2020) studied that SI positively influenced the attitude towards using AI-based mental health apps. Therefore, based on the evidence found in the previous literature, following hypotheses have been proposed:

H5a: 'Social influence has a significant impact on attitude towards using AI-based mental health apps.'

H5b: 'Social influence has a significant impact on intention to use AI-based mental health apps'.

Trust in AI Mechanism

Trust plays an important role in adoption of new technologies (Bitkina et al., 2020). Trust, in the realm of AI-based health solutions, can be conceptualised as users' belief that the system will act reliably, securely and ethically (Kleine et al., 2023). Researchers tested the impact of trust on the use of a new information system and various online services such as mobile wallet (Singh & Sinha, 2020), biometric technology (Pai et al., 2018) and health websites (Boon-itt, 2019). In the context of AI-enabled mental health applications, trust becomes even more pivotal due to the personalised and data-intensive nature of the services provided. Previous research explored positive association of trust on attitude and intention both (Gefen et al., 2003; Beldad & Hegner, 2018; Choung et al., 2023). Therefore, following hypotheses have been proposed for this study:

H6a: 'Trust in AI mechanism has a positive impact on attitude towards using AI-based mental health apps'.

H6b: 'Trust in AI mechanism has a positive impact on intention to use AI-based mental health apps'.

Attitude

Attitude is one of the key variables being explored in the field of consumer behaviour research (Maghnati & Ling, 2013). According to Van Birgelen et al. (2003), attitude is 'a psychological inclination that is shown by assessing a specific entity with varying degrees of favour or disfavour'. In the context of AI, Dwivedi et al. (2017) define attitude as 'an individual's positive or negative feelings about using AI for organisational decision-making'. Existing studies provide enough evidence towards the notion that a positive attitude toward technology is linked to a greater ITU it (Alqasa et al., 2014; Hasan, 2023; Yeoh et al., 2024). Similarly in the context of using AI-based mental health apps, attitude was found to greatly influence the usage intention towards it (Holtz et al., 2020; Lu et al., 2023; Nogueira-Leite et al., 2024). Therefore, following hypothesis has been hypothesised for the present study:

H7: 'Attitude has a significant impact on intention to use AI-based mental health apps'.

Mediating Role of Attitude

Mediating role of attitude towards ITU technology has been tested and verified in previous studies (Khurana et al., 2020; Singh & Tewari, 2021). Recent studies have also tested the mediating role of attitude in the context of adopting healthcare apps (Ofori et al., 2021; Ahadzadeh et al., 2021; Chawla & Joshi, 2023). Therefore, in the light of previous research this study explores the mediation effect of attitude on ITU AI-based mental health apps. For this, following hypotheses have been proposed:

H8a: 'Attitude mediates the relationship between perceived usefulness and intention to use AI-based mental health apps'.
H8b: 'Attitude mediates the relationship between perceived ease of use and intention to use AI-based mental health apps'.
H8c: 'Attitude mediates the relationship between hedonic motivation and intention to use AI-based mental health apps'.
H8d: 'Attitude mediates the relationship between price value and intention to use AI-based mental health apps'.
H8e: 'Attitude mediates the relationship between social influence and intention to use AI-based mental health apps'
H8f: 'Attitude mediates the relationship between trust and intention to use AI-based mental health apps'

Fig. 7.1 depicts a framework that represents the hypothetical relationships between the variables.

Methodology

Gen Z and Millennials who were aware of these applications and their features were taken into consideration as the population to study how likely it was for young people to use AI-based mental health apps. A representative sample was selected from which the data were collected. Since data were collected only from youngsters informed about such apps, the sampling method was purposive sampling.

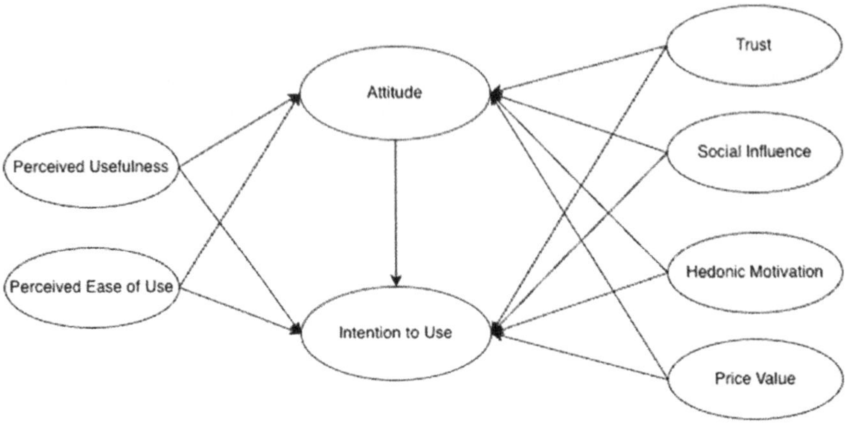

Fig. 7.1. Research Framework. *Source:* Author's own source.

A questionnaire was utilised to gather primary data for the study from the respondents. The questions on the questionnaire were designed to be closed-ended. A 5-point Likert scale, with 1 denoting strongly disagree and 5 denoting strongly agree, was used for the questions. There were multiple sections on the questionnaire: the demographic portion was the first, and the measurement of items section was the second. The demographic section's questions gathered information on the respondents' age, gender and other personal details. The following range of items was used to measure the study's latent variables: PEU with four items, PU with three items, trust measured with four items, SI measured with four items, HM with four items, PV with three items, Attitude with three items and ITU measured with three items. The measuring items for latent variables were taken from a variety of sources and have been listed in the Appendix section.

Results

Descriptive Statistics

The descriptive analysis of the study's respondents shows that the majority were male (62.77%), with females comprising 37.23%. Most respondents belonged to the Gen Z age group (67.88%), followed by Millennials (32.12%). In terms of household income, 42.34% earned above 10 lakhs while 10.22% earned below 2.5 lakhs. Educationally, the majority held a Master's degree (53.28%), with 42.34% having a Bachelor's degree, and a small percentage (2.92%) holding a Doctoral degree. In terms of employment, students made up the largest segment (58.76%), followed by those employed (34.67%), with small proportions of unemployed (3.65%) and self-employed (2.92%) individuals. These results of the descriptive analysis are summarised in Table 7.1.

Table 7.1. Descriptive Statistics.

Variable	Frequency (*n*)	Percentage (%)
Gender		
Male	172	62.77
Female	102	37.23
Others		
Age		
Gen Z (Born 1997–2012)	186	67.88
Millennial (Born 1981–1996)	88	32.12
Annual Household Income		
Below 2.5 lakhs	28	10.22
2.5–5 lakhs	38	13.87
5-7.5 lakhs	38	13.87
7.5–10 lakhs	54	19.71
Above 10 lakhs	116	42.34
Education		
High school, diploma or less	4	1.46
Bachelor's degree	116	42.34
Master's degree	146	53.28
Doctoral degree	8	2.92
Employment		
Student	161	58.76
Working	95	34.67
Unemployed	10	3.65
Self employed	8	2.92

Source: Author's own source.

The model's reliability was analysed through Cronbach's alpha, composite reliability (CR) and factor loadings, as presented in Table 7.2. Cronbach alpha, which assesses internal consistency, showed values ranging from 0.706 to 0.862, indicating acceptable reliability. CR, which measures internal consistency, ranged from 0.829 to 0.916, exceeding the recommended threshold of 0.70, thus confirming strong reliability among the constructs. Construct validity was measured through average variance extracted (AVE) and factor loadings. According to the guidelines by (Hair et al., 2010, 2013), the minimum threshold for both AVE and factor loadings is 0.50. In this study, AVE values ranged from 0.548 to 0.784, with factor loadings between 0.648 and 0.897, all meeting the required threshold. These

Table 7.2. Reliability and Validity Assessment.

Paths	Factor Loading	Cronbach Alpha	Composite Reliability	AVE	VIF
Perceived Ease of Use		0.734	0.829	0.548	
PEU1 → PEU	0.784				1.315
PEU2 → PEU	0.706				1.441
PEU3 → PEU	0.73				1.574
PEU4 → PEU	0.74				1.332
Perceived Usefulness		0.706	0.835	0.627	
PU1 → PU	0.794				1.472
PU2 → PU	0.784				1.464
PU3 → PU	0.798				1.273
Price Value		0.707	0.85	0.739	
PV1 → PV	Removed				
PV2 → PV	0.863				1.296
PV3 → PV	0.856				1.296
Trust		0.74	0.837	0.563	
TRS1 → TRS	0.648				1.296
TRS2 → TRS	0.801				1.618
TRS3 → TRS	0.808				1.632
TRS4 → TRS	0.734				1.317
Social Influence		0.821	0.881	0.651	
SI1 → SI	0.838				1.695
SI2 → SI	0.869				2.332
SI3 → SI	0.85				2.317
SI4 → SI	0.652				1.365
Hedonic Motivation		0.805	0.885	0.721	
HM1 → HM	0.9				2.29
HM2 → HM	0.842				1.991
HM3 → HM	0.802				1.498
Attitude		0.805	0.885	0.719	
ATT1 → ATT	0.805				1.641
ATT2 → ATT	0.884				2.185
ATT3 → ATT	0.854				1.743

Table 7.2. *(Continued)*

Paths	Factor Loading	Cronbach Alpha	Composite Reliability	AVE	VIF
Intention to Use		0.862	0.916	0.784	
ITU1 → ITU	0.869				1.854
ITU2 → ITU	0.889				2.558
ITU3 → ITU	0.897				2.601

Source: Author's own source.

findings confirm that the model is both valid and reliable. The variance inflation factor (VIF) values for the items ranged from 1.273 to 2.601, all of which are below the critical threshold of 5.0. This indicates that the structural model does not suffer from multicollinearity issues, meaning that there is no significant correlation among the predictors that could negatively impact the model's results (Hair et al., 2017; Ringle et al., 2015).

The discriminant validity of the model was assessed using both the Fornell–Larcker Criterion (FLC) and the Heterotrait–Monotrait Ratio (HTMT), and the results confirm that the constructs are distinct and well-defined. The FLC states that discriminant validity is proven when the correlations between any construct and any other construct (off-diagonal values) are less than the square root of the AVE for each construct (represented by the diagonal values) (Fornell & Larcker, 1981). In the provided data, each construct's diagonal value exceeds its correlations with other constructs. This satisfies the requirements for discriminant validity. Furthermore, the HTMT analysis, which examines the ratio of correlations between constructs, shows that all HTMT values are less than the threshold of 0.85, which is generally recommended to confirm discriminant validity. The highest HTMT value is 0.87 between ATT and ITU, but it remains below the stricter threshold of 0.90, further supporting the model's discriminant validity. The results of HTMT and the FLC are shown in Table 7.3.

Hypothesis Evaluation

The study utilised PLS-SEM to assess the relationships between various constructs and the ITU AI-based mental health apps (Table 7.4). The analysis provided insights into the direct, mediating, and total effects of PEU, PU, trust (TRS) SI, HM, PV and attitude (ATT) on ITU. The findings revealed that PEU had a significant positive effect on attitude ($\beta = 0.281, p < 0.01$), suggesting that when users perceive a technology or service as easy to use, their attitude towards it becomes more favourable. This is consistent with the TAM, which posits that ease of use enhances users' perceptions and, consequently, their attitudes. However, PEU did not show a significant direct effect on ITU ($\beta = 0.025, p > 0.05$), indicating that while ease of use shapes attitudes, it does not directly translate into

Table 7.3. Discriminant Validity Analysis.

	ATT	HM	ITU	PEU	PU	PV	SI	TRS
Heterotrait Monotrait Ratio (HTMT)								
ATT								
HM	0.471							
ITU	0.87	0.543						
PEU	0.673	0.444	0.525					
PU	0.724	0.451	0.603	0.807				
PV	0.682	0.401	0.689	0.448	0.558			
SI	0.566	0.476	0.637	0.241	0.4	0.642		
TRS	0.839	0.3	0.662	0.469	0.767	0.504	0.635	
Fornell-Larcker Criterion (FLC)								
ATT	0.848							
HM	0.386	0.849						
ITU	0.735	0.459	0.885					
PEU	0.553	0.362	0.448	0.74				
PU	0.554	0.339	0.481	0.575	0.792			
PV	0.49	0.29	0.514	0.33	0.371	0.86		
SI	0.488	0.369	0.556	0.198	0.332	0.481	0.807	
TRS	0.661	0.239	0.535	0.36	0.574	0.352	0.495	0.751

Source: Author's own source.

Table 7.4. Hypothesis Evaluation and SEM Analysis.

HN	Hypothesised Paths	β	M	SD	t Value	p Values	Results
Direct Effect							
H1a	PU → ATT	0.03	0.036	0.059	0.512	0.304	Not Supported
H1b	PU → ITU	0.031	0.042	0.059	0.529	0.298	Not Supported
H2a	PEU → ATT	0.281	0.277	0.057	4.962	0	Supported
H2b	PEU → ITU	0.025	0.025	0.048	0.524	0.3	Not Supported
H3a	HM → ATT	0.089	0.095	0.05	1.78	0.038	Supported

Table 7.4. *(Continued)*

HN	Hypothesised Paths	β	M	SD	t Value	p Values	Results
H3b	HM → ITU	0.144	0.142	0.068	2.136	0.016	Supported
H4a	PV → ATT	0.164	0.159	0.056	2.935	0.002	Supported
H4b	PV → ITU	0.118	0.126	0.058	2.055	0.02	Supported
H5a	SI → ATT	0.107	0.108	0.048	2.238	0.013	Supported
H5b	SI → ITU	0.182	0.18	0.051	3.59	0	Supported
H6a	TRS → ATT	0.41	0.409	0.057	7.163	0	Supported
H6b	TRS → ITU	0.019	0.014	0.058	0.333	0.37	Not Supported
H7	ATT → ITU	0.488	0.481	0.076	6.444	0	Supported
Mediating Effect							
H8a	PU → ATT → ITU	0.015	0.016	0.028	0.524	0.3	Not Supported
H8b	PEU → ATT → ITU	0.137	0.135	0.039	3.481	0	Supported
H8c	HM → ATT → ITU	0.044	0.044	0.023	1.886	0.03	Supported
H8d	PV → ATT → ITU	0.08	0.077	0.03	2.631	0.004	Supported
H8e	SI → ATT → ITU	0.052	0.052	0.024	2.165	0.015	Supported
H8f	TRS → ATT → ITU	0.2	0.197	0.043	4.69	0	Supported
Total Effect							
	PU → ITU	0.046	0.058	0.064	0.724	0.234	Not Supported
	PEU → ITU	0.162	0.16	0.059	2.762	0.003	Supported
	HM → ITU	0.188	0.187	0.065	2.894	0.002	Supported
	PV → ITU	0.198	0.203	0.064	3.077	0.001	Supported
	SI → ITU	0.235	0.232	0.058	4.071	0	Supported
	TRS → ITU	0.219	0.211	0.071	3.112	0.001	Supported

Source: Author's own source.

an ITU the technology. HM emerged as another significant factor, influencing both attitude ($\beta = 0.089, p < 0.05$) and ITU ($\beta = 0.144, p < 0.05$) suggesting that the enjoyment or pleasure derived from using a technology plays a critical role in forming positive attitudes and encouraging usage intentions. Trust had the most substantial direct effect on attitude ($\beta = 0.41, p < 0.01$), highlighting that trust is a key determinant of positive user attitudes. However, similar to PEU, trust did not have a significant direct impact on ITU ($\beta = 0.019, p > 0.05$), indicating that while trust significantly influences attitudes, it does not directly lead to the ITU the technology. In contrast, constructs like PU, while theoretically important, did not exhibit significant direct effects on either attitude or ITU. Both the paths from PU to ATT ($\beta = 0.03, p > 0.05$) and from PU to ITU ($\beta = 0.031, p > 0.05$) were not supported.

The study also explored the mediating role of attitude in the relationships between the constructs and ITU AI-based mental health apps. Attitude served as a significant mediator in several key relationships. For instance, the relationship between PEU and ITU was significantly mediated by attitude ($\beta = 0.137, p < 0.01$), suggesting that while PEU does not directly influence ITU, it has an indirect impact. Similarly, the relationships between SI ($\beta = 0.052, p < 0.015$), HM ($\beta = 0.044, p < 0.03$), PV ($\beta = 0.08, p < 0.004$) and ITU were also mediated by attitude.

When considering both direct and indirect pathways, the total effects of the constructs on ITU were also analysed. Constructs like PEU, HM, PV, SI and trust all had significant total effects on ITU, even if their direct effects were not always significant. For instance, the total effect of PEU on ITU was significant ($\beta = 0.162$, $p < 0.01$) despite the non-significant direct effect. This result indicates that the influence of PEU on ITU is fully realised when considering the mediating role of ATT. Similarly, SI and trust had significant total effects on ITU ($\beta = 0.235, p < 0.01$ and $\beta = 0.219, p < 0.01$, respectively), emphasising that SI and trust contribute to the ITU, particularly when their effects are mediated by attitudes. While some constructs, like PEU and trust, may not directly influence intention, their impact is significant when mediated through attitude. Fig. 7.2 represents the hypotheses results of the PLS-SEM analysis.

Discussion

The current study investigates the factors influencing the adoption of AI-based mental health applications among Gen Z and Millennials, utilising an extended TAM. The findings provide insight on how several constructs – PU, PEU, SI, HM, pricing value (PV) and attitude (ATT) – impact respondents' intentions to use these apps. The results show that PU has no substantial direct effect on either attitude or ITU AI-based mental health apps. This outcome contradicts the core premise of the original TAM, which posits that PU is a critical determinant of technology adoption (Davis, 1989). A possible explanation for this deviation could be the unique context of AI-based mental health apps, where users may prioritise emotional engagement or trust over perceived effectiveness. The significant positive impact of PEU on attitude ($\beta = 0.281, p < 0.01$), however, aligns with the TAM and other studies (Jeon & Park, 2015; Cho, 2016). This suggests that when users perceive AI-based mental health apps as easy to use, their attitude towards these apps improves, even if PU does not directly influence their behavioural intentions. The lack of a significant direct effect of PEU ($\beta = 0.025$,

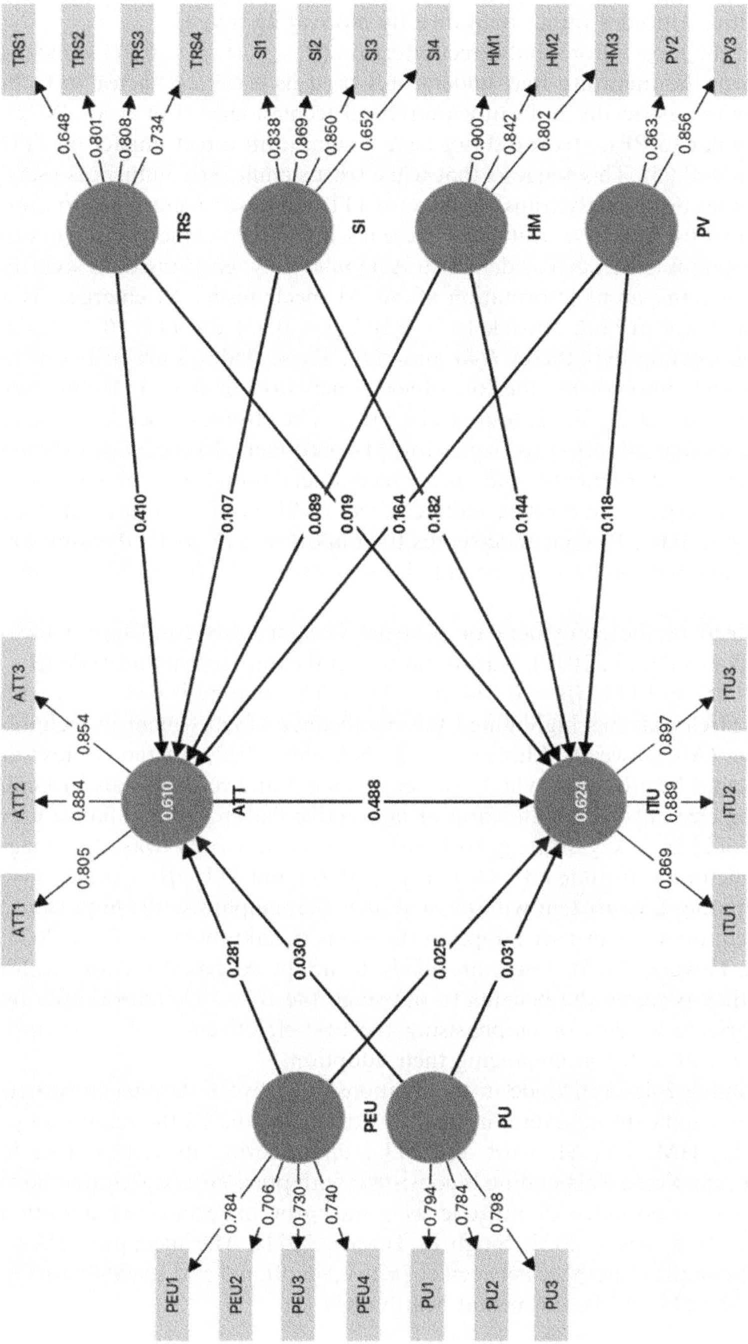

Fig. 7.2. Hypothesis Evaluation and SEM Analysis. *Source:* Author's own source.

$p > 0.05$) further highlights that ease of use impacts user intentions indirectly by shaping positive attitudes rather than directly motivating usage.

Trust had the most substantial direct effect on ($\beta = 0.41$, $p < 0.01$), which is consistent with the literature that underscores trust as a critical factor in technology adoption, especially in healthcare-related technologies (Liu et al., 2022). However, similar to PEU, trust did not have a significant direct impact on ITU ($\beta = 0.019$, $p > 0.05$). This suggests that while trust significantly influences users' attitudes, it does not directly translate into the ITU AI-based mental health apps unless mediated by a positive attitude. Future research could explore strategies to build and maintain trust, such as demonstrating reliability, ensuring data security and providing transparent information about AI mechanisms. SI emerged as a significant predictor of both attitude ($\beta = 0.107$, $p < 0.05$) and ITU ($\beta = 0.182$, $p < 0.01$), supporting hypotheses *H4a* and *H4b*. These findings are in line with previous research emphasising the role of social networks in shaping technology adoption (Li et al., 2024; Venkatesh et al., 2012). The strong influence of social factors suggests that adoption strategies for AI-based mental health apps should leverage social endorsements and peer recommendations to enhance user acceptance. Moreover, the positive indirect effect of SI on ITU through attitude ($\beta = 0.052$, $p < 0.05$) further underscores the importance of social dynamics in the decision-making process of potential users especially from the younger generation.

HM, defined as the enjoyment or pleasure obtained from utilising a technology (Venkatesh et al., 2012), was found to significantly impact attitude ($\beta = 0.089$, $p < 0.05$) and ITU ($\beta = 0.144$, $p < 0.05$). This finding is consistent with previous research that has highlighted the significance of enjoyment in technology adoption (Al-Azawei & Alowayr, 2020; Schmidt, 2022). In the context of AI-based mental health apps, where user engagement and retention are critical, incorporating elements of gamification or interactive features that enhance user enjoyment could be a key strategy to boost adoption rates. PV was also a significant predictor of attitude ($\beta = 0.164$, $p < 0.01$) and ITU ($\beta = 0.118$, $p < 0.05$). This finding is consistent with prior studies that emphasise the importance of cost–benefit analyses in user adoption decisions (Chakraborty & Paul, 2023; Valentine & Powers, 2013). Users are likely to adopt AI-based mental health apps when they perceive the benefits to outweigh the costs. Therefore, offering affordable pricing models or emphasising the cost-effectiveness of these apps could be a crucial factor in enhancing their adoption.

The mediating role of attitude in the relationship between various constructs and ITU was significant in several instances. Attitude mediated the relationships between PEU, HM, PV, SI, trust and ITU, underscoring its critical role in shaping user intentions. This finding is consistent with previous research that have emphasised the importance of attitude as a mediator in technology adoption models (Chawla & Joshi, 2023; Singh & Tewari, 2021). The mediating effects highlight the complex interplay between cognitive, emotional and social factors in determining the ITU AI-based mental health apps.

Implications and Conclusion

This study produces several key theoretical implications. Examining the effect of attitude as a mediator in the ITU such technology helps refine and expand existing theories in technology acceptance, behavioural psychology and mental health interventions. This study contributes to a more nuanced understanding of how AI-based technologies influence attitudes, and ITU, offering insights that can guide future research and theoretical development. One of the central theoretical implications lies in expanding the traditional TAM to better capture the nuances of AI-based mental health apps. Further in this study, attitude is positioned as a mediator between the factors influencing the adoption of AI-based mental health apps. This mediation effect highlights the importance of understanding how attitudes are formed and altered in response to AI-based technologies, specifically in the sensitive area of mental health.

As the younger generation increasingly adopts digital solutions, mental health apps driven by AI have become an important tool to address mental well-being. Understanding the factors that drive their adoption and usage intention has profound implications for app developers, healthcare providers, policymakers and educators. This research contributes valuable insights into improving the effectiveness, acceptance and overall impact of AI-based mental health solutions. Attitude plays a mediating role in the adoption of AI-based mental health apps, making it crucial to foster positive perceptions about both AI and mental health apps through public awareness campaigns. Educational initiatives targeting the younger generation should emphasise the benefits of mental health care and how AI can enhance these services. Another key practical implication is the need for AI-based mental health app developers to focus on user experience about trust. The younger generation, though technologically savvy, is increasingly aware of data privacy issues. Therefore, mental health app developers must prioritise transparency in how AI uses personal data, clearly communicating privacy policies and security measures. Building trust is essential to shaping a positive attitude towards the app, which directly influences the ITU the app.

Limitations and Future Research Directions

While this study provides valuable insights into the adoption of AI-based mental health apps among the younger generation, it is not without its limitations. First one is, the study primarily focuses on younger users, which limits the generalisability of the findings to other age groups. Older adults or individuals with different technology exposure may exhibit different adoption behaviours and attitudes towards AI-based mental health apps. Also, the study relies heavily on self-reported data for assessing attitudes, perceptions and intentions. Future research can incorporate actual behavioural data from app usage patterns. Further, this study provides a cross-sectional snapshot of users' attitudes and intentions, which may evolve over time. Future researchers can use longitudinal research design to overcome this limitation.

References

Ahadzadeh, A. S., Wu, S. L., Ong, F. S., & Deng, R. (2021). The mediating influence of the unified theory of acceptance and use of technology on the relationship between internal health locus of control and mobile health adoption: Cross-sectional study. *Journal of Medical Internet Research*, *23*(12), e28086.

Ahmed, S., Alqasmi, I., Ashrafi, D. M., Choudhury, M. M., Rahman, M. K., & Mohiuddin, M. (2024). Determining the intention to use app-based medicine service in an emerging economy. *International Journal of Healthcare Management*, *17*(3), 468–482.

AIHW. (2024, July 24). *Prevalence and impact of mental illness—Mental health*. Australian Institute of Health and Welfare. https://www.aihw.gov.au/mental-health/overview/prevalence-and-impact-of-mental-illness

Al-Adwan, A. S., & Sammour, G. (2020). What makes consumers purchase mobile apps: Evidence from Jordan. *Journal of Theoretical and Applied Electronic Commerce Research*, *16*(3), 562–583.

Al-Azawei, A., & Alowayr, A. (2020). Predicting the intention to use and hedonic motivation for mobile learning: A comparative study in two middle eastern countries. *Technology in Society*, *62*, 101325.

Alam, M. M. D., Alam, M. Z., Rahman, S. A., & Taghizadeh, S. K. (2021). Factors influencing mHealth adoption and its impact on mental well-being during COVID-19 pandemic: A SEM-ANN approach. *Journal of Biomedical Informatics*, *116*, 103722.

Almaiah, M. A., Alhumaid, K., Aldhuhoori, A., Alnazzawi, N., Aburayya, A., Alfaisal, R., Salloum, S. A., Lutfi, A., Al Mulhem, A., Alkhdour, T., Awad, A. B., & Shehab, R. (2022). Factors affecting the adoption of digital information technologies in higher education: An empirical study. *Electronics*, *11*(21), 3572.

Alqasa, K. M., Mohd Isa, F., Othman, S. N., & Zolait, A. H. S. (2014). The impact of students' attitude and subjective norm on the behavioural intention to use services of banking system. *International Journal of Business Information Systems*, *15*(1), 105–122.

Alsyouf, A., Lutfi, A., Alsubahi, N., Alhazmi, F. N., Al-Mugheed, K., Anshasi, R. J., Alharbi, N. I., & Albugami, M. (2023). The use of a technology acceptance model (TAM) to predict patients' usage of a personal health record system: The role of security, privacy, and usability. *International Journal of Environmental Research and Public Health*, *20*(2), 1347.

Ancis, J. R. (2020). The age of cyberpsychology: An overview. *Technology, Mind, and Behavior*, *1*(1). https://doi.org/10.1037/tmb0000009

Azhar, M., Ali, R., Hamid, S., Akhtar, M. J., & Rahman, M. N. (2022). Demystifying the effect of social media eWOM on revisit intention post-COVID-19: An extension of theory of planned behavior. *Future Business Journal*, *8*(1), 49.

Beldad, A. D., & Hegner, S. M. (2018). Expanding the technology acceptance model with the inclusion of trust, social influence, and health valuation to determine the predictors of German users' willingness to continue using a fitness app: A structural equation modeling approach. *International Journal of Human-Computer Interaction*, *34*(9), 882–893.

Bitkina, O. V., Jeong, H., Lee, B. C., Park, J., Park, J., & Kim, H. K. (2020). Perceived trust in artificial intelligence technologies: A preliminary study. *Human Factors and Ergonomics in Manufacturing & Service Industries*, *30*(4), 282–290.

Boon-itt, S. (2019). Quality of health websites and their influence on perceived usefulness, trust and intention to use: An analysis from Thailand. *Journal of Innovation and Entrepreneurship*, *8*(4), 1–18.

Cao, G., Duan, Y., Edwards, J. S., & Dwivedi, Y. K. (2021). Understanding managers' attitudes and behavioral intentions towards using artificial intelligence for organizational decision-making. *Technovation*, *106*, 102312.

Casu, M., Triscari, S., Battiato, S., Guarnera, L., & Caponnetto, P. (2024). AI Chatbots for mental health: A scoping review of effectiveness, feasibility, and applications. *Applied Sciences*, *14*(13). Article 13. https://doi.org/10.3390/app14135889

Chakraborty, D., & Paul, J. (2023). Healthcare apps' purchase intention: A consumption values perspective. *Technovation*, *120*, 102481.

Chang, H. J., Eckman, M., & Yan, R. N. (2011). Application of the Stimulus-Organism-Response model to the retail environment: The role of hedonic motivation in impulse buying behavior. *International Review of Retail Distribution & Consumer Research*, *21*(3), 233–249.

Chauhan, S., & Jaiswal, M. (2017). A meta-analysis of e-health applications acceptance: Moderating impact of user types and e-health application types. *Journal of Enterprise Information Management*, *30*(2), 295–319.

Chawla, D., & Joshi, H. (2023). Role of mediator in examining the influence of antecedents of mobile wallet adoption on attitude and intention. *Global Business Review*, *24*(4), 609–625.

Cho, J. (2016). The impact of post-adoption beliefs on the continued use of health apps. *International Journal of Medical Informatics*, *87*, 75–83.

Choung, H., David, P., & Ross, A. (2023). Trust in AI and its role in the acceptance of AI technologies. *International Journal of Human-Computer Interaction*, *39*(9), 1727–1739.

Clement, S., Schauman, O., Graham, T., Maggioni, F., Evans-Lacko, S., Bezborodovs, N., Morgan, C., Rüsch, N., Brown, J. S. L., & Thornicroft, G. (2015). What is the impact of mental health-related stigma on help-seeking? A systematic review of quantitative and qualitative studies. *Psychological Medicine*, *45*(1), 11–27. https://doi.org/10.1017/S0033291714000129

Davis, F. D. (1989). Perceived usefulness, perceived ease of use, and user acceptance of information technology. *MIS Quarterly*, *13*(3), 319–340.

Dwivedi, Y. K., Rana, N. P., Janssen, M., Lal, B., Williams, M. D., & Clement, M. (2017). An empirical validation of a unified model of electronic government adoption (UMEGA). *Government Information Quarterly*, *34*(2), 211–230.

Fiske, A., Henningsen, P., & Buyx, A. (2019). Your robot therapist will see you now: ethical implications of embodied artificial intelligence in psychiatry, psychology, and psychotherapy. *Journal of Medical Internet Research*, *21*(5), e13216. https://doi.org/10.2196/13216

Fitzpatrick, K. K., Darcy, A., & Vierhile, M. (2017). Delivering cognitive behavior therapy to young adults with symptoms of depression and anxiety using a fully automated conversational agent (Woebot): A randomized controlled trial. *JMIR Mental Health*, *4*(2), e7785. https://doi.org/10.2196/mental.7785

Fornell, C., & Larcker, D. F. (1981). Evaluating structural equation models with unobservable variables and measurement error. *Journal of Marketing Research*, *18*(1), 39–50. https://doi.org/10.2307/3151312

Grand View Research. (2022). *Organic Personal Care Market Size & Share Report, 2030*. https://www.grandviewresearch.com/industry-analysis/organic-personal-care-market

Gefen, D., Karahanna, E., & Straub, D. W. (2003). Trust and TAM in online shopping: An integrated model. *MIS Quarterly*, 51–90.

Hair, J. F., Black, W. C., Babin, B. J., & Anderson, R. E. (2013). *Multivariate data analysis*. Pearson Education Limited.

Hair, J., Hult, G., & Ringle, C. (2017). *A Primer on Partial Least Squares Structural Equation Modeling (PLS-SEM)* (2nd ed.). Sage Publications.

Hair, J., William, C., Barry, J., & Anderson, R. (2010). *Multivariate data analysis*. Prentice Hall.

Han, H., Hsu, L. T. J., & Sheu, C. (2010). Application of the theory of planned behavior to green hotel choice: Testing the effect of environmental friendly activities. *Tourism Management*, *31*(3), 325–334.

Hasan, A. A. T. (2023). Determinants of intentions to use the foodpanda mobile application in Bangladesh: The role of attitude and fear of COVID-19. *South Asian Journal of Marketing*, *4*(1), 17–32.

Holtz, B. E., McCarroll, A. M., & Mitchell, K. M. (2020). Perceptions and attitudes toward a mobile phone app for mental health for college students: Qualitative focus group study. *JMIR Formative Research*, *4*(8), e18347.

Hong, J. W. (2022). I was born to love AI: The influence of social status on AI self-efficacy and intentions to use AI. *International Journal of Communication*, *16*, 20.

Hong, S., Thong, J. Y., & Tam, K. Y. (2006). Understanding continued information technology usage behavior: A comparison of three models in the context of mobile internet. *Decision Support Systems*, *42*(3), 1819–1834.

Iyortsuun, N. K., Kim, S.-H., Jhon, M., Yang, H.-J., & Pant, S. (2023). A review of machine learning and deep learning approaches on mental health diagnosis. *Healthcare*, *11*(3). Article 3. https://doi.org/10.3390/healthcare11030285

Jacinto Convit. (2021, October 28). *Mental health in developed vs developing countries*. Jacinto Convit World Organization. https://www.jacintoconvit.org/social-science-series-5-mental-health-in-developed-vs-developing-countries/

Jain, R., Munde, A., & Ansari, Z. A. (2024). Determinants of adoption of mobile health applications: A machine learning approach. *Procedia Computer Science*, *235*, 1568–1576.

Jeon, E., & Park, H. A. (2015). Factors affecting acceptance of smartphone application for management of obesity. *Healthcare Informatics Research*, *21*(2), 74–82.

Kelly, S., Kaye, S. A., & Oviedo-Trespalacios, O. (2023). What factors contribute to the acceptance of artificial intelligence? A systematic review. *Telematics and Informatics*, *77*, 101925.

Khazaei, H. (2019). The influence of personal innovativeness and price value on intention to use of electric vehicles in Malaysia. *European Online Journal of Natural and Social Sciences*, *8*(3), 483–494.

Khurana, A., Kumar, V. R., & Sidhpuria, M. (2020). A study on the adoption of electric vehicles in India: The mediating role of attitude. *Vision*, *24*(1), 23–34.

Kim, H. M., Xu, Y., & Wang, Y. (2022). Overcoming the mental health stigma through m-health apps: Results from the healthy minds study. *Telemedicine and e-Health*, *28*(10), 1534–1540.

Kleine, A. K., Kokje, E., Gaube, S., & Lermer, E. (2023). Attitudes toward the adoption of two AI-enabled mental health tools among prospective psychotherapists: A cross-sectional study. *JMIR Human Factors*. https://doi.org/10.2196/46859

Leso, B. H., & Cortimiglia, M. N. (2022). The influence of user involvement in information system adoption: An extension of TAM. *Cognition, Technology & Work*, *24*(2), 215–231.

Li, X., Han, J., & Lin, H. (2024). The effects of psychological flexibility and night shifts on mental health and well-being in nurses. *PLoS One*, *19*(11), e0313634. https://doi.org/10.1371/journal.pone.0313634

Liu, X., He, X., Wang, M., & Shen, H. (2022). What influences patients' continuance intention to use AI-powered service robots at hospitals? The role of individual characteristics. *Technology in Society*, *70*, 101996.

Lu, H. H., Lin, W. S., Raphael, C., & Wen, M. J. (2023). A study investigating user adoptive behavior and the continuance intention to use mobile health applications during the COVID-19 pandemic era: Evidence from the telemedicine applications utilized in Indonesia. *Asia Pacific Management Review*, *28*(1), 52–59.

Luo, J., Ahmad, S. F., Alyaemeni, A., Ou, Y., Irshad, M., Alyafi-Alzahri, R., Alsanie, G., & Unnisa, S. T. (2024). Role of perceived ease of use, usefulness, and financial strength on the adoption of health information systems: The moderating role of hospital size. *Humanities and Social Sciences Communications*, *11*(1), 1–12.

Maghnati, F., & Ling, K. C. (2013). Exploring the relationship between experiential value and usage attitude towards mobile apps among the smartphone users. *International Journal of Business and Management*, *8*(4), 1.

Marangunić, N., & Granić, A. (2015). Technology acceptance model: A literature review from 1986 to 2013. *Universal Access in the Information Society*, *14*, 81–95.

Miner, A. S., Milstein, A., & Hancock, J. T. (2017). Talking to machines about personal mental health problems. *JAMA*, *318*(13), 1217–1218. https://doi.org/10.1001/jama.2017.14151

Nadella, G. S., Meduri, S. S., Gonaygunta, H., & Podicheti, S. (2023). Understanding the role of social influence on consumer trust in adopting AI tools. *International Journal of Sustainable Development in Computing Science*, *5*(2), 1–18.

Natarajan, T., Balasubramanian, S. A., & Kasilingam, D. L. (2017). Understanding the intention to use mobile shopping applications and its influence on price sensitivity. *Journal of Retailing and Consumer Services*, *37*, 8–22.

Nogueira-Leite, D., Marques-Cruz, M., & Cruz-Correia, R. (2024). Individuals' attitudes toward digital mental health apps and implications for adoption in Portugal: Web-based survey. *BMC Medical Informatics and Decision Making*, *24*(1), 99.

Ofori, P. P., Antwi, E. A., & Owusu-Ansah, K. A. (2021). The mediating effects of satisfaction and attitude on consumers' intent toward adoption of social media healthcare information. *Journal of Health and Social Sciences*, *6*(3), 391–402.

Oexle, N., Müller, M., Kawohl, W., Xu, Z., Viering, S., Wyss, C., Vetter, S., & Rüsch, N. (2018). Self-stigma as a barrier to recovery: A longitudinal study. *European Archives of Psychiatry and Clinical Neuroscience*, *268*(2), 209–212. https://doi.org/10.1007/s00406-017-0773-2

Psychology Today. (2023, March). Generative AI could help solve the U.S. mental health crisis. *Psychology Today*. https://www.psychologytoday.com/au/blog/the-doctor-of-the-future/202303/generative-ai-could-help-solve-the-us-mental-health-crisis

Pai, C. K., Wang, T. W., Chen, S. H., & Cai, K. Y. (2018). Empirical study on Chinese tourists' perceived trust and intention to use biometric technology. *Asia Pacific Journal of Tourism Research*, *23*(9), 880–895.

Palos-Sanchez, P. R., Saura, J. R., Rios Martin, M. A., & Aguayo-Camacho, M. (2021). Toward a better understanding of the intention to use mHealth apps: Exploratory study. *JMIR mHealth and uHealth*, *9*(9), e27021.

Ringle, C., da Silva, D., & Bido, D. (2015). *Structural Equation Modeling with the SmartPLS*. (SSRN Scholarly Paper 2676422). https://papers.ssrn.com/abstract=2676422

Salimon, M. G., Yusoff, R. Z. B., & Mohd Mokhtar, S. S. (2017). The mediating role of hedonic motivation on the relationship between adoption of e-banking and its determinants. *International Journal of Bank Marketing*, *35*(4), 558–582.

Sarker, P., Dwivedi, Y. K., & Hughes, L. (2023, November). Investigating social commerce factors: Motivation, price value, habit, risk and attitude. In *Conference on e-Business, e-Services and e-Society* (pp. 207–223). Springer Nature Switzerland.

Schmidt, A. (2022). *The factors influencing the adoption of mental health applications* Doctoral dissertation.

Singh, N., & Sinha, N. (2020). How perceived trust mediates merchant's intention to use a mobile wallet technology. *Journal of Retailing and Consumer Services*, *52*, 101894.

Singh, R., & Tewari, A. (2021). Modeling factors affecting online learning adoption: Mediating role of attitude. *International Journal of Educational Management*, *35*(7), 1405–1420.

Spiegel, B. M. R., Liran, O., Clark, A., Samaan, J. S., Khalil, C., Chernoff, R., Reddy, K., & Mehra, M. (2024). Feasibility of combining spatial computing and AI for mental health support in anxiety and depression. *NPJ Digital Medicine*, *7*(1), 22. https://doi.org/10.1038/s41746-024-01011-0

Statista. (2024, July). *Meditation and mental wellness apps*. Statista. https://www.statista.com/topics/11045/meditation-and-mental-wellness-apps/

Taylor, C. B., Graham, A. K., Flatt, R. E., Waldherr, K., & Fitzsimmons-Craft, E. E. (2021). Current state of scientific evidence on Internet-based interventions for the treatment of depression, anxiety, eating disorders and substance abuse: An overview of systematic reviews and meta-analyses. *European Journal of Public Health*, *31*(31 Suppl. 1), i3–i10. https://doi.org/10.1093/eurpub/ckz208

Teo, A. C., Tan, G. W. H., Ooi, K. B., Hew, T. S., & Yew, K. T. (2015). The effects of convenience and speed in m-payment. *Industrial Management & Data Systems*, *115*(2), 311–331.

Valentine, D. B., & Powers, T. L. (2013). Generation Y values and lifestyle segments. *Journal of Consumer Marketing*, *30*(7), 597–606.

Van Birgelen, M., de Ruyter, K., & Wetzels, M. (2003). The impact of attitude strength on customer-oriented priority setting by decision-makers: An empirical investigation. *Journal of Economic Psychology*, *24*(6), 763–783.

Venkatesh, V., Thong, J. Y., & Xu, X. (2012). Consumer acceptance and use of information technology: Extending the unified theory of acceptance and use of technology. *MIS Quarterly*, 157–178.

Vidal-Silva, C., Sánchez-Ortiz, A., Serrano-Malebrán, J., Arriagada, V., Flores, M., Godoy, M., & Vargas, C. (2024). Social influence, performance expectancy, and price value as determinants of telemedicine services acceptance in Chile. *Heliyon*, *10*(5).

Vries, H. D., Backbier, E., Kok, G., & Dijkstra, M. (1995). The impact of social influences in the context of attitude, self-efficacy, intention, and previous behavior as predictors of smoking onset 1. *Journal of Applied Social Psychology*, *25*(3), 237–257.

WHO. (2022, June). WHO highlights urgent need to transform mental health and mental health care. https://www.who.int/news/item/17-06-2022-who-highlights-urgent-need-to-transform-mental-health-and-mental-health-care

WHO. (2024, May). World Health Organization: Mental health. https://www.who.int/health-topics/mental-health

Wies, B., Landers, C., & Ienca, M. (2021). Digital mental health for young people: A scoping review of ethical promises and challenges. *Frontiers in Digital Health*, *3*, 697072. https://doi.org/10.3389/fdgth.2021.697072

Yang, S. (2013). Understanding undergraduate students' adoption of mobile learning model: A perspective of the extended UTAUT2. *Journal of Convergence Information Technology*, *8*(10), 969.

Yeoh, R., Kim, H. K., Kang, H., Lin, Y. A., Ho, A. D., & Ho, K. F. (2024). What determines intentions to use mobile fitness apps? The independent and joint influence of social norms. *International Journal of Human-Computer Interaction*, *40*(2), 121–130.

Yu, C. S. (2012). Factors affecting individuals to adopt mobile banking: Empirical evidence from the UTAUT model. *Journal of Electronic Commerce Research*, *13*(2), 104.

Appendix

Table A1. Latent Variables and Measurement Items.

Variables	Measurement Items	Sources
Perceived Ease of Use		
PEU1	AI-based Mental Health apps will be easy to use.	Gefen and Straub (2000)
PEU2	It will be easy to become skilful at using AI-based Mental Health apps.	
PEU3	Learning to operate AI-based Mental Health apps would be easier for me.	
PEU4	AI-based Mental Health apps will be flexible to interact with.	
Perceived Usefulness		
PU1	Using AI-based Mental Health apps will be useful in everyday life.	Kang and Hwang (2022)
PU2	Using AI-based Mental Health apps can increase the effectiveness of my work.	
PU3	Using a healthcare wearable device will help me accomplish my mental health goals faster.	
Trust		
TRS1	AI-based Mental Health apps are trustworthy.	Sebastián et al. (2022)
TRS2	I trust AI-based Mental Health apps for their ability to perform their functions.	
TRS3	AI-based Mental Health apps will be capable of performing assigned tasks.	
TRS4	AI-based Mental Health apps will instil trust in me.	
Social Influence		
SI1	People who are important to me encourage me to interact with AI-based Mental Health apps.	Sebastián et al. (2022)
SI2	People whose opinions I value, prefer that I interact with AI-based Mental Health apps.	
SI3	People who influence my behaviour want me to utilise AI-based Mental Health apps.	

Table A1. *(Continued)*

Variables	Measurement Items	Sources
SI4	People in my social networks who interact with AI-based Mental Health apps have a high profile.	
Hedonic Motivation		
HM1	Using AI-based Mental Health apps will be fun.	Sebastián et al. (2022)
HM2	Using AI-based Mental Health apps will be enjoyable.	
HM3	Using AI-based Mental Health apps will be entertaining.	
Price Value		
PV1	AI-based Mental Health apps charge reasonably/are free.	Sebastián et al. (2022)
PV2	I am willing to pay for using AI-based Mental Health apps.	
PV3	The cost of AI-based Mental Health apps is manageable.	
Attitude		
ATT1	Using AI-based Mental Health apps is a good idea.	Cao et al. (2021)
ATT2	I like the idea of using AI-based Mental Health apps.	
ATT3	Using AI-based Mental Health apps would be pleasant.	
Intention to Use		
ITU1	I intend to use AI-based Mental Health apps in the future.	Sebastián et al. (2022)
ITU2	I will continue to use AI-based Mental Health apps regularly in my everyday life.	
ITU3	My plan is to continue on using AI-based Mental Health apps.	

Source: Author's own source.

Chapter 8

Revolutionizing Health Care With AI-Powered Contactless Remote Patient Monitoring: The Case of Dozee

Subhransu Nag and Kumar Chokalingam

Turtle Shell Technologies Private Limited, India

Abstract

The advent of Artificial Intelligence (AI) is transforming health care, particularly in remote patient monitoring (RPM). This chapter explores the clinical and business impact of Dozee, an AI-powered noninvasive RPM system designed to fill critical gaps in patient care, especially in non-ICU settings. By continuously tracking vital signs, Dozee enables early detection of deteriorating health conditions, triggering timely interventions. Its AI-powered Early Warning System (EWS) can predict health complications up to 16 hours in advance, thereby enhancing patient outcomes. The system's scalability and cloud integration facilitate its use across hospitals and home care settings, offering an efficient, noninvasive alternative to traditional monitoring methods. Additionally, Dozee's regulatory compliance ensures the highest standards of patient data safety and system reliability. This chapter discusses how Dozee's innovative technology is driving the adoption of AI in health care, leading to operational efficiencies, cost savings, and enhanced patient experiences. The case of Dozee exemplifies the future of value-based care in an increasingly digital and data-driven healthcare landscape.

Keywords: Remote patient monitoring (RPM); AI-driven health care; contactless monitoring; Early Warning System (EWS); noninvasive patient monitoring; healthcare innovation; Dozee; digital health transformation; cloud-based healthcare solutions; healthcare resource optimization

Digital Transformation and Artificial Intelligence for Operational Excellence in Healthcare, 145–163

doi:10.1108/978-1-83662-314-420251023

Introduction

Modern health care is transforming through technology, evolving patient expectations, and proactive care models. One such technology reshaping health care is remote patient monitoring (RPM), which has enabled continuous monitoring of patients in diverse care settings, such as hospitals, postacute care facilities, and home environments (Serrano et al., 2023; Tan et al., 2024; Vegesna et al., 2017). RPM has become even more relevant in the post-COVID-19 era (Mishra, 2022; Mishra & Sharma, 2024), as healthcare systems prioritize continuous, contactless patient care and early intervention. RPM capabilities have been further enhanced by integrating with the emerging technologies Internet of Things (IoT) and Artificial Intelligence (AI) (Dubey & Tiwari, 2023; Kantipudi et al., 2021; Shaik et al., 2023). These integrations have provided RPM with the capacity for real-time monitoring, predictive analytics, and early intervention strategies to improve clinical outcomes.

Patient monitoring has traditionally been resource-intensive, relying on manual assessments, periodic spot checks, and reactive clinical decision-making (Ghosh et al., 2017). In ICU settings, patients benefit from round-the-clock surveillance through multi-parameter bedside monitors, allowing for early detection and immediate response to critical health deteriorations(Moreno et al., 2009; Sundrani et al., 2023). However, most hospital beds (90–95%) are in general wards and non-ICU areas, where advanced monitoring is not easily accessible. Instead, nurses and healthcare staff conduct intermittent vital sign checks, often every 4–6 hours (Ghosh et al., 2017), leaving significant gaps in patient surveillance that can result in missed early warning signs, delayed interventions, and preventable complications (Sun et al., 2015).

Studies have shown that many patient deteriorations leading to ICU admissions or fatalities could have been prevented with continuous monitoring and timely intervention (Downey, Randell, et al., 2018; Eddahchouri et al., 2022; Grønbaek et al., 2023; Stellpflug et al., 2021; van Rossum et al., 2023; Vincent et al., 2018; Watkins et al., 2016). A large proportion of adverse clinical events, such as sepsis, respiratory failure, and cardiac arrest, often present with subtle physiological changes hours before they escalate into critical conditions (Sessler & Saugel, 2019). However, traditional, manual-based monitoring methods are inherently limited in capturing these early warning signs (Cardona-Morrell et al., 2016; Downey, Chapman, et al., 2018; Peelen et al., 2023), especially in understaffed hospitals (Drennan & Ross, 2019) where healthcare professionals are burdened with increasing patient loads.

This growing challenge has amplified the demand for AI-powered RPM solutions, which can bridge the gap between ICU-level monitoring and non-ICU patient care. By leveraging AI-driven analytics, cloud-based data integration, and advanced sensor technology, these solutions provide uninterrupted patient surveillance, allowing healthcare providers to detect health deteriorations early, allocate resources more efficiently, and reduce the strain on hospital staff.

AI is transforming RPM by introducing advanced data analytics, pattern recognition, and automated risk stratification. AI-driven RPM systems offer several key advantages (Shaik et al., 2023). One of the most significant benefits is their ability to function as Early Warning Systems (EWSs), using predictive models to detect early signs of patient deterioration hours in advance. This proactive approach enables clinicians to intervene before emergencies arise rather than responding after the fact. Additionally, AI-powered technology supports continuous monitoring, eliminating the need for wearables or invasive probes and ensuring patient comfort without interruptions. By analyzing vast amounts of patient data in real time, these systems facilitate data-driven decision-making, providing healthcare professionals with actionable insights and trend analyses for swift, informed interventions. Moreover, AI-based RPM solutions enhance operational efficiency by automating routine monitoring tasks, reducing the burden on nurses and clinicians while ensuring comprehensive patient oversight and allowing medical staff to focus on critical cases.

This chapter delves deeper into Dozee (Kedia et al., 2023; Pavithra et al., 2024; Saran et al., 2018, 2019, 2022; Yadav et al., 2024), a pioneering AI-powered solution that offers continuous, noninvasive monitoring of vital signs, supported by an AI-driven EWS. It examines Dozee's impact on improving patient safety and operational efficiency in hospitals, especially in non-ICU settings, where traditional monitoring methods are limited. The discussion covers important features like the system's contactless sensor technology, real-time data tracking, and seamless cloud integration. Additionally, the chapter highlights the system's regulatory compliance, the significant reduction in ICU admissions, and the enhanced bed utilization achieved through early detection and timely interventions. Furthermore, it addresses the challenges of adopting AI-powered monitoring systems in health care and explores the scalability and flexibility of Dozee across various care environments, from hospitals to home care settings. The chapter also outlines the business model driving Dozee's success and its ability to integrate seamlessly into healthcare operations, ultimately revolutionizing patient monitoring and contributing to value-based care models.

Dozee: Revolutionizing Continuous, Noninvasive Remote Patient Monitoring

Dozee is at the forefront of healthcare innovation, offering continuous, noninvasive monitoring of vital signs powered by AI. By combining advanced AI algorithms with ballistocardiography (BCG) technology, Dozee enables healthcare providers to detect potential health issues early and act proactively, making it especially valuable in non-ICU settings where constant monitoring is often limited. Dozee is transforming healthcare delivery, providing a seamless, contactless monitoring experience that drives better outcomes and enhances patient safety.

Working Mechanism of Dozee

Contactless Sensor Technology and AI-Driven Signal Processing

At the core of Dozee is a thin, flexible sensor mat, equipped with piezoelectric sensors placed under a mattress (Fig. 8.1). These sensors, which work on the

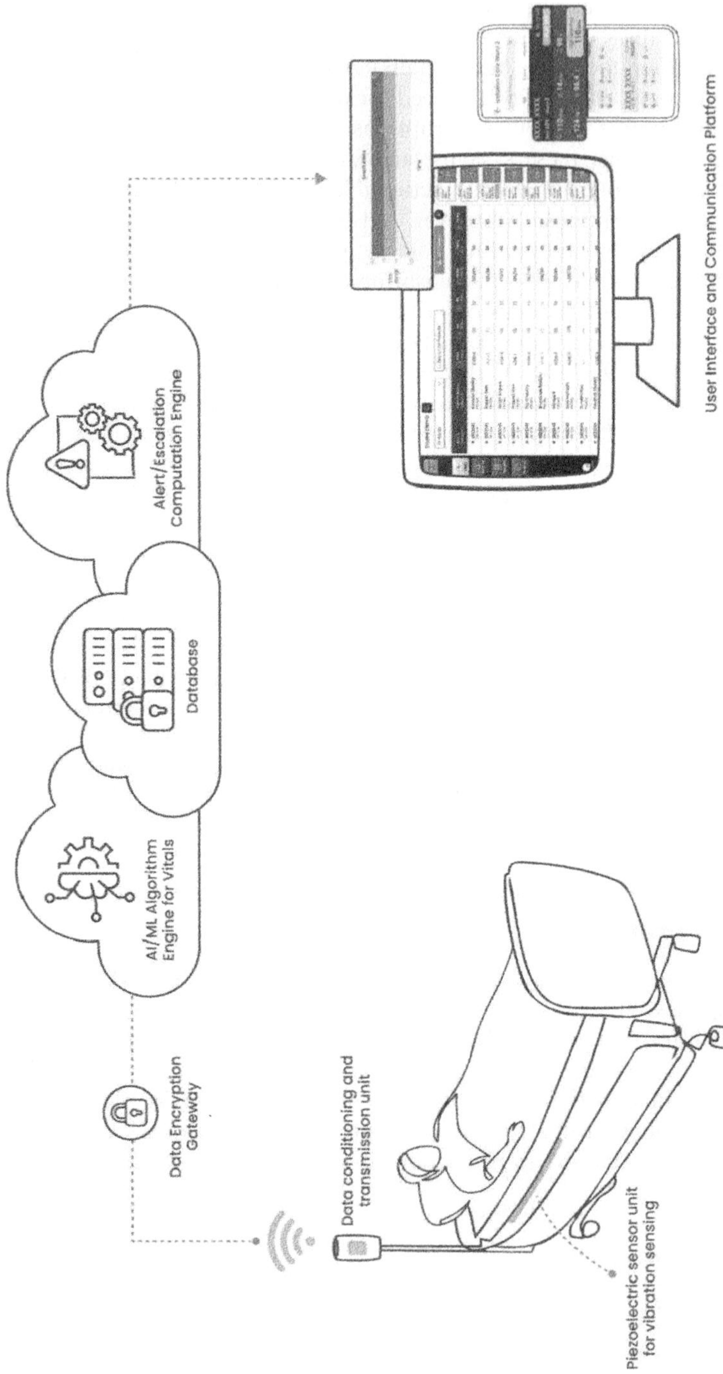

Fig. 8.1. Illustration of the Dozee's Remote Patient Monitoring System. *Source:* Author's own source.

principle of BCG, capture the body's micro-vibrations generated by physiological processes, ensuring patient comfort without the need for wearable devices or invasive equipment. The vibration data are processed through advanced AI algorithms to compute these vital signs – heart rate (HR), respiration rate (RR), and blood pressure (BP) contactlessly, while also detecting bed exits to help prevent falls. This contactless approach ensures that long-term monitoring is unobtrusive, making it ideal for both clinical and home environments.

AI-Powered Early Warning System

Dozee's AI-driven EWS continuously analyzes vital signs, detecting subtle health changes that may signal complications. By triggering real-time alerts for deviations like sudden HR or breathing changes, it enables timely interventions, especially in non-ICU settings where continuous monitoring is limited. Additionally, its bed exit detection enhances safety by preventing falls, particularly for high-risk patients.

Contact-Based Accessories for Enhanced Monitoring

Dozee's versatility is further enhanced with contact-based accessories that result in comprehensive patient monitoring (Fig. 8.2).

- *Pulse oximetry:* Dozee integrates with a pulse oximeter to measure oxygen saturation (SpO_2), delivering essential data on respiratory health.
- *Body temperature sensors:* Real-time body temperature monitoring is enabled through contact-based sensors.
- *Heart rhythm analysis (ECG):* By enabling ECG monitoring, Dozee provides insights into heart rhythm abnormalities, such as arrhythmias, critical for patients with cardiovascular conditions.

Continuous Data Monitoring and Cloud Integration

Dozee securely transmits BCG data to a cloud-based platform, where it is processed to get the vitals which are then displayed on a user-friendly dashboard. This dashboard allows healthcare providers to monitor patients from anywhere, offering real-time vital trends and historical data for deeper insights. With seamless cloud integration, Dozee supports RPM across hospitals and home care settings. Its intuitive dashboard provides easy access to patient information, and it can integrate smoothly with existing hospital systems, ensuring vital sign data fits effortlessly into clinical workflows.

Commitment to Regulatory Excellence and Compliance

Operating in the healthcare industry demands rigorous adherence to regulatory and compliance standards, and Dozee excels in meeting these requirements.

Fig. 8.2. Dozee's Comprehensive Patient Monitoring. *Source:* Author's own source.

The system ensures full compliance with international healthcare regulations, encompassing patient data privacy, device safety, and certifications such as Food And Drug Administration (FDA) 510K clearance, ISO 13485:2016, ISO 27001:2022, CDSCO approval, SOC2, and HIPAA.

Rapid Expansion and Growing Trust in Dozee's Healthcare Solutions Across India

The adoption of Dozee in India has seen remarkable growth, as reflected by the increasing number of hospitals and beds utilizing the platform (Fig. 8.3). From FY22 to FY24, the number of hospitals increased from 60 to 200, and the total number of beds rose from about 6,000 to more than 14,000. This exponential rise highlights the growing trust and acceptance of Dozee's AI-driven remote monitoring solutions across healthcare facilities, enabling better patient outcomes and optimized resource allocation in hospitals.

Operational Excellence and Value Addition Brought by Dozee in Hospitals

The implementation of Dozee in hospitals offers transformative benefits by optimizing patient care, improving operational efficiency, and enhancing overall healthcare outcomes. Dozee not only automates routine tasks but also provides

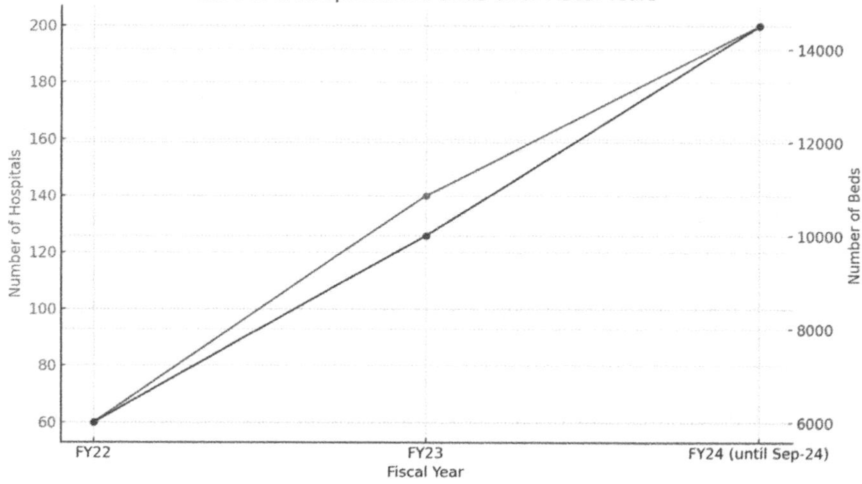

Fig. 8.3. Growth of Hospitals and Beds Using Dozee Over Fiscal Years. *Source:* Author's own source.

real-time, actionable insights, leading to significant value addition across various hospital operations. Below is a comprehensive look at how Dozee fosters operational excellence and creates value in hospitals:

Enhancing Patient Safety in Non-ICU Settings

Continuous monitoring is essential for early detection of critical conditions and improved patient outcomes. Traditional periodic checks leave gaps where deterioration may go unnoticed, but Dozee's real-time monitoring ensures timely detection of vital sign changes. Studies show that patients monitored with Dozee received earlier interventions, with its AI-driven EWS predicting deterioration up to 16 hours in advance (Pavithra et al., 2025; Yadav et al., 2024). Research also indicates EWS-based continuous monitoring can detect worsening conditions 8.3 hours ahead, compared to 5.2 hours with periodic EWSs (Peelen et al., 2023). Dozee's alerts, with over 90% sensitivity (Pavithra et al., 2025; Yadav et al., 2024), enable proactive care, reducing ICU admissions and easing hospital strain where manual monitoring was not feasible (Rajanna et al., 2023; Unlocking the potential of connected, 2022). An independent study by Sattva Consultants estimates that for every 100 Dozee-powered beds, approximately 144 lives are saved annually (Unlocking the potential of connected, 2022).

Operational Efficiency and Workflow Optimization

Reducing Manual Workload With Automated Monitoring

Dozee automates vital sign collection, reducing the time healthcare staff spend on routine checks by 80%. Traditionally, nurses spent around 50 minutes per patient daily on vitals, but with Dozee, this dropped to just 10 minutes, saving approximately 2.5 hours per nurse per day (Unlocking the potential of connected, 2022). Additionally, 70% of nurses reported reduced workload and stress, thanks to the automation and digitization provided by Dozee (Unlocking the potential of connected, 2022). At Ramaiah Hospital, its implementation led to a 56% reduction in routine checks and a 45.9% decrease in time spent on coordination, allowing nurses to dedicate 43% more time to direct patient care (Pavithra et al., 2024). By streamlining monitoring, Dozee reduces workload, minimizes errors, and enhances hospital efficiency and patient outcomes (Pavithra et al., 2024).

Workflow Optimization and Enhanced Communication and Coordination Through Real-Time Data Access

Dozee enhances hospital workflows by providing real-time patient data through a centralized dashboard, eliminating manual checks and data entry. This enables healthcare providers to monitor multiple patients remotely, improving efficiency. Hospitals using Dozee saw a 46% reduction in communication time, leading to faster interventions and better coordination among medical teams (Pavithra et al., 2024). Dozee's centralized data ensures healthcare teams have real-time patient information, reducing administrative workload and enabling faster decision-making. Doctors can instantly access vitals, and nurses can prioritize tasks efficiently, improving coordination and patient care. Its real-time data access also streamlines shift handovers, minimizing miscommunication and ensuring continuity of care. Enhanced coordination between departments enables quicker interventions, reducing complications and improving overall hospital efficiency.

Enhanced Data Accuracy and Decision-Making

Improving Accuracy Through Continuous Monitoring

Dozee ensures continuous, accurate vital sign monitoring, eliminating errors and inconsistencies common in manual checks. In busy hospitals, its 24/7 automated system provides real-time data, reducing missed or delayed readings and enhancing clinical decision-making. Healthcare professionals trust Dozee's data for clinical decisions (Pavithra et al., 2024) as it provides a comprehensive view of a patient's condition, enabling more informed and timely interventions.

By automating data collection and analysis, Dozee improves reliability, minimizes human error, and ensures consistent patient monitoring across shifts (Pavithra et al., 2024; Unlocking the potential of connected, 2022).

Real-Time Data for Proactive Decision-Making

Dozee provides healthcare providers with real-time access to patient data through centralized dashboards and mobile applications. This allows healthcare teams to continuously monitor patients, even from a distance, enabling timely interventions and proactive decision-making. The Dozee's EWS, which continuously analyzes patient data, adds an extra layer of predictive capability by identifying trends that may indicate early signs of deterioration.

Resource Optimization and Cost Savings

Optimizing Staffing and Reducing Workload

Dozee helps optimize staffing by reducing the workload of healthcare professionals. Nurses are no longer required to conduct routine manual checks, freeing them up to focus on more critical tasks. In hospitals using Dozee, this resulted in substantial time savings, allowing hospitals to maintain high standards of care while optimizing the use of their staff (Pavithra et al., 2024; Unlocking the potential of connected, 2022).

Cost Savings Through Reduced ICU Admissions and Length of Stay

The continuous monitoring provided by Dozee reduces ICU admissions by enabling early intervention for deteriorating patients. By catching warning signs earlier, hospitals can treat patients in general wards rather than transferring them to ICUs, which reduces the costs associated with critical care. Hospitals saw a 26% drop in ICU treatment costs and a 14% decrease in general ward expenses. Additionally, Dozee helps reduce the average length of hospital stays by up to 1.3 days in ICUs and 0.7 days in general wards (Unlocking the potential of connected, 2022).

Enhanced Bed Utilization and Patient Turnover

Dozee improves bed utilization by reducing the length of hospital stays and facilitating faster patient recovery and discharge. This leads to more efficient patient turnover and enables hospitals to treat more patients without needing to expand their infrastructure. For every 100 beds equipped with Dozee, hospitals can treat an additional 3,700 patients annually (Unlocking the potential of connected, 2022).

Improved Patient Experience and Satisfaction

Noninvasive Monitoring for Patient Comfort

Dozee's contactless monitoring enhances patient comfort by eliminating the need for physical checks. Its under-mattress sensor continuously tracks vital signs without disturbance, benefiting elderly and long-term patients. Both patients and healthcare providers report improved care quality, with its unobtrusive design ensuring better rest and overall well-being (Pavithra et al., 2024).

Reducing Patient Stress Through Continuous Monitoring

Patients feel reassured knowing that their vital signs are being continuously monitored, even in the absence of healthcare staff. The sensor technology used is comfortable, with 74.2% of patients reporting that they felt safer (Pavithra et al., 2024). This enhanced sense of safety reduces anxiety and stress, leading to an improved overall patient experience. Continuous monitoring allows for a more peaceful recovery environment, contributing to faster recovery times.

Facilitating Value-Based Health Care

The healthcare industry is increasingly adopting a value-based care model that prioritizes patient outcomes and treatment quality over the volume of services provided. This approach encourages healthcare providers to focus on delivering effective, high-quality care that improves patient safety, enhances health results, and reduces costs. Dozee's monitoring system aligns with this model by enabling early detection of health deterioration, preventing severe medical complications, and optimizing the use of healthcare resources.

Scalability and Flexibility

Dozee's scalable system transforms standard hospital beds into step-down ICU beds, making it ideal for resource-limited settings. Its flexibility allows seamless integration across public and private hospitals, expanding monitoring capabilities without major infrastructure investments. During the COVID-19 surge, Dozee helped hospitals increase critical care capacity by converting regular beds into connected ICU beds. Beyond hospitals, its adaptability extends to long-term care, home health care, and other settings, proving its versatility in enhancing patient monitoring at scale.

Enhanced Compliance and Reporting

Dozee's contactless monitoring ensures continuous tracking of vital signs, aiding compliance with hospital and government regulations, especially in high-risk wards. By automating monitoring and data logging, it prevents compliance gaps, simplifies reporting, and streamlines audits. Hospitals benefit from accurate records, reduced administrative workload, and real-time data for better decision-making and care planning.

Business Model of Dozee

Revenue Streams

Dozee's business model is built around multiple revenue streams. The primary revenue source is subscription-based services offered to hospitals and healthcare facilities, providing access to Dozee's monitoring platform and data analytics. Dozee provides healthcare providers with data-driven insights, empowering them to make well-informed decisions about patient care. These insights may also be monetized through partnerships with research institutions and insurance companies seeking to improve healthcare delivery models.

Target Markets and Customers

Dozee's primary target markets include hospitals and long-term care facilities. The company prioritizes non-ICU settings, where continuous monitoring is crucial but resources are often limited. Dozee also targets home healthcare providers, offering solutions for postdischarge monitoring and chronic disease management. Internationally, the company is expanding its presence in regions like the United States, Middle East, Africa, and Southeast Asia, where healthcare systems are rapidly adopting digital health solutions.

Partnerships and Collaborations

Key to Dozee's success are its partnerships with hospitals and healthcare institutions, which help drive the adoption of its AI-based monitoring system.

Collaborations with research institutions, like AIIMS Jodhpur, Apollo Applied Research, and NIMHANS, have been instrumental in validating the clinical effectiveness of the system. Partnerships with technology providers ensure the continuous improvement of the platform's capabilities. These collaborations not only support the scalability of Dozee's solution but also strengthen its competitive position in the market.

Market Landscape and Competitive Analysis

Global RPM Market Overview

The global RPM market is rapidly growing, driven by an aging population, rising chronic diseases, and advancements in AI, IoT, and wearables. With a projected 13.7% CAGR, it is expected to reach $116.84 billion by 2031 (https://www.meticulousresearch.com/product/remote-patient-monitoring-market-5343#:). The COVID-19 pandemic further accelerated adoption, emphasizing the need for continuous, contactless care.

As health care shifts toward value-based models, key trends include AI-powered analytics, RPM expansion in home care, and cloud-based data management. Hospitals increasingly adopt scalable, AI-driven solutions like Dozee for noninvasive, continuous monitoring to improve patient outcomes and resource efficiency.

Competitive Landscape in RPM

The RPM market is characterized by fierce competition, with both well-established medical device manufacturers and newer digital health companies vying for market share. Leading companies in this space, such as Philips Healthcare, GE Healthcare, Masimo, and Medtronic, provide wearable and semi-invasive solutions to advance RPM. These competitors have established strong presences in the healthcare industry, but Dozee's distinct advantage lies in its contactless monitoring technology and AI-driven EWS.

Comparison With Competitors

Philips Healthcare. Philips is one of the largest players in the healthcare industry, offering comprehensive RPM solutions that include wearable devices and patient-centric telehealth platforms. Their monitoring devices are used extensively in hospitals, with a strong focus on multi-parameter patient monitoring for both in-clinic and at-home care. Philips' solutions emphasize integration with existing hospital systems, offering a seamless flow of data to healthcare providers. However, unlike Dozee's contactless technology, Philips relies heavily on wearables, which require consistent maintenance and patient compliance.

Masimo. Masimo is a leader in advanced pulse oximetry and wearable patient monitoring systems. The company offers wireless, noninvasive devices designed to monitor oxygen levels, pulse rate, and respiratory rate. While Masimo's devices are widely used in hospitals, the reliance on wearables introduces challenges in terms of patient comfort and long-term compliance. This is where Dozee's contactless system provides a significant edge, particularly in non-ICU settings where patient comfort and ease of use are critical.

GE Healthcare. GE offers a broad range of monitoring solutions, primarily focused on critical care and ICU patients. Their systems are known for high accuracy and comprehensive monitoring of vital signs. However, GE's systems are typically more suited to ICU settings, making them less adaptable to general wards or home healthcare environments. Dozee, on the other hand, is tailored for non-ICU settings and long-term care, addressing a gap in continuous monitoring without requiring expensive, high-maintenance ICU-level equipment.

Dozee's Competitive Advantage

While the market is crowded with solutions from established players, Dozee differentiates itself with the following competitive advantages:

- *Contactless Monitoring:* Unlike wearable devices that can be intrusive and require regular interaction from patients or caregivers, Dozee's system provides HR, RR, and BP contactlessly. This noninvasive approach makes it particularly appealing in long-term care environments, where patient compliance with wearables may decrease over time.
- *AI-Driven Early Warning System:* The integration of AI to predict and alert healthcare providers of potential patient deterioration well before a critical event occurs gives Dozee a significant edge. While many competitors offer real-time monitoring, the ability to provide predictive alerts based on data analysis is a unique feature that sets Dozee apart.
- *Cost-Effective Model:* Dozee's subscription-based model provides a scalable and affordable solution for healthcare providers. This contrasts with the high upfront costs associated with many traditional RPM systems that require significant investments in wearable devices and supporting infrastructure.
- *Scalability:* Dozee's system is highly adaptable and can be scaled easily to general wards, long-term care facilities, and home health care, providing a flexible solution for diverse patient needs and care settings.

Barriers to Adoption of AI-Powered RPM Systems Like Dozee

Despite the clear advantages that AI-powered RPM systems like Dozee offer, several barriers hinder widespread adoption in healthcare settings. Recognizing and addressing these obstacles is essential for broader adoption and acceptance.

Technological Integration and Infrastructure Limitations

A major barrier to adopting advanced remote monitoring is outdated healthcare infrastructure, as many hospitals lack systems that support AI-driven solutions.

Integrating Dozee with hospital IT, EHR, and clinical workflows can be complex and require significant investment.

Reliable internet access is also crucial for real-time data transmission. In rural or underdeveloped areas, poor network infrastructure can limit Dozee's effectiveness, impacting real-time communication of critical patient data.

Data Security and Privacy Concerns

The rise of AI-powered RPM systems like Dozee brings concerns about data security and patient privacy. The systems collect vast amounts of sensitive patient data, including vital signs and health history, which must be stored, transmitted, and processed securely. The biggest challenge revolves data security and unauthorized access to personal health information. Compliance with established regulations (HIPAA, GDPR, and local laws) is key to protecting privacy and minimizing risks. Ensuring secure data management adds complexity to adoption, making healthcare institutions cautious about integration.

Cost and Financial Considerations

The high initial cost of AI-driven RPM systems like Dozee can be a barrier, especially for smaller or resource-limited healthcare institutions. While these systems reduce costs long-term, upfront expenses for hardware, software, and training can be significant. Limited insurance coverage and evolving reimbursement models further complicate adoption.

Regulatory and Compliance Challenges

Regulatory hurdles for AI-driven healthcare technology, such as FDA and Medicines and Healthcare products Regulatory Agency approvals, add costs and delay market entry. Ensuring transparency and explainability is crucial for provider and regulator confidence. The lengthy approval process slows adoption for developers and healthcare institutions.

Resistance and Lack of Familiarity

Healthcare providers may resist AI-driven solutions like Dozee, preferring familiar workflows over new technology. Overcoming this requires education, clear clinical benefits, and strong evidence of AI's reliability. Skepticism and lack of training can further slow adoption, highlighting the need for proper onboarding.

Patient Trust and Acceptance

Patient trust can be a barrier to AI-driven monitoring, with concerns about privacy, data security, and reduced direct care. Transparent communication about benefits, safety, and improved healthcare accuracy can help build confidence and acceptance.

Training and Workforce Adaptation

Successful AI-powered RPM adoption depends on effective staff training, which can be costly and time-consuming. Healthcare providers must balance this with workflow adjustments, as real-time AI insights may disrupt established routines. In high-pressure environments, adapting to new protocols can be challenging, slowing adoption.

Ethical Considerations in AI-Based Monitoring

AI-driven healthcare systems raise ethical concerns related to patient autonomy, bias in AI algorithms, and equitable access to technology. Ensuring that AI models are trained on diverse datasets and do not introduce biases that may impact certain patient groups is critical. Guidelines and oversight mechanisms are needed to govern the responsible use of AI in health care.

Overcoming the Barriers

To drive the adoption of *AI-powered remote monitoring systems* like Dozee, stakeholders need to address these barriers through strategic initiatives such as:

- *Building robust integration solutions* that allow AI-driven systems to seamlessly interface with existing healthcare infrastructure.
- *Strengthening data security protocols* and ensuring compliance with global privacy regulations.
- *Demonstrating ROI* through case studies and pilots that highlight long-term cost savings and improved patient outcomes.
- *Streamlining regulatory approval* processes by working closely with regulatory bodies and adhering to transparent AI standards.
- *Education and awareness programs* to help healthcare professionals and patients understand the value and safety of AI-based monitoring.
- *Auditing AI algorithms for bias and fairness*, is needed to ensure equitable access to quality health care.

By addressing these barriers, AI-based RPM systems, like Dozee, can achieve broader adoption, transforming patient care and healthcare systems globally.

Opportunities for Growth

Despite barriers to the adoption of RPM, there are significant opportunities for growth in the RPM market, particularly for companies like Dozee. Home care is one example where there is an increasing need for continuous monitoring of patients with chronic conditions. By providing real-time monitoring and EWSs, Dozee can help prevent hospital readmissions and reduce the burden on healthcare systems. Another growth opportunity lies in partnerships with government health programs and insurance providers. There is a growing interest in solutions that can reduce costs through early intervention and preventative care. By partnering with these organizations, Dozee can expand its reach and provide its technology to a broader audience.

Future Trends

The future of RPM lies in advancing AI, machine learning, and predictive analytics to enhance health predictions, enable earlier interventions, and improve clinical decisions. In addition, the growing trend toward personalized medicine presents new opportunities for AI-driven platforms like Dozee to offer tailored monitoring solutions that address the unique needs of individual patients. As healthcare providers increasingly adopt value-based care models, the demand for AI-driven RPM solutions is expected to grow, further driving innovation in the market.

Conclusion

AI-powered RPM systems like Dozee are transforming health care by enhancing patient safety, optimizing hospital resources, and reducing healthcare costs. By enabling early detection of critical conditions, these systems improve clinical outcomes while easing the burden on healthcare providers. Despite barriers like integration challenges, regulatory complexities, and cultural resistance, strategic investments in interoperability, data security, training, and reimbursement models can drive widespread adoption. Dozee's noninvasive monitoring system has proven to be a game-changer in non-ICU settings, offering continuous vital sign monitoring and early warning alerts. Its scalable model, coupled with AI-driven analytics and cloud integration, enhances patient outcomes and operational efficiencies. As AI continues to reshape health care, Dozee is well-positioned to drive a more proactive, efficient, and value-based healthcare system, ensuring accessible, high-quality monitoring across diverse settings.

References

Cardona-Morrell, M., Prgomet, M., Turner, R. M., Nicholson, M., & Hillman, K. (2016, October). Effectiveness of continuous or intermittent vital signs monitoring in preventing adverse events on general wards: A systematic review and meta-analysis. *International Journal of Clinical Practice*, *70*(10), 806–824. https://doi.org/10.1111/ijcp.12846

Downey, C. L., Chapman, S., Randell, R., Brown, J. M., & Jayne, D. G. (2018). The impact of continuous versus intermittent vital signs monitoring in hospitals: A systematic review and narrative synthesis. *International Journal of Nursing Studies*, *84*, 19–27. https://doi.org/10.1016/j.ijnurstu.2018.04.013

Downey, C., Randell, R., Brown, J., & Jayne, D. G. (2018). Continuous versus intermittent vital signs monitoring using a wearable, wireless patch in patients admitted to surgical wards: Pilot cluster randomized controlled trial. *Journal of Medical Internet Research*, *20*(12), e10802. https://doi.org/10.2196/10802

Drennan, V. M., & Ross, F. (2019, June 19). Global nurse shortages-the facts, the impact and action for change. *British Medical Bulletin*, *130*(1), 25–37. https://doi.org/10.1093/bmb/ldz014

Dubey, A., & Tiwari, A. (2023, May 3). Artificial intelligence and remote patient monitoring in US healthcare market: A literature review. *Journal of Market Access & Health Policy*, *11*(1), 2205618. https://doi.org/10.1080/20016689.2023.2205618

Eddahchouri, Y., Peelen, R. V., Koeneman, M., Touw, H. R. W., van Goor, H., & Bredie, S. J. H. (2022, May). Effect of continuous wireless vital sign monitoring on unplanned ICU admissions and rapid response team calls: A before-and-after study. *British Journal of Anaesthesia*, *128*(5), 857–863. https://doi.org/10.1016/j.bja.2022.01.036

Ghosh, E., Eshelman, L., Yang, L., Carlson, E., & Lord, B. (2017, November 21). Description of vital signs data measurement frequency in a medical/surgical unit at a community hospital in United States. *Data in Brief*, *16*, 612–616. https://doi.org/10.1016/j.dib.2017.11.053

Grønbaek K. K., Rasmussen S. M., Langer N. H.., Vincentz M., Oxbøll A. B., Søgaard M., Awada, H. N., Jensen, T. O., Jensen, M. T., Sørensen, H. B. D., Aasvang, E. K., & Meyhoff, C. S. (2023, May). Continuous monitoring is superior to manual measurements in detecting vital sign deviations in patients with COVID-19. *Acta Anaesthesiologica Scandinavica*, *67*(5), 640–648. https://doi.org/10.1111/aas.14221

Kantipudi, M. V. V. P., Moses, C. J., Aluvalu, R., & Kumar, S. (2021). Remote patient monitoring using IoT, cloud computing and AI. In *Hybrid artificial intelligence and IoT in healthcare* (pp. 51–74). Springer Singapore. https://doi.org/10.1007/978-981-16-2972-3_3

Kedia S., Ur Rahman I., Kaushal A., Mahizhvannan E., Jain R. S., Radhakrishna R., Rao, S., Chokalingam, K., Rawooth, M., Kadambi, P., & Parchani, G. (2023). Clinical validation of an indigenous micro-vibration vital parameter monitor dozee VS. In *2023 15th International Conference on COMmunication Systems & NETworkS (COMSNETS)*. p. 141–146. https://doi.org/10.1109/COMSNETS56262.2023.10041343

Mishra, V. (2022, December 20). Analysis of systemic and behavioral barriers to COVID-19 vaccination in rollout phase. *International Journal of Healthcare Management*, *17*, 1–10. https://doi.org/10.1080/20479700.2022.2157934

Mishra, V., & Sharma, M. G. (2024, June 25). Factors affecting implementation of digital lean in healthcare in the post-COVID world – mixed-method approach. *The TQM Journal*, *36*(6), 1651–1664. https://doi.org/10.1108/tqm-08-2023-0251

Moreno, R. P., Rhodes, A., & Donchin, Y., & European Society of Intensive Care. (2009, August 21). Patient safety in intensive care medicine: The declaration of Vienna. *Intensive Care Medicine*, *35*(10), 1667–1672. https://doi.org/10.1007/s00134-009-1621-2

Pavithra, L. S., Priyanka, T. G., & Khurdi, S. (2025). Effectiveness of remote patient monitoring equipped with an early warning system in tertiary care hospital wards: A retrospective cohort study. *Journal of Medical Internet Research*, *27*, e56463.

Pavithra, L. S., Khurdi, S., Priyanka, T. G., Patrisia, M. S., & Pavithra, L. S. (2024, June 4). Impact of remote patient monitoring systems on nursing time, healthcare providers, and patient satisfaction in general wards. *Cureus, 16*(6). https://www.cureus.com/articles/255710-impact-of-remote-patient-monitoring-systems-on-nursing-time-healthcare-providers-and-patient-satisfaction-in-general-wards

Peelen, R. V., Eddahchouri, Y., Koeneman, M., Melis, R., van Goor, H., & Bredie, S. J. H. (2023, May 8). Comparing continuous with periodic vital sign scoring for clinical deterioration using a patient data model. *Journal of Medical Systems, 47*(1), 60. https://doi.org/10.1007/s10916-023-01954-z

Rajanna A. H., Bellary V. S., Puranic S. K., Nayana, C., Nagaraj, J. R., Eshanye, D. A., & Preethi, K. (2023, September 1). Continuous remote monitoring in moderate and severe COVID-19 patients. *Cureus*. https://www.cureus.com/articles/165057-continuous-remote-monitoring-in-moderate-and-severe-covid-19-patients.pdf

Saran, V., Kumar, G., & Dhawan, U. (2018). Unsupervised identification of cardiac contraction through ballistocardiography. In *2018 IEEE-EMBS*. https://ieeexplore.ieee.org/abstract/document/8626652/

Saran, V., Kumar, R., Kumar, G., Chokalingam, K., Rawooth, M., & Parchani, G. (2022). Validation of dozee, a ballistocardiography-based device, for contactless and continuous heart rate and respiratory rate measurement. In *Conference Proceeding IEEE Engineering in Medicine and Biology Society*. 2022 July, 1939–1943. https://doi.org/10.1109/EMBC48229.2022.9871007

Saran, V., Kumar, G., & Parchani, G. (2019). Unsupervised extraction of respiration cycles through ballistocardiography. In *Advanced informatics for computing research* (pp. 136–147). Springer Singapore. https://doi.org/10.1007/978-981-15-0108-1_14

Serrano, L. P., Maita, K. C., Avila, F. R., Torres-Guzman, R. A., Garcia, J. P., Eldaly, A. S., Haider, C. R., Felton, C. L., Paulson, M. R., Maniaci, M. J., & Forte, A. J. (2023, December 15). Benefits and challenges of remote patient monitoring as perceived by health care practitioners: A systematic review. *The Permanente Journal, 27*(4), 100–111. https://doi.org/10.7812/TPP/23.022

Sessler, D. I., & Saugel, B. (2019, January 3). Beyond "failure to rescue": The time has come for continuous ward monitoring. *British Journal of Anaesthesia, 122*(3), 304–306. https://doi.org/10.1016/j.bja.2018.12.003

Shaik, T., Tao, X., Higgins, N., Li, L., Gururajan, R., Zhou, X., & Acharya, U. R. (2023). Remote patient monitoring using artificial intelligence: Current state, applications, and challenges. *arXiv [cs.CY]*. http://arxiv.org/abs/2301.10009

Stellpflug C., Pierson L., Roloff D., Mosman E., Gross T., Marsh S., Willis, V., & Gabrielson, D. (2021, April 1). Continuous physiological monitoring improves patient outcomes. *American Journal of Nursing, 121*(4), 40–46. https://doi.org/10.1097/01.NAJ.0000742504.44428.c9

Sun Z., Sessler D. I., Dalton J. E., Devereaux P. J., Shahinyan A., Naylor A. J., Hutcherson, M. T., Finnegan, P. S., Tandon, V., Darvish-Kazem, S., Chugh, S., Alzayer, H., & Kurz, A. (2015, September). Postoperative hypoxemia is common and persistent: A prospective blinded observational study. *Anesthesia & Analgesia, 121*(3), 709–715. https://doi.org/10.1213/ANE.0000000000000836

Sundrani, S., Chen, J., Jin, B. T., Abad, Z. S. H., Rajpurkar, P., & Kim, D. (2023, April 4). Predicting patient decompensation from continuous physiologic monitoring in the emergency department. *npj Digital Medicine, 6*(1), 60. https://doi.org/10.1038/s41746-023-00803-0

Tan, S. Y., Sumner, J., Wang, Y., & Wenjun Yip, A. (2024, July 18). A systematic review of the impacts of remote patient monitoring (RPM) interventions on safety, adherence, quality-of-life and cost-related outcomes. *npj Digital Medicine*, *7*(1), 192. https://doi.org/10.1038/s41746-024-01182-w

Unlocking the potential of connected healthcare in India (2022). Sattva Consulting. https://www.sattva.co.in/publication/unlocking-the-potential-of-connected-healthcare-in-india/

van Rossum M. C., Bekhuis R. E., Wang Y., Hegeman J. H., Folbert E. C., Vollenbroek-Hutten M. M., Kalkman, C. J., Kouwenhoven, E. A., & Hermens, H. J. (2023, August 30). Early warning scores to support continuous wireless vital sign monitoring for complication prediction in patients on surgical wards: Retrospective observational study. *JMIR Perioperative Medicine*, *6*, e44483. https://doi.org/10.2196/44483

Vegesna, A., Tran, M., Angelaccio, M., & Arcona, S. (2017, January). Remote patient monitoring via non-invasive digital technologies: A systematic review. *Telemedicine Journal and e-Health*, *23*(1), 3–17. https://doi.org/10.1089/tmj.2016.0051

Vincent J. L., Einav S., Pearse R., Jaber S., Kranke P., Overdyk F. J., Whitaker, D. K., Gordo, F., Dahan, A., & Hoeft, A. (2018, May). Improving detection of patient deterioration in the general hospital ward environment. *European Journal of Anaesthesiology*, *35*(5), 325–333. https://doi.org/10.1097/EJA.0000000000000798

Watkins, T., Whisman, L., & Booker, P. (2016, January). Nursing assessment of continuous vital sign surveillance to improve patient safety on the medical/surgical unit. *Journal of Clinical Nursing*, *25*(1–2), 278–281. https://doi.org/10.1111/jocn.13102

Yadav A., Dandu H., Parchani G., Chokalingam K., Kadambi P., Mishra R., Jahan, A., Teboul, J., & Latour, J. M. (2024, August 29). Early detection of deteriorating patients in general wards through continuous contactless vital signs monitoring. *Frontiers in Medical Technology*, *6*. https://doi.org/10.3389/fmedt.2024.1436034

https://www.meticulousresearch.com/product/remote-patient-monitoring-market-5343#:

Chapter 9

Navigating the Economic Impact of Artificial Intelligence in the Healthcare Sector: A Systematic Review

Sharif Mohd, Rajbeer Kaur and Teena Singh

New Delhi Institute of Management, India

Abstract

Artificial Intelligence (AI) is revolutionizing health care by improving operational efficiency and cost-effectiveness. This study applies a Preferred Reporting Items for Systematic Reviews and Meta-Analyses (PRISMA)-based systematic review to examine the economic impact of AI in healthcare by reviewing studies published from 2019 to 2024. The review evaluates AI's involvement in a variety of healthcare areas using a range of approaches, such as cost-effectiveness assessments, extensive clinical trials, and predictive modeling. According to the studies, AI significantly improves screening effectiveness and diagnostic accuracy, particularly in instances of glaucoma, breast cancer, and diabetic retinopathy. This innovation helps save money by enabling early detection and more efficient use of resources. Even while AI is more affordable, its full-scale implementation is hampered by significant financing and regulatory obstacles. Creating uniform assessment methods will improve the accuracy of economic analyses and offer more precise information on the wider cost effects of AI in health care. To fully realize AI's potential for cost savings and improved patient outcomes, healthcare stakeholders must solve the present AI's adoption barriers. To overcome economic and regulatory obstacles and promote smooth integration, more study would be required. Well-executed AI-driven solutions have the potential to significantly increase healthcare access, particularly in unprivileged regions, which will eventually result in a more efficient and equitable healthcare system.

Keywords: Artificial Intelligence; health care; cost-effectiveness; economic impact; PRISMA; cost-saving potential

Digital Transformation and Artificial Intelligence for Operational Excellence in Healthcare, 165–188

doi:10.1108/978-1-83662-314-420251026

Introduction

Alan Turing's groundbreaking work in the mid-20th century laid the foundation for Artificial Intelligence (AI) (Copeland, 2004). In 1935, he introduced the universal Turing machine, demonstrating how machines could modify their programs (Hodges, 2012). His cryptanalysis efforts at Bletchley Park during World War II further shaped his ideas on machine intelligence (Copeland, 2006; Michie, 1991). By 1947, he proposed machine learning, expanding on this in his 1948 report, Intelligent Machinery (Hodges, 2012; Turing, 1947). His vision continues to influence modern AI, including neural networks and heuristic problem-solving (Turing, 1950).

AI has since revolutionized health care, enabling early disease detection, advanced medical imaging, and personalized treatments (Secinaro et al., 2021). During the COVID-19 pandemic, AI-driven virtual care became crucial (Islam, 2024). However, challenges remain, including ethical concerns, privacy issues, and governance needs (Kuwaiti et al., 2023). Health technology assessments are essential for optimizing AI applications in health care (Petersson et al., 2022).

AI and Health care

AI is revolutionizing the healthcare sector, improving efficiency, enhancing patient outcomes, and simplifying administrative tasks. Its impact spans across various domains, from clinical diagnostics to medical education, significantly reducing workloads and allowing healthcare professionals to focus more on patient care (Spear et al., 2023). One notable development is AI-assisted imaging, which has substantially improved diagnostic accuracy. Studies show that AI enhances clinicians' ability to detect pneumothoraxes by 11.4%, a breakthrough that is especially beneficial for less experienced practitioners (Novak et al., 2024). Additionally, AI-driven tools, like MUFASA, utilize machine learning to optimize medical affairs, providing actionable insights that improve engagement with healthcare professionals (Ng & Zhang, 2023).

Predictive analytics powered by deep neural networks (DNNs) is another key innovation, enabling the classification of diseases and the analysis of vast patient datasets to aid decision-making (Abut et al., 2024). AI systems refine diagnostic precision and personalize treatment plans, leading to better patient outcomes (Alberto Mazzoli et al., 2023). Generative AI technologies, such as MidJourney, are also being explored for developing educational materials, particularly for high-stakes scenarios like cardiac arrest training (Alberto Mazzoli et al., 2023). Despite these advancements, AI integration into clinical environments presents challenges, including concerns about data accuracy and algorithmic biases that may compromise reliability (Kulkarni & Singh, 2023).

AI has the potential to match or surpass human performance in various healthcare tasks, improving accessibility, security, and efficiency, which ultimately enhances quality of life (Alia et al., 2023; Davenport & Kalakota, 2019). Several AI applications, particularly in analyzing patient data, diagnosing diseases, and recommending treatments, have already shown maturity (Davenport & Kalakota, 2019). Additionally, AI tools aggregate real-time medical information, aiding healthcare professionals (Secinaro et al., 2021). Projections suggest the healthcare AI market will grow significantly, reaching $99.5 billion by 2027 (Joshi, 2019; Sunarti et al., 2021).

However, integrating AI with existing healthcare infrastructures poses challenges, as many organizations still rely on outdated legacy systems that are not compatible with modern AI technologies. This lack of interoperability leads to inefficiencies and data silos, hindering AI's seamless integration into clinical workflows (Sharma, 2020; Smith et al., 2021). Ethical concerns also play a significant role in AI adoption, raising questions about accountability, transparency, and potential biases in decision-making (Secinaro et al., 2021; Shamszare & Choudhury, 2023). The need for explainable AI is critical to ensure that healthcare professionals trust and understand AI-generated recommendations (Mani, 2024; Reddy, 2024). Without transparency in AI systems, clinicians may hesitate to rely on them, fearing they could compromise patient safety or ethical standards (van de Sande et al., 2022).

Resistance to change among healthcare professionals is another barrier to AI adoption. Many clinicians worry that AI may replace their roles or increase their workload due to the additional training required for effective implementation (Chaibi & Zaiem, 2022; Shamszare & Choudhury, 2023). A lack of understanding of AI's capabilities and benefits further contributes to skepticism in clinical settings (Kelly et al., 2019; Lai et al., 2020). Overcoming these challenges requires fostering a culture of acceptance and providing sufficient training to ensure healthcare professionals feel empowered rather than threatened by AI technologies (Castagno & Khalifa, 2020; Sarker, 2023).

Financial concerns significantly influence AI adoption in health care. The costs of software, training, and maintenance can be a barrier, particularly for smaller healthcare providers (Chan & Petrikat, 2023; Cheng et al., 2022). Additionally, the unclear return on investment discourages organizations from fully committing to AI solutions (van Leeuwen et al., 2023). There is a need for a robust evaluation framework to assess the economic viability and impact of AI in healthcare settings (Abdul, 2024). Further research is essential to guide investment and policy decisions. Studies suggest that existing literature on AI's financial impact lacks depth, necessitating a more systematic and comprehensive approach (Vithlani et al., 2023; Wolff et al., 2020). This systematic review aims to bridge that gap by analyzing current research on AI's economic role in health care, assessing study quality and identifying future research directions.

Method

This study is organized into six key sections: introduction, methods, results, discussion, future research directions, and conclusion. The Methods section examines existing literature on the economic impact of AI systems relative to traditional healthcare approaches. The Results section presents a summary of the economic impacts identified in these studies. The Discussion section evaluates the strengths and limitations of the findings and offers recommendations for future research. The aim is to clarify the value of AI in health care, supporting informed decisions regarding the adoption and implementation of AI technologies.

Literature Search Strategy

Our literature review approach was designed to focus on recent trends in AI developments, particularly in the healthcare sector. To ensure relevance, we prioritized collecting current and appropriate studies on the economic impacts of AI in health care, with a specific emphasis on publications between 2019 and 2024. The search was carried out using the Scopus databases, selected for their comprehensive coverage of economic and health research. Our search strategy involved the use of keywords such as "Artificial Intelligence," "Economic Impact," "Healthcare," and "Cost Saving," resulting in search combinations like "AI AND Cost Saving AND Healthcare" and "Artificial Intelligence AND Economic Impact AND Healthcare." We restricted our search to publications available in English. Adhering to the Preferred Reporting Items for Systematic Reviews and Meta-Analyses (PRISMA) guidelines (Moher et al., 2009), we structured our review and identified relevant studies, as illustrated in Fig. 9.1. This framework also guided the development of our search strategy.

In our selection process, we utilized the PRISMA flow diagram (Fig. 9.1) to determine which articles to include or exclude from the Scopus databases. Initially, we screened the titles and abstracts to identify articles that addressed the economic impacts of AI in health care, such as cost-effectiveness or cost savings. Following this, we examined the full texts of potentially relevant articles. For inclusion, studies needed to include a cost evaluation related to AI in health care, such as cost-effectiveness, cost-utility, or cost–benefit analysis. Articles that did not provide a cost evaluation were excluded from further review.

Results

In our literature review, we examined 151 studies on AI's economic impact in health care, narrowing the selection to 59 focused on cost-related factors. From these 59 studies, we identified 22 studies that specifically looked at the economic impacts of AI in health care. These studies ranged from basic cost assessments to complex economic models, providing valuable insights into AI's healthcare implications.

Cost-Effectiveness and Economic Efficiency

In the realm of specific medical applications, several studies underscore AI's potential for enhancing cost-efficiency. Rizvi Anza et al. (2023) and Huang et al. (2022) both demonstrate that AI applications in diabetic retinopathy (DR) screening offer more cost-effective solutions compared to traditional methods. Rizvi et al. (2023) advocate for further economic evaluations in low- and

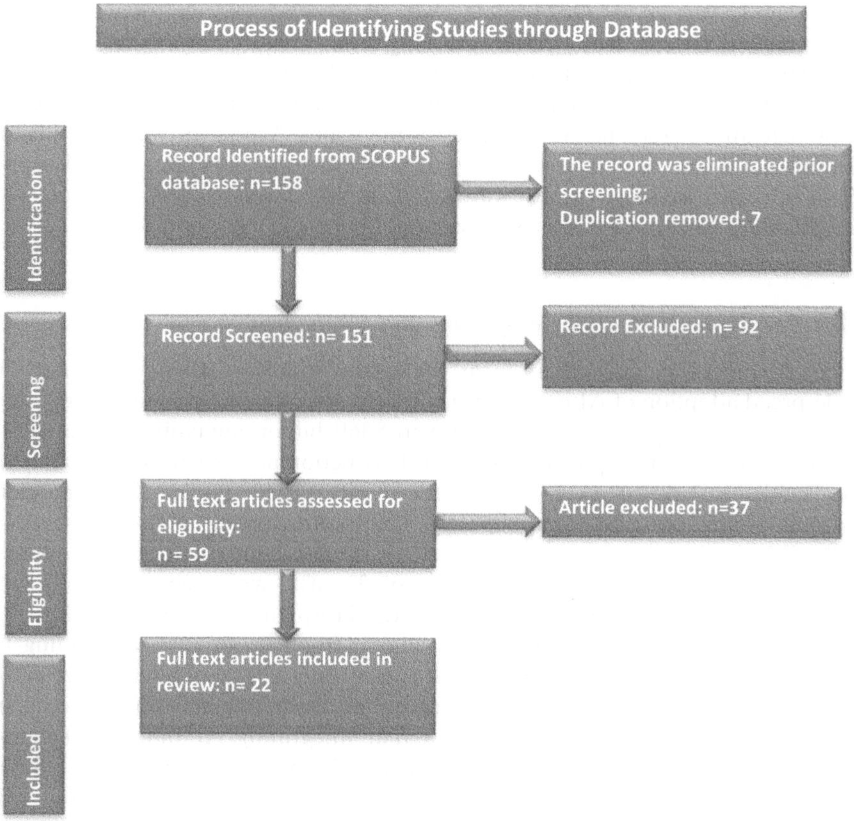

Fig. 9.1. PRISMA Flow Chart.

middle-income countries to better understand AI's potential benefits in these settings. Meanwhile, Huang et al. (2022) provide evidence of significant cost savings in rural China, indicating that AI can drive economic efficiency across diverse healthcare environments. In oncology, Zhang (2023) illustrates how machine learning models can improve diagnostic accuracy for breast cancer. This improvement not only enhances patient outcomes but also reduces the financial burden associated with misdiagnoses and subsequent treatments. Similarly, Areia et al. (2022) demonstrate that AI-assisted colonoscopy for colorectal cancer is a cost-effective approach. By improving early detection and reducing both incidence and mortality rates, AI has the potential to yield substantial long-term savings in cancer treatment.

Further insights into the economic impact of AI in screening are provided by Xiao et al. (2021) and Wu et al. (2024). Xiao et al. (2021) reveal that AI's effectiveness in reducing severe glaucoma cases and preventing associated blindness could lead to significant long-term cost reductions in health care. On the other hand, Wu et al. (2024) note that while AI screening for cataracts is cost-effective, Direct Health (DH) screening remains more economical in certain contexts. This indicates that while AI offers notable benefits, it must be carefully evaluated against other screening methods to determine the most cost-effective approach. Juuso Heinonen (2021) assesses the Klinik Access software in Finland, finding that it can result in cost savings of 8–20 euros per patient episode. Despite these potential savings, the software's low uptake suggests that the economic benefits may be constrained if barriers to adoption are not addressed.

Cost Reduction in Healthcare Systems and Challenges

A recent report by researchers from McKinsey and Harvard projects that the widespread adoption of AI in the US healthcare system could generate substantial financial benefits, potentially saving up to $360 billion annually. This analysis highlights significant opportunities for cost reduction across various segments of the healthcare industry. According to the report, private payers could see their overall costs decrease by approximately 7%–9%, translating to savings between $80 billion and $110 billion over the next five years. Similarly, physician groups are expected to achieve cost reductions of 3%–8%, which corresponds to an estimated $20 billion to $60 billion in savings. Hospitals, too, could benefit from AI integration, with potential savings ranging from 4% to 11%, amounting to between $60 billion and $120 billion each year (Pifer, 2023). Abd Rahman et al. (2023) explore the impact of machine learning on reducing maintenance costs in healthcare facilities. Their study shows that integrating AI into maintenance routines can lead to significant financial savings by predicting equipment failures before they occur and scheduling timely maintenance. This proactive approach minimizes downtime and extends the lifespan of medical equipment, ultimately enhancing overall healthcare management and reducing operational expenses. Khanna et al. (2022) extend this discussion by examining the broader implications of AI in healthcare diagnostics and treatment. Their research highlights how AI technologies can streamline processes, leading to notable cost reductions. By automating routine diagnostic tasks and optimizing treatment protocols, AI not only improves efficiency but also lowers overall costs, reinforcing the notion that AI has the potential to transform healthcare operations on a large scale. Supporting this view, Mori et al. (2020) provide specific evidence of cost savings through AI integration in colonoscopy procedures. Their findings demonstrate that AI can enhance the accuracy of colonoscopies, leading to fewer missed diagnoses and reducing the need for repeat procedures. This result in significant cost savings for both healthcare providers and patients, showcasing AI's potential to drive economic efficiencies in specialized medical procedures.

However, the probable economic benefits of AI are not without challenges. Singh Sikarwar et al. (2022) identify numerous obstacles to the implementation of AI and the Internet of Medical Things (IoMT), including regulatory hurdles and inadequate research funding. These obstacles could hinder the extensive implementation of AI technologies and delay the realization of their full economic potential. Addressing these challenges is essential for unlocking the benefits that AI can offer to the healthcare sector. Gomez Rossi et al. (2022) and Smak Gregoor et al. (2023) further explore the variability in AI's cost-effectiveness across different medical specialties. Their studies reveal that while AI can significantly enhance diagnostic capabilities, its economic benefits are not uniform. For example, the advantages of AI in dermatology and ophthalmology depend heavily on the specific context and application. This suggests that the economic impact of AI should be assessed on a case-by-case center, considering the unique needs and conditions of each medical field.

Innovative Approaches and Future Potential

Karabeg et al. (2024) and Monlezun et al. (2022) provide compelling evidence of how AI can drive economic benefits within specialized medical fields. Karabeg et al. (2024) focus on DR, a condition that demands frequent monitoring and intervention. Their research demonstrates that AI can streamline diagnostic processes, leading to substantial cost savings by reducing the need for manual assessments and improving early detection rates. This not only enhances patient outcomes but also optimizes resource allocation within healthcare systems. Similarly, Monlezun et al. (2022) examine AI's application in cardio-oncology, a complex field that combines cancer treatment with cardiovascular care. Their findings suggest that AI can improve cost-efficiency by integrating and analyzing vast amounts of patient data, thereby facilitating more accurate and timely interventions. This results in reduced treatment costs and better management of cardiovascular complications in cancer patients.

In another significant contribution, Hanna Jonsson and Luyolo Mazomba (2019) explore the potential of AI and big data within the Swedish healthcare system. They argue that with strategic adjustments to existing systems, AI could substantially enhance economic outcomes. By leveraging AI to analyze large datasets, the healthcare system could achieve more personalized and efficient care, ultimately leading to significant cost reductions and improved patient experiences. Poveda et al. (2022) further show the economic benefits of AI through its role in value-based contracting. Their research highlights how AI, particularly when combined with natural language processing (NLP), can refine decision-making processes and resource management. By optimizing contracts based on real-time data and predictive analytics, AI can improve healthcare delivery efficiency and ensure better alignment of resources with patient needs. Below is a summary of the results derived from the five articles listed in Table 9.1, in conjunction with the critical appraisal checklist for economic evaluations.

Discussion

This discussion highlights the economic benefits and challenges of AI in health care. AI improves cost-effectiveness and efficiency, especially in low- and middle-income countries. For example, Rizvi et al. (2023) and Huang et al. (2022)

Table 9.1. Summary of Literature Reviewed.

Author(s) Name and Pub. Year	Study Location	Study Objective	AI Technology Used	Healthcare Area	Type of Method/ Evaluation Employed	Key Findings
Zhang (2023)	Maryland	Role of machine learning and its applications in healthcare sector.	Decision Tree model, Random Forest model and Support Vector Classifier model	Breast Cancer Diagnosis	Machine Learning in the Diagnostic Testing Process	The study found that machine learning improves breast cancer diagnosis, boosting accuracy from 97.1% to 97.7% by reducing required criteria from nine to five.
Khanna et al. (2022)		To assess the impact of Artificial Intelligence (AI) on healthcare expenditures.	—	Diagnosis and Treatment	PRISMA	Study reveals significant cost reductions through the utilization of AI tools in diagnosis and treatment.
Mori et al. (2020)	Japan, England, Norway, and the United States.	This study evaluates financial savings from integrating AI in colonoscopy procedures.	—	Colonoscopy Screening	Large-Scale, Single-Center Clinical Trial	Result shows that the implementation of AI to facilitate the diagnose-and-leave approach leads to significant cost

						savings in colonoscopy procedures.
Xiao et al. (2021)	China	To explore the impact of glaucoma screening with AI.	One-way sensitivity analysis	Glaucoma Screening	Markov Model	The study confirmed that AI-assisted screening effectively reduced PACG cases, lowering PACS by 163, PAC by 79, and PACG by 45, while also preventing visual blindness in 10 patients.
Juuso (2021)	Finland	This study explores the cost efficiency and financial structures of the triage software "Klinik Access."	Klinik Access software and its functionalities	Preliminary Diagnoses	Regression Analyses	The study found Klinik users are younger females with fewer health concerns, shorter care episodes, and savings of €8–20 per episode, though uptake remains low at 16%.

(Continued)

Table 9.1. *(Continued)*

Author(s) Name and Pub. Year	Study Location	Study Objective	AI Technology Used	Healthcare Area	Type of Method/ Evaluation Employed	Key Findings
Abd Rahman et al. (2023)	Malaysia	To lower healthcare facility costs through smart healthcare management.	Machine Learning And Deep Learning	Healthcare Management System	Predictive Model	The model improves device maintenance, cutting annual costs by MYR 326,330.88, showing promise for healthcare management integration.
van Leeuwen et al. (2021)	UK	This study evaluates the cost-effectiveness of AI software in detecting intracranial LVO in stroke patients.	AI Software for Radiology	Vessel Occlusion Detection in Acute Stroke	Markov-Based Model	This study shows how early health technology assessment (HTA) of AI tools for detecting LVO can improve outcomes and reduce costs.

Chandna Palak (2022)	India	To determine the role of innovations in healthcare management in providing cost-effective and sustainable solutions.	AI	Telemedicine and Diagnosis	Empirical	Research showed that participants recognized AI's role in improving healthcare effectiveness, leading to more accurate diagnoses and cost savings.
Huang et al. (2022)	China	To assess the cost-effectiveness of AI-based screening for diabetic retinopathy (DR) in rural China.	AL	DR	Markov Model	The analysis shows AI-based screening is more cost-effective than traditional methods, offering a viable alternative for DR screening in rural China.
Areia et al. (2022)	US	This study examines AI detection tools in screening colonoscopy,	AI-assisted colonoscopy	Colorectal Cancer Screening	Markov Model Microsimulation	Study indicates that employing AI detection tools during screening colonoscopy is a

(Continued)

Table 9.1. *(Continued)*

Author(s) Name and Pub. Year	Study Location	Study Objective	AI Technology Used	Healthcare Area	Type of Method/ Evaluation Employed	Key Findings
		focusing on their impact on colorectal cancer incidence, mortality, and cost-effectiveness.				cost-effective approach for reducing both the incidence and mortality rates associated with colorectal cancer.
Hanna and Mazomba (2019)	Swedish R	This study explores how big data solutions can generate revenue opportunities within the Swedish healthcare system.	Big Data	Healthcare Delivery Process	Grounded Theory Approach	The findings suggest that Sweden's healthcare system currently lacks support for big data solutions, but with necessary improvements, future revenue growth is possible.
van Leeuwen et al. (2021)	United Kingdom	To assess the potential value of AI software in the field of radiology.	AI software in radiology	Vessel Occlusion Detection	Markov-Based Model	The study found that AI tools for detecting LVO in emergency settings improve

						outcomes, reduce costs, and highlight the role of early health technology assessment in radiology.
Karabeg et al. (2024)	Norway, COST	The study aims to conduct a preliminary cost analysis for identifying DR in diabetic women in Oslo.	EyeArt Automated DR Detection System	Ophthalmologist Assessment Of DR	Survey Method	The findings suggest that the Eye Art AI system serves as a dependable, economical, and effective resource for DR grading in clinical settings.
Singh Sikarwar et al., 2022	Indian Investment and funding	The adoption of AI and the Internet of Medical Things (IoMT) by healthcare professionals.	AI And IoMT	Healthcare Workforce	Descriptive Analysis	The study identified challenges in integrating AI and IoMT, including regulatory gaps, uncertain ROI from limited research, and issues with data management and

(Continued)

Table 9.1. *(Continued)*

Author(s) Name and Pub. Year	Study Location	Study Objective	AI Technology Used	Healthcare Area	Type of Method/ Evaluation Employed	Key Findings
						operational inefficiencies requiring ongoing processing.
Arya et al. (2024)	Canada CBA	Discrepancies and gaps in access to medical interpreting services.	Medical Interpreting Services and AI Tools	Access To Medical	Cost–Benefit Analysis	The analysis highlights how medical interpreting improves healthcare quality, supporting patient autonomy and emphasizing clinicians' and interpreters' critical roles in decision-making.
Smak Gregoor et al. (2023)	Netherland	Examine the impact on dermatological healthcare utilization.	AI-based mHealth App	Skin Cancer Detection	Cost-Effectiveness Analysis	The findings show AI in mHealth improves identification of cutaneous (pre)

						malignancies, but the benefit must be balanced against increased healthcare use for benign skin conditions.
Wu et al. (2024)	China	To evaluate the cost-effectiveness and cost-utility of different cataract screening methods.	Telescreening, AI Screening and DH Screening	Eye Health	Decision-Analytic Markov Models	The findings suggest DH screening outperforms no screening, tele-screening, and AI screening in China, proving cost-effective and supporting annual screening as a viable public health initiative.
Monlezun et al. (2022)	United States	Investigate how AI and propensity score (PS) methodologies are integrated into clinical and cost-effectiveness analyses.	Deep Learning And Machine Learning	Cardio-Oncology Cardiac Arrests	Multivariable Regression and Cohort Analysis	The findings reveal that AI-assisted evaluations offer insights into mortality reductions from cardiac interventions,

(Continued)

Table 9.1. *(Continued)*

Author(s) Name and Pub. Year	Study Location	Study Objective	AI Technology Used	Healthcare Area	Type of Method/ Evaluation Employed	Key Findings
						improving equitable healthcare outcomes when integrated into digital systems.
Kaczmarek et al. (2021)	Poland	To investigate the multifaceted prevention approach for infections related to cardiac implantable electronic devices.	Cardiac implantable electronic device	Cardiac Implantable	Retrospective Observational Study and Analysis of Cost-Effectiveness	The use of GCS to reduce infections related to CIEDs is both practical and secure, significantly lowering infection rates while remaining cost-effective in our prevention strategy.
Poveda et al. (2022)	United Kingdom	Value-based contracting (VBC) in the pharmaceutical market,	NLP and Big Data Analysis	Value-Based Contracts and Payment of a Drug	Real-World Evidence (RWE)	The findings suggest that NLP and AI technologies enhance

		highlighting the impact of AI and natural language processing (NLP).				Value-Based Care by improving decision-making in treatment and contracts, leading to better patient outcomes and efficient resource use.
Gomez Rossi et al. (2022)	United States and Germany	This study evaluates AI's cost-effectiveness in assisting disease detection and classification in dermatology, dentistry, and ophthalmology.	(AI) Algorithms Dermatology	Dentistry and Ophthalmology	Markov Models and Sensitivity Analyses	The study found that AI as a decision-support tool in dermatology, dentistry, and ophthalmology offers marginal cost-effectiveness benefits influenced by use cases and implementation costs.

Source: Author's Complied.

showed that AI in DR screening cuts costs while Zhang (2023) found machine learning enhances breast cancer diagnosis, reducing misdiagnoses and unnecessary treatments.

Further evidence supports AI's economic advantages across different medical fields. Areia et al. (2022) and Mori et al. (2020) demonstrated that AI-assisted colonoscopy enhances colorectal cancer screening efficiency while lowering costs. Additionally, Xiao et al. (2021) found that AI-driven glaucoma screening reduces severe cases and long-term healthcare expenses. In stroke care, van Leeuwen et al. (2021) showed that AI tools improve large vessel occlusion detection, enabling timely interventions and reducing emergency care costs.

However, despite these benefits, challenges persist. Regulatory barriers, insufficient funding and low adoption rates hinder AI's full potential (Heinonen, 2021; Singh Sikarwar et al., 2022). Addressing these requires policymakers to establish clear regulatory frameworks while investing in AI-driven healthcare initiatives (Mesko, 2020). Clinicians must integrate AI tools into practice, supported by continuous training (Jiang et al., 2017). Healthcare administrators and developers should prioritize usability, security and compliance to drive adoption (Davenport & Kalakota, 2019). Overcoming these barriers will maximize AI's economic impact while ensuring equitable access and ethical implementation.

Gaps in the Literature

The economic implications of AI in the healthcare sector represent a dynamic field of study, with significant findings already highlighting its potential for enhancing cost efficiency and operational effectiveness. Nonetheless, there are notable deficiencies in the existing literature, indicating areas where future investigations could yield important insights. Current research tends to concentrate on particular regions or healthcare frameworks, such as low- and middle-income nations or affluent environments like the United States and the United Kingdom. For instance, studies by Rizvi et al. (2023) and Huang et al. (2022) examine the role of AI in DR screening in low- and middle-income countries and rural China, respectively. However, there is a scarcity of research assessing the economic performance of AI across a variety of healthcare environments and populations worldwide. The economic ramifications of AI within different cultural, economic and infrastructural contexts remain insufficiently investigated. While many studies emphasize short-term cost-effectiveness and immediate financial benefits, there is a lack of understanding regarding the long-term economic impacts of AI adoption, including the sustainability of cost reductions and the enduring advantages of AI integration into healthcare systems. Although some research employs advanced models such as Markov models or decision trees, comprehensive economic models that encompass multiple AI applications within a single healthcare framework are lacking. Research frequently isolates AI applications; however, a comprehensive perspective that considers the aggregate economic effects of various AI technologies could yield more profound insights. Additionally, many studies depend on theoretical frameworks and simulations, revealing a gap in empirical evidence demonstrating AI's performance in real-world healthcare settings. This includes insights into user experiences, challenges related to system integration, and the actual cost savings achieved following AI implementation.

Future Research Directions

Future research should focus on cross-regional and cross-national studies to better understand how AI impacts healthcare economics in different settings. Comparative studies can provide valuable insights into how regional factors influence AI's effectiveness and economic benefits. Additionally, longitudinal research is crucial for assessing the long-term financial effects of AI in health care, tracking cost reductions, shifts in patient outcomes over time, and the sustainability of AI-driven efficiencies.

Developing integrated economic models that incorporate multiple AI applications within a single healthcare system can offer a more comprehensive understanding of AI's overall financial impact. Researchers should also explore how various AI technologies interact and collectively contribute to cost savings and operational improvements. Conducting thorough cost–benefit analyses is essential to account for not only immediate savings but also the costs of implementation, training, and potential disruptions during adoption.

Future studies should examine how AI can help bridge healthcare disparities and improve access to care for marginalized populations. Ensuring AI solutions promote equity and meet diverse community needs is critical. Additionally, researchers must explore the ethical and regulatory aspects of AI in health care, considering their influence on economic outcomes to maximize AI's benefits while ensuring responsible implementation.

Conclusion

AI is transforming health care by enhancing cost-effectiveness, optimizing resource allocation, and improving patient outcomes. Our study examines the economic impact of AI in health care, identifying both its benefits and the challenges that hinder widespread adoption. A review of 22 relevant studies highlights AI's potential to reduce costs in various medical applications, including DR screening, breast cancer diagnosis, and colonoscopy procedures. AI-driven screening for glaucoma and stroke detection has also demonstrated significant economic advantages by enabling early intervention and reducing long-term healthcare expenses.

Despite these benefits, barriers such as regulatory challenges, insufficient funding, and low adoption rates limit AI's full potential. Addressing these economic barriers requires targeted strategies. Policymakers should establish clear regulatory frameworks to ensure compliance and ethical implementation while increasing investment in AI-driven healthcare initiatives. Clinicians must receive continuous training to integrate AI into medical practice effectively while healthcare administrators should focus on streamlining operations and reducing costs through AI adoption. Additionally, AI developers must collaborate with healthcare professionals to create practical, user-friendly solutions. Future research should explore long-term economic impacts, cross-regional cost evaluations, and strategies to enhance equity in AI-driven health care. By overcoming these challenges, AI can drive sustainable cost reductions and improve healthcare accessibility worldwide.

References

Abd Rahman, N. H., Mohamad Zaki, M. H., Hasikin, K., Abd Razak, N. A., Ibrahim, A. K., & Lai, K. W. (2023). Predicting medical device failure: A promise to reduce healthcare facilities cost through smart healthcare management. *PeerJ Computer Science*, *9*(e1279), e1279. https://doi.org/10.7717/peerj-cs.1279

Abdul, S., Adeghe, E. P., Adegoke, B. O., Adegoke, A. A., & Udedeh, E. H. (2024). AI-enhanced healthcare management during natural disasters: Conceptual insights. *Engineering Science & Technology Journal*, *5*(5), 1794–1816. https://doi.org/10.51594/estj.v5i5.1155

Abut, S., Okut, H., Zackula, R., & James Kallail, K. (2024). Deep neural networks and applications in medical research. In M. Domínguez-Morales, J. Civit-Masot, L. Muñoz-Saavedra, & R. Damaševičius (Eds.), *Artificial intelligence*. IntechOpen.

Alberto Mazzoli, C., Semeraro, F., & Gamberini, L. (2023). Enhancing cardiac arrest education: Exploring the potential use of mid journey. *Resuscitation*, *189*(109893), 109893. https://doi.org/10.1016/j.resuscitation.2023.109893

Alia, O., Abdelbakib, W., Shrestha, A., Elbasib, E., Alryalat, M. A. A., & Dwivedi, Y. K. (2023). A systematic literature review of artificial intelligence in the healthcare sector: Benefits, challenges, methodologies, and functionalities. *Journal of Innovation & Knowledge*, *8*. 100333. https://doi.org/10.1016/j.jik.2023.100333

Areia, M., Mori, Y., Correale, L., Repici, A., Bretthauer, M., Sharma, P., Taveira, F., Spadaccini, M., Antonelli, G., Ebigbo, A., Kudo, S.-E., Arribas, J., Barua, I., Kaminski, M. F., Messmann, H., Rex, D. K., Dinis-Ribeiro, M., & Hassan, C. (2022). Cost-effectiveness of artificial intelligence for screening colonoscopy: A modelling study. *The Lancet Digital Health*, *4*(6), e436–e444. https://doi.org/10.1016/S2589-7500(22)00042-5

Arya, A. N., Hyman, I., Holland, T., Beukeboom, C., Tong, C. E., Talavlikar, R., & Eagan, G. (2024). Medical interpreting services for refugees in Canada: Current state of practice and considerations in promoting this essential human right for all. *International Journal of Environmental Research and Public Health*, *21*(5), 588. https://doi.org/10.3390/ijerph21050588

Castagno, S., & Khalifa, M. (2020). Perceptions of artificial intelligence among healthcare staff: A qualitative survey study. *Frontiers in Artificial Intelligence*, *3*, 578983. https://doi.org/10.3389/frai.2020.578983

Chaibi, A., & Zaiem, I. (2022). Doctor resistance of artificial intelligence in healthcare. *International Journal of Healthcare Information Systems and Informatics*, *17*(1), 1–13. https://doi.org/10.4018/ijhisi.315618

Chan, C. Y. T., & Petrikat, D. (2023). Strategic applications of artificial intelligence in healthcare and medicine. *Journal of Medical and Health Studies*, *4*(3), 58–68. https://doi.org/10.32996/jmhs.2023.4.3.8

Chandna, P. (2022). To determine the role of innovations in healthcare management in providing cost-effective and sustainable solutions. *NeuroQuantology*, *20*(4), 2176–2182.

Cheng, M., Li, X., & Xu, J. (2022). Promoting healthcare workers' adoption intention of artificial-intelligence-assisted diagnosis and treatment: The chain mediation of social influence and human-computer trust. *International Journal of Environmental Research and Public Health*, *19*(20), 13311. https://doi.org/10.3390/ijerph192013311

Copeland, B. J. (2004). *The essential Turing: Seminal writings in computing, logic, philosophy, artificial intelligence, and artificial life*. Oxford University Press.

Copeland, B. J. (2006). *Colossus: The secrets of Bletchley Park's code-breaking computers*. Oxford University Press.

Davenport, T., & Kalakota, R. (2019). The potential for artificial intelligence in healthcare. *Future Healthcare Journal*, *6*, 94–98. https://doi.org/10.7861/futurehosp.6-2-94

Gomez Rossi, J., Rojas-Perilla, N., Krois, J., & Schwendicke, F. (2022). Cost-effectiveness of artificial intelligence as a decision-support system applied to the detection and grading of melanoma, dental caries, and diabetic retinopathy. *JAMA Network Open*, *5*(3), e220269. https://doi.org/10.1001/jamanetworkopen.2022.0269

Hanna, J., & Mazomba, L. (2019). *An exploratory study of how big data solutions can be integrated into the Swedish healthcare system*, n.d., sec. Master's Thesis in Business Administration. UMEA School of Busness Economics and Statistics.

Heinonen, J. (2021). Overcoming barriers to AI adoption in healthcare: Funding, regulation, and implementation strategies. *Health Policy and Technology*, *10*(3), 100546. https://doi.org/10.1016/j.hlpt.2021.100546

Hodges, A. (2012). *Alan turing: The enigma*. Princeton University Press.

Huang, X.-M., Yang, B.-F., Zheng, W.-L., Liu, Q., Xiao, F., Ouyang, P.-W., Li, M.-J., Li, X.-Y., Meng, J., Zhang, T.-T., Cui, Y.-H., & Pan, H.-W. (2022). Cost-effectiveness of artificial intelligence screening for diabetic retinopathy in rural China. *BMC Health Services Research*, *22*(1). https://doi.org/10.1186/s12913-022-07655-6

Islam, M. M. (2024). Exploring the impact of artificial intelligence in healthcare. *Deleted Journal*, *2*(1), 171–188. https://doi.org/10.60087/jaigs.v2i1.p188

Jiang, F., Jiang, Y., Zhi, H., Dong, Y., Li, H., Ma, S., Wang, Y., Dong, Q., Shen, H., & Wang, Y. (2017). Artificial intelligence in healthcare: Past, present and future. *Stroke and Vascular Neurology*, *2*(4), 230–243. https://doi.org/10.1136/svn-2017-000101

Joshi, N. (2019). *7 Types of artificial intelligence*. [Online]. https://www.forbes.com/sites/cognitiveworld/2019/06/19/7-types-of-artificial-intelligence/#433c0504233e

Juuso, H. (2021). *Cost benefits and mechanisms of imple-menting an AI triage solution in a primary healthcare center- Case Klinik Access at Myyrmäki health center*. Master Programme thesis. Alto University.

Kaczmarek, K., Strzelecki, A., Ptaszyński, P., Wranicz, J. K., & Cygankiewicz, I. (2021). The safety, efficacy, and cost-effectiveness of gentamycin-collagen sponge in multicomponent prevention strategy of cardiac implantable electronic device infections — A single-center experience. *Kardiologia Polska*, *79*(10), 1079–1085. https://doi.org/10.33963/kp.a2021.0089

Karabeg, M., Petrovski, G., Hertzberg, S. N. W., Erke, M. G., Fosmark, D. S., Russell, G., Moe, M. C., Volke, V., Raudonis, V., Verkauskiene, R., Sokolovska,

J., Haugen, I.-B. K., & Petrovski, B. E. (2024). A pilot cost-analysis study comparing AI-based EyeArt® and ophthalmologist assessment of diabetic retinopathy in minority women in Oslo, Norway. *International Journal of Retina and Vitreous*, *10*(1). https://doi.org/10.1186/s40942-024-00547-3

Kelly, C. J., Karthikesalingam, A., Suleyman, M., Corrado, G., & King, D. (2019). Key challenges for delivering clinical impact with artificial intelligence. *BMC Medicine*, *17*(1), 195. https://doi.org/10.1186/s12916-019-1426-2

Khanna, N. N., Maindarkar, M. A., Viswanathan, V., Fernandes, J. F. E., Paul, S., Bhagawati, M., Ahluwalia, P., Ruzsa, Z., Sharma, A., Kolluri, R., Singh, I. M., Laird, J. R., Fatemi, M., Alizad, A., Saba, L., Agarwal, V., Sharma, A., Teji, J. S., Al-Maini, M., … Suri, J. S. (2022). Economics of artificial intelligence in healthcare: Diagnosis vs. Treatment. *Healthcare*, *10*(12), 2493. https://doi.org/10.3390/healthcare10122493

Kulkarni, P. A., & Singh, H. (2023). Artificial intelligence in clinical diagnosis: Opportunities, challenges, and hype. *JAMA, The Journal of the American Medical Association*, *330*(4), 317. https://doi.org/10.1001/jama.2023.11440

Kuwaiti, A. A., Nazer, K., Al-Reedy, A., Al-Shehri, S., Al-Muhanna, A., Subbarayalu, A. V., Muhanna, D. A., & Al-Muhanna, F. A. (2023). A review of the role of artificial intelligence in healthcare. *Journal of Personalized Medicine*, *13*(6), 951. https://doi.org/10.3390/jpm13060951

Laï, M.-C., Brian, M., & Mamzer, M.-F. (2020). Perceptions of artificial intelligence in healthcare: Findings from a qualitative survey study among actors in France. *Journal of Translational Medicine*, *18*(1), 14. https://doi.org/10.1186/s12967-019-02204-y

Mani, Z., & Albagawi, B. (2024). AI frontiers in emergency care: The next evolution of nursing interventions. *Frontiers in Public Health*, *12*, 1439412. https://doi.org/10.3389/fpubh.2024.1439412

Mesko, B. (2020). The role of artificial intelligence in precision medicine. *Expert Review of Precision Medicine and Drug Development*, *5*(5), 239–241.

Michie, D. (1991). Machine intelligence: A personal view. In M. Boden (Ed.), *The philosophy of artificial intelligence* (pp. 45–57). Oxford University Press.

Moher, D., Liberati, A., Tetzlaff, J., & Altman, D. G., & The PRISMA Group. (2009). Preferred reporting Items for systematic reviews and meta-analyses: The PRISMA statement. *PLoS Medicine*, *6*(7), e1000097. https://doi.org/10.1371/journal.pmed.1000097

Monlezun, D. J., Sinyavskiy, O., Peters, N., Steigner, L., Aksamit, T., Girault, M. I., Garcia, A., Gallagher, C., & Iliescu, C. (2022). Artificial intelligence-augmented propensity score, cost effectiveness and computational ethical analysis of cardiac arrest and active cancer with novel mortality predictive score. *Medicina*, *58*(8), 1039. https://doi.org/10.3390/medicina58081039

Mori, Y., Kudo, S.-E., East, J. E., Rastogi, A., Bretthauer, M., Misawa, M., Sekiguchi, M., Matsuda, T., Saito, Y., Ikematsu, H., Hotta, K., Ohtsuka, K., Kudo, T., & Mori, K. (2020). Cost savings in colonoscopy with artificial intelligence-aided polyp diagnosis: An add-on analysis of a clinical trial (with video). *Gastrointestinal Endoscopy*, *92*(4), 905–911.e1. https://doi.org/10.1016/j.gie.2020.03.3759

Ng, K. K. Y., & Zhang, P. C. (2023). Advancing medical affair capabilities and insight generation through machine learning techniques. *Journal of Pharmaceutical Policy and Practice*, *16*(1). https://doi.org/10.1186/s40545-023-00670-w

Novak, A., Ather, S., Gill, A., Aylward, P., Maskell, G., Cowell, G. W., Espinosa Morgado, A. T., Duggan, T., Keevill, M., Gamble, O., Akrama, O., Belcher, E., Taberham, R., Hallifax, R., Bahra, J., Banerji, A., Bailey, J., James, A., Ansaripour, A., … Gleeson, F. (2024). Evaluation of the impact of artificial intelligence-assisted image interpretation on the diagnostic performance of clinicians in identifying pneumothoraces on plain chest X-ray: A multi-case multi-reader study. *Emergency Medicine Journal: Engineering Management Journal*. emermed-2023-213620. https://doi.org/10.1136/emermed-2023-213620

Petersson, J., Erlingsdóttir, G., & Marklund, B. (2022). Health technology assessment in the era of artificial intelligence: A scoping review of AI applications in health care. *Frontiers in Digital Health*, *4*, 812214.

Pifer, R. (2023). Artificial intelligence could save healthcare industry $360B a year. *Healthcare Dive*. https://www.healthcaredive.com/news/artificial-intelligence-healthcare-savings-harvard-mckinsey-report/641163/

Poveda, J. L., Bretón-Romero, R., Del Rio-Bermudez, C., Taberna, M., & Medrano, I. H. (2022). How can artificial intelligence optimize value-based contracting? *Journal of Pharmaceutical Policy and Practice*, *15*(1). https://doi.org/10.1186/s40545-022-00475-3

Reddy, S., Lebrun, A., Chee, A., & Kalogeropoulos, D. (2024). Discussing the role of explainable AI and evaluation frameworks for safe and effective integration of large language models in healthcare. *Telehealth and Medicine Today*, *9*(2). https://doi.org/10.30953/thmt.v9.485

Rizvi, A., Rizvi, F., Lalakia, P., Hyman, L., Frasso, R., Sztandera, L., & Das, A. V. (2023). Is artificial intelligence the cost-saving lens to diabetic retinopathy screening in low- and middle-income countries? *Cureus*. https://doi.org/10.7759/cureus.45539

Sarker, M. (2023). Assessing the integration of ai technologies in enhancing patient care delivery in u.s. hospitals. *Journal of Knowledge Learning and Science Technology*, *2*(2), 338–351. https://doi.org/10.60087/jklst.vol2.n2.p351

Secinaro, S., Calandra, D., Secinaro, A., Muthurangu, V., & Biancone, P. (2021). The role of artificial intelligence in healthcare: A structured literature review. *BMC Medical Informatics and Decision Making*, *21*, 125. https://doi.org/10.1186/s12911-021-01488-9

Shamszare, H., & Choudhury, A. (2023). Clinicians' perceptions of artificial intelligence: Focus on workload, risk, trust, clinical decision making, and clinical integration. *Healthcare*, *11*(16). https://doi.org/10.3390/healthcare11162308

Sharma, R. (2020). Artificial intelligence in healthcare: A review. *Turkish Journal of Computer and Mathematics Education (TURCOMAT)*, *11*(1), 1663–1667. https://doi.org/10.61841/turcomat.v11i1.14628

Singh Sikarwar, T., Mehta, S., Yadav, S., & Arora, D. (2022). Factors of adoption of artificial intelligence and internet of medical things amongst healthcare workers: A descriptive analysis. *International Journal of Systematic Innovation*, *7*(3). https://doi.org/10.6977/IJoSI.202209_7(3).0002

Smak Gregoor, A. M., Sangers, T. E., Bakker, L. J., Hollestein, L., Uyl - de Groot, C. A., Nijsten, T., & Wakkee, M. (2023). An artificial intelligence based app for skin cancer detection evaluated in a population based setting. *npj Digital Medicine*, *6*(1). https://doi.org/10.1038/s41746-023-00831-w

Smith, M., Sattler, A., Hong, G., & Lin, S. (2021). From code to bedside: Implementing artificial intelligence using quality improvement methods. *Journal of*

General Internal Medicine, *36*(4), 1061–1066. https://doi.org/10.1007/s11606-020-06394-w

Spear, J., Ehrenfeld, J. M., & Miller, B. J. (2023). Applications of artificial intelligence in health care delivery. *Journal of Medical Systems*, *47*(1). https://doi.org/10.1007/s10916-023-02018-y

Sunarti, S., Rahman, F. F., Naufal, M., Risky, M., Febriyanto, K., & Masnina, R. (2021). Artificial intelligence in healthcare: Opportunities and risk for future. *Gaceta Sanitaria*, *35*, S67–S70. https://doi.org/10.1016/j.gaceta.2020.12.019

Turing, A. M. (1947). *Lecture on the automatic computing engine.*

Turing, A. M. (1950). *Lecture on the automatic computing engine.*

van de Sande, D., Van Genderen, M. E., Smit, J. M., Huiskens, J., Visser, J. J., Veen, R. E. R., van Unen, E., Ba, O. H., Gommers, D., & van Bommel, J. (2022). Developing, implementing and governing artificial intelligence in medicine: A step-by-step approach to prevent an artificial intelligence winter. *BMJ Health & Care Informatics*, *29*(1), e100495. https://doi.org/10.1136/bmjhci-2021-100495

van de Sande, J. C., van der Molen, D. R., Gommers, D. A. M., & De Bruin, M. L. (2022). Transparency and trust in artificial intelligence in healthcare: The importance of explainability. *BMJ Health & Care Informatics*, *29*(1), e100495.

van Leeuwen, J., Wouters, M., & van der Heijden, B. (2023). Barriers to adopting artificial intelligence in healthcare: A managerial perspective on return on investment and organizational readiness. *Journal of Health Management and Economics*, *7*(2), 115–128.

van Leeuwen, K. G., Meijer, F. J. A., Schalekamp, S., Rutten, M. J. C. M., van Dijk, E. J., van Ginneken, B., Govers, T. M., & de Rooij, M. (2021). Cost-effectiveness of artificial intelligence aided vessel occlusion detection in acute stroke: An early health technology assessment. *Insights into Imaging*, *12*(1). https://doi.org/10.1186/s13244-021-01077-4

Vithlani, P., Sharma, V., Singh, R., & Patel, D. (2023). Evaluating the economic implications of AI-driven healthcare solutions: A systematic review. *Frontiers in Pharmacology*, *14*, 1220950. https://doi.org/10.3389/fphar.2023.1220950

Wolff, J., Pauling, J., Keck, A., Baumbach, J., & Möller, D. (2020). The economic impact of artificial intelligence in health care: Systematic review. *Journal of Medical Internet Research*, *22*(2), e16866. https://doi.org/10.2196/16866

Wu, X., Wu, Y., Tu, Z., Cao, Z., Xu, M., Xiang, Y., Lin, D., Jin, L., Zhao, L., Zhang, Y., Liu, Y., Yan, P., Hu, W., Liu, J., Liu, L., Wang, X., Wang, R., Chen, J., Xiao, W., … Lin, H. (2024). Cost-effectiveness and cost-utility of a digital technology-driven hierarchical healthcare screening pattern in China. *Nature Communications*, *15*(1). https://doi.org/10.1038/s41467-024-47211-w

Xiao, X., Xue, L., Ye, L., Li, H., & He, Y. (2021). Health care cost and benefits of artificial intelligence-assisted population-based glaucoma screening for the elderly in remote areas of China: A cost-offset analysis. *BMC Public Health*, *21*(1). https://doi.org/10.1186/s12889-021-11097-w

Zhang, J. (2023). Using AI to improve breast cancer diagnosis and its effects on health care cost. *Scholarly Review Journal, SR Online: Showcase*, (Summer 2023 Pt 2). https://doi.org/10.70121/001c.121754

Chapter 10

Performance Incentives as a Tool to Motivate Employees: A Study in the Indian Healthcare Sector

Moumita Acharyya[a] *and Jennifer A. Pope*[b]

[a]TERI School of Advanced Studies, India
[b]Grand Valley State University, USA

Abstract

Incentive programs are used to reward performance, reinforce positive behavior, introduce interest in employees, and most importantly motivate them. Employee incentive programs offer a diversity of rewards that may be monetary or non-monetary. Organizations are investing billions of dollars into employee incentive programs. However, not all programs have arrived at the desired results. Successfully implemented programs have shown results that boost performance. The primary objective of carrying out this research study is to analyze the effect of performance incentive plans on the motivation level of employees in the organizations. Thus to understand what all factors in an incentive plan motivate, satisfy and develop a sense of loyalty in the employees, the research study was conducted with a structured questionnaire drafted to collect primary data from the organization's employees. To have more reliable source for the research study, three different organizations operating in the same healthcare sector were chosen. A sample of 30 employees of each organization having undergone at least one appraisal cycle in their respective companies participated in the research study. Apart from primary data, secondary data from already conducted research, articles, and books were used to draft the entire report. Data collected were analyzed quantitatively using statistical software SPSS 17.0 and arrived at meaningful conclusions.

However, the conclusions made from this research study cannot be generalized on a large scale because of unavailability of incentive plans of the organization taken into consideration out security constraints in the

Digital Transformation and Artificial Intelligence for Operational Excellence in Healthcare, 189–209

Published under exclusive licence by Emerald Publishing Limited
doi:10.1108/978-1-83662-314-420251028

organizations. Moreover, sample size could have been increased to obtain more trustworthy results.

Keywords: Performance incentive; motivation; job performance; reward; healthcare

Introduction

In today's highly competitive and dynamic environment, most organizational theorists mention that employees are an integral part of any organization because a large part of the daily operations are managed by them. In simple words, the overall success of an organization in achieving its strategic objectives relies heavily on the performance level of employees of the organization. Thus, it is crucial to identify the factors influencing performance first.

Employee performance is derived from ability and motivation, where ability can be described in the form of the skills, training, and resources required for performing a task and motivation is an inner force that drives individuals to act. All firms, irrespective of the size of organization and the size of industry or sector, require motivated employees to function effectively. Human resources are assets that ensure the productivity and performance of an organization. Motivated employees are contented, dedicated and work enthusiastically. The outcome of a motivated workforce includes employee retention, loyalty, and harmony. All such factors contribute significantly to the growth and development of the organization. Consequently, one of the most compelling challenges facing today's organizations is how to make sure that employees are highly motivated.

As far as the issue of employee motivation is concerned, employee incentive programs have been found to be the most adopted technique among organizations.

The purpose of incentive programs is to reward performance, reinforce positive behavior, introduce interest in employees, and most importantly motivate them. These programs offer a diversity of rewards that may be monetary or non-monetary. Research conducted each year shows that organizations are investing billions of dollars into employee incentive programs. However, not all programs have arrived at the desired results. Successfully implemented programs have shown results that boost performance.

Motivation is a critical dimension of capacity, defined as "the ability of people, institutions and societies to perform functions, solve problems and set and achieve objectives". Incentive plans are important in developing capacities and to translating developed capacities into improved performance. The focus of this research study is on judging the perception of employees toward incentive programs (monetary and non-monetary incentive programs) that influence motivation and behavior of people for developmental outcomes. Incentive systems and motivations are critical for capacity development as they enable individuals and organizations to perform their functions effectively, efficiently, and sustain ably.

Incentive programs have existed since the start of the 19th century. Since then, the idea of what an incentive program has changed for both the employer and the employee. Incentive programs are used as simply a method of payment, but for employees, it is a source of inducing motivation.

Today, the definition of an incentive program is used as a two-sided sword as it includes not only a way of paying employees but a way of reducing costs for the employer while at the same time, rewarding the employee for making the extra effort.

Rationale of the Study

The purpose of incentive programs is to reward performance, reinforce positive behavior, introduce interest in employees, and most importantly motivate them. Employee incentive programs offer a diversity of rewards that may be monetary or non-monetary. Research conducted each year shows that organizations are investing billions of dollars into employee incentive programs. However, not all programs have arrived at the desired results. Successfully implemented programs have shown results that boost performance.

Thus, problem statement for this study is defined as to analyze the effect of performance incentive plans on the motivation level of employees in the organizations.

Literature Review

Employee motivation and performance incentives have been widely studied in organizational behavior literature. Deci et al. (2022) revisited the role of extrinsic rewards in education and workplace motivation, arguing that while financial incentives boost short-term productivity, they may undermine intrinsic motivation if not well-structured. This aligns with Eisenberger et al. (2023), who emphasized that perceived organizational support enhances employee loyalty and job satisfaction, particularly when rewards are seen as fair and justified.

Choi et al. (2022) examined how job changes affect life satisfaction and found that performance incentives play a significant role in employees' decisions to stay or leave an organization. Similarly, Kim and Lee (2023) highlighted the impact of performance-based bonuses in sales and customer service sectors, demonstrating that targeted financial rewards significantly improve productivity. However, they caution against over-reliance on monetary incentives, which can lead to burnout and reduced long-term commitment.

Recent studies also suggest that hybrid incentive models are gaining traction. Gentry and Sparks (2023) explored the balance between financial rewards and career development opportunities in the technology sector. Their findings indicate that employees respond best to a mix of salary bonuses, career growth programs, and skill enhancement opportunities. Likewise, Zhang et al. (2022) found that long-term financial incentives foster employee loyalty, particularly in knowledge-based industries where retention is crucial.

Park and Lee (2022) examined how career development opportunities influence job performance and organizational commitment, reinforcing the argument that non-monetary incentives, such as training and mentorship, significantly contribute to employee satisfaction. Their research study complements findings from Deci et al. (2022), suggesting that organizations should design incentives that balance extrinsic rewards with intrinsic motivation to sustain long-term engagement.

Importance of Performance Incentives as a Motivational Tool

Workplace motivation strategies are commonly adopted by organizations to improve profitability by increasing motivation and productivity, reducing absenteeism and turnover, and to retain talented and skilled employees (Holcomb & Johnson, 2023). Typical motivation techniques such as incentives, rewards, and recognition are often used complementarily to motivate employees.

The main difference between incentive and reward is that while an incentive is defined as something that triggers a particular course of action, a reward is given following a desired behavior to increase the probability that the behavior will be repeated. In other words, when an incentive is offered for meeting specific goals, the employee is likely to expend more energy and effort into the job, and thereafter, the incentive will be given to the employee as a reward when the goal is met, but it all stems from an incentive. By and large, organizations use rewards as incentives to stimulate desired behavior. Recognition, on the other hand, is to show appreciation for the employee's efforts and positive contributions and at the same time, reinforce and encourage similar future behavior. Recognition takes place only after the behavior has occurred and it may be offered in conjunction with the reward. On the whole, both incentives and recognition are useful mechanisms to induce positive attitude and motivate employees. For the purpose of this study, the concept of incentives, rewards, and recognition will be studied under the category of "incentives."

The classification of incentives provides a framework of the breakdown of organizational rewards, as proposed by Pattanayak is presented in Table 10.1.

Monetary Incentives, Tangible Non-Monetary Incentives, and Intangible Non-Monetary Incentives

Monetary incentives refer to financial rewards given to employees in terms of bonuses, stock options, insurances, paid leave, etc. Tangible non-monetary incentives involve the indirect payment of money in the form of tangible rewards such as gift cards, watches, garments, plaques/trophies, electronic appliances, decorative items, vacation trips etc. and services such as bus service, club privileges, meal treats, celebration parties, internet services, etc. Intangible non-monetary incentives include the use of social rewards and task-related rewards. Social-related rewards concern the organization's social practices such

Table 10.1. Different Type of Incentives.

Monetary Incentives	Tangible Non-Monetary	Intangible Non-Monetary
Direct compensation: • Base salary • Commission • Bonus *Indirect compensation:* • Insurance for health/ disability/life • Profit sharing plans • Retirement plans • Employee Stock Ownership Plan (ESOP) • Educational reimbursement • Overtime policy • Paid leave • Unpaid leave • Subsidized utilities • Subsidized housing • Travel expenses • Childcare	*Treats: Free meal treats* • Free food/beverage • Festival bashes • Coffee breaks • Picnics • Birthday treats *Awards* • Plaques or trophies • Certificates or scrolls • Letters of appreciation *Knick-knacks:* • Decorative • Tie pins or brooches • Calendars or diaries • Watch • Electronic items such as cameras, mp3, mobile phones, appliances, software • Newspaper or magazine subscription *Tokens:* • Tickets to movies/sports events/concerts • Gift certificates • Accessories/garments bearing company logo • Anniversary/birthday gifts	*Social rewards:* • Informal recognition • Verbal recognition or praise • Formal recognition at office get-togethers • Feedback • Friendly greetings • Pat on the back • Solicitations of advice/ suggestions • Club privileges • Use of company facilities, equipment, supplies for personal projects *Task-related rewards:* • More responsibility • Meaningful work • Job rotation • Special assignments • Training • Representing the company at public forums • Participation in decision-making • Growth opportunities • Autonomy over work • Promotion • Flexible hours

Source: Created by author.

as employees being courteous and respectful to one another, managers recognizing employees for their hard work, etc. Task-related rewards have the potential to address the intrinsic motivation of employees. It includes career advancement, job design, skills training, and autonomy over work.

Throughout the years, many researchers have advocated the use of incentives to motivate employee performance. One such example was an interesting study conducted by Condly, Clark, and Stolovitch in 2003. The following are some important highlights from this study:

- Incentive programs have the potential to improve performance by as much as 44% if administered properly to address the problems of performance and motivation.
- Incentive programs increase the level of engagement from employees.
- Employees motivated by incentives see a performance surge by 27% when asked to persevere toward a goal.
- Incentive programs can be incorporated into the organization's attraction and retention strategies.
- Long-term incentive programs were discovered to generate higher performance outcomes than short-term incentive programs.
- Contrary to the belief that extrinsic rewards hinder intrinsic motivation, the study found that employees who are rewarded for exceeding targets are inclined to invest more time and effort on a task that leads to satisfaction.
- Incentive programs help to boost morale and build employee loyalty.
- To sum up, according to the research done by Condly et al. (2003), incentives do seem to have great benefits and a high potential to motivate employees.

Employees tend to view monetary incentives as part of the total remuneration package. An illustration will be used to substantiate this point.

In 1999, Wirthlin Worldwide conducted a poll to find out how employees spent their most recent monetary incentive yielded the following results: 29% used the money to settle bills and 11% used the money to purchase household items (American Express Incentive Services, 2008). This implies that monetary incentives have quite a limited impact as it is normally spent on daily necessities, and the derivation of money is easily forgotten, thus losing the effectiveness as a motivator. On the other hand, tangible non-monetary incentives such as a ticket to a sports event, a gift certificate, a subscription to a magazine or a vacation trip can be used to fulfill the "wants" of employees. Allowing employees to select the type of desired tangible non-monetary incentives can make them feel valued by their organization and in return feel more motivated to work.

Tangible non-monetary incentives are typically viewed upon as luxury items especially if the purchase cannot be justified had the employee bought it. For example, lower income strata families may not have expendable income to enjoy pleasurable activities with their family. Offering tangible non-monetary incentives such as a night out at a movie theater or a family dinner at a nice restaurant may be valuable to them. Shilpa and Patrick (2003) found that the team-based objectives and incentives model supports enhancements in teamwork, motivation, and performance among health professionals while reinforcing intrinsic motivation (Chen & Huang, 2022). However, they also found that personality mediated the role of organizational roles and motivation for healthcare workers serving in poor regions of India.

Lastly, employees need social acknowledgment for something good they have done.

Tangible non-monetary incentives serve this purpose particularly better than monetary incentives as the latter is, firstly, a socially unacceptable manner of seeking recognition from peers, and, secondly, people are uncomfortable and unlikely to flaunt their monetary rewards in front of others. Conversely, the physicality of a tangible non-monetary incentive like a wall plaque is palpable to everyone, and the employee has no reason to feel embarrassed raving about it. In addition, tangibility provides a lasting reminder of achievement, and most importantly, how the reward was achieved.

Items such as office desk decorations, plaques, or everyday merchandise are a strong way to remind employees the reason behind the incentive. On the other hand, the Incentive Federation Study revealed two thirds of the respondents felt that cash incentive is easily forgotten.

Motivation and Job Performance

Motivation is defined as "the forces within a person that affect his or her direction, intensity, and persistence of voluntary behavior" (McShane & Von Glinow, 2000).

Mol (in 2005) believes the definition of motivation will be when the employee is assigned to a task that he/she dislikes, yet willing to do so merely for the sake of being rewarded, then he/she is said to be moved. But when the employee engages in a task because he/she takes delight in the work, then motivation is said to occur.

Another factor influencing motivation and job performance is the employee's ability to successfully carry out a task. 'Ability' refers to the inherent aptitude and learned competencies to perform well at work. Inherent aptitude includes the employee's mental willingness and ability to quickly acquire new competencies. In this respect, organizations can help employees with good aptitude scores to further develop their expertise through participating in various skill enhancement courses.

Robbins and Coulter (2005) suggest that motivation refers to "the processes that account for an individual's willingness to exert high levels of effort to reach organizational goals, conditioned by the effort's ability to satisfy some individual need." If managers today are to assume responsibility to lead employees toward attaining organizational goals, it is then crucial for them to comprehend the psychological process of motivation.

The key elements of the above definition are direction, intensity, and persistence. The 'direction' element refers to a compelling force to achieve a specific objective. This means that when a motivated employee recognizes the need to achieve something, then all efforts will be focused on reaching that goal. The 'intensity' element represents the magnitude of the effort allocated to the objective. In other words, one employee may exert more effort than another employee to accomplish certain tasks. The last element "persistence" refers to the time duration in which an effort is sustained. A highly persistent employee will not concede before reaching the objective. In addition, motivation can be described as intentional when the employee chooses to act on his/her own will.

Factors of Motivation: Intrinsic and Extrinsic Motivation

Motivation is a critical driver of job performance, and it is typically categorized into two types: extrinsic and intrinsic motivation. Extrinsic motivation refers to external factors that influence an individual's behavior, such as rewards, recognition, and compensation. In contrast, intrinsic motivation is driven by internal factors like personal satisfaction, interest in the task, and a sense of accomplishment. Motivation is an integral component of human experience (Morris, 2022). While motivated behavior is often examined with respect to extrinsic reinforcers, not all actions are driven by reactions to external stimuli; some are driven by 'intrinsic' motivation. Intrinsically motivated behaviors are computationally similar to extrinsically motivated behaviors, in that they strive to maximize reward value and minimize punishment (Gottlieb, Lopes, & Oudeyer (2016).

There are two types of motivation present in the workplace: intrinsic and extrinsic (Adams, 2007). This means that job-related variables affecting motivation have intrinsic and extrinsic motivational value that drives employees to perform. Given that most employees are intrinsically and extrinsically motivated simultaneously, a conclusion can be made that intrinsic and extrinsic motivation are not mutually exclusive.

Extrinsic Motivation

Extrinsic motivation has long been recognized as a powerful determinant of job performance. Rewards, whether monetary or non-monetary, can significantly boost an employee's drive to perform tasks efficiently. Recent studies have explored how different forms of extrinsic motivation affect job performance across various industries and job roles. For instance, a study by Nguyen et al. (2023) found that financial incentives, such as bonuses and pay raises, have a direct positive effect on job performance in sales-driven environments. Similarly, a study by Choi et al. (2022) highlighted the importance of recognition and career advancement opportunities as extrinsic motivators that enhance job satisfaction and performance in the healthcare sector.

However, some research indicates that the impact of extrinsic motivation may not be universally positive. Excessive reliance on extrinsic rewards can potentially undermine intrinsic motivation, leading to a decrease in overall job performance. A study by Deci et al. (2022) suggested that while extrinsic rewards can boost performance in the short term, they may lead to diminished intrinsic motivation over time, particularly in roles that require creativity and problem-solving.

Intrinsic Motivation

Intrinsic implies that motivation comes from within the individual; in other words, this type of motivation is self-generated. When employees are intrinsically motivated, the individual will strive to satisfy the three innate psychological needs, namely needs for, autonomy, competence, and relatedness (Deci & Ryan, 2000). Such employees like to have substantial freedom to make decisions, a channel to express creativity, opportunities for advancement, recognition for good work, be treated in a polite and thoughtful manner, and possess the passion to take on tasks that are both challenging and meaningful of which feel an inherent sense of accomplishment upon successful completion. For instance, an employee who has encountered an intriguingly difficult problem is unlikely to surrender just because the problem appears to be unsolvable. Instead, the employee will put forth his/her best efforts, say by investing more time or taking the task home, as he/she views the problem as challenging and worthwhile to complete. In fact, many researchers have acknowledged and proven that intrinsic motivation does have a positive long-term effect and is regarded as the "true motivators".

Intrinsic motivation is increasingly recognized as a crucial factor for sustained job performance, especially in roles that require creativity, innovation, and deep engagement. When employees are intrinsically motivated, they are more likely to find their work meaningful, which in turn enhances their performance. Recent research by Ryan and Deci (2024) supports this view, demonstrating that intrinsic motivation is closely linked to higher job satisfaction, greater commitment, and improved performance, particularly in knowledge-intensive industries.

Moreover, studies have shown that intrinsic motivation can lead to long-term job performance benefits. For example, a longitudinal study by Grant and Parker (2009) found that employees who are intrinsically motivated tend to exhibit higher levels of creativity and problem-solving skills, which contribute to better performance over time. The research study also indicates that intrinsic motivation is strongly associated with lower turnover rates, as employees who are internally driven are more likely to stay committed to their organizations.

One type of intrinsic motivation some organizations have introduced are goal-based prosocial rewards. This means that the employees donate their reward to a charity once they reach that goal. Berger et al. (2003) found that these types of rewards are motivating when the goals are relatively easy to achieve but lose their motivation as the goal becomes harder to reach.

Tangible incentives and social rewards contribute to extrinsic motivation, and task-related incentives are job factors that lead to intrinsic motivation. Intrinsically motivated employees engage in tasks without requiring the need for external directives such as monetary or tangible incentives as they are generally motivated by the nature of their job. This is achievable because some characteristics of the job allow the employees to gain a sense of accomplishment and innate pleasure simply by performing the task.

Having an intrinsically motivated workforce brings about immense benefits to the organization. Firstly, task-related non-monetary incentives such as skill development training, special assignments, growth opportunities, and promotion are considered powerful motivators for employees to satisfy their need for esteem and self-actualization. Secondly, the employee's inherent motivation to perform at optimum level does not require extensive supervision at work, allowing the organization to channel resources to more critical issues. Thirdly, organizations may reduce the spending on extrinsic incentives which can be quite expensive.

The recent literature emphasizes the complex interaction between extrinsic and intrinsic motivation in influencing job performance. While both types of motivation are important, their effectiveness can vary depending on the nature of the task, the individual's personality, and the organizational context. A study by Gagné and Deci (2005) suggests that the most effective motivation strategies are those that combine both extrinsic and intrinsic elements, tailored to the specific needs of employees and the nature of their work.

For instance, in a study by Eisenberger et al. (2023), it was found that offering extrinsic rewards for tasks that employees are already intrinsically motivated to perform can enhance their motivation and performance, as long as the rewards are perceived as supportive rather than controlling. Conversely, extrinsic rewards that are perceived as controlling can undermine intrinsic motivation, leading to lower performance in the long term.

Research Methodology

Objectives of the Study

The main objective of this dissertation report is "*To analyze the effect of performance incentive plans on the motivation level of employees in the organizations*".

The secondary objectives are:

- To determine whether demographics has an influence on preference for *monetary incentive*.
- To determine whether *loyalty* build due to incentives has an influence on *employee satisfaction*.
- To determine whether the *opportunity for being creative* due to performance-based incentive has an influence on *employee satisfaction*.
- To determine whether *employee satisfaction* due to incentive plans has an influence on him/her going an *extra mile with his/her efforts*.

Research Design

Research design is a conceptual structure within which research is conducted. A research design is the detailed blueprint used to guide a research study toward its objectives. A survey was conducted among 90 healthcare professionals, including doctors, nurses, and administrative staff, from various hospitals across India. The survey consisted of structured questionnaires designed to assess the impact of performance incentives on job motivation and satisfaction. Data were analyzed using statistical tools such as regression analysis and correlation models to determine the relationship between performance incentives and employee motivation. The methodology section provides detailed information on data collection methods, sampling techniques, ethical considerations, and analytical procedures used in the study.

Research Technique

The report is based on *primary as well as secondary data.* However, a major emphasis is made on collecting the data via primary data collection tools in order to avoid the overhearing factor in the study of the preferences of the respondents.

Primary Data: Primary data are a term for data collected on a source which has not been subjected to processing or any other manipulation; it is also known as raw data. It is the new data, which is gathered to solve the problem at hand, as compared to the secondary data which is previously gathered data.

- *Primary data (i.e. quantitative) were obtained using a well-drafted, self-administered questionnaire.*

Secondary Data: Apart from the primary data, the secondary data were collected referring to various reports and published data. The sources of secondary data included various academic journals, magazines, research articles and other reports to get an insight of the work already done.

Sampling Technique

Target Population: Employees of healthcare sector, who have undergone at least one appraisal cycle in their respective organizations.

Sampling Procedure: The sampling procedure followed is *Convenience Sampling.* Convenience sampling is a process wherein the samples are chosen completely on the basis of the convenience of the researcher. The entire market research has been done using convenience sampling only.

Sample Size: The sample size for the project is limited to 90 employees (30 employees each in three organizations).

Data Collection: The data collection was done using the survey method. A survey has been done on the sample elements using a self-administered questionnaire.

Data Analysis: The data have been analyzed using statistical software: SPSS 17.0. The analysis done using SPSS was used to arrive at a meaningful conclusion of the research study.

Sample Design: The data shall be presented with the help of bar graph, pie charts, line graphs and other presentation formats.

Results

Reliability Test

According to the test conducted in Table 10.2, the questionnaire used for the research is 97% reliable.

Table 10.2. Reliability Scores.

Reliability Statistics	
Cronbach's Alpha	**No of Items**
0.972	23

T-*Tests Conducted*

H0: Continuous recognition and incentives do not build a sense of loyalty toward the organization and develops a strong desire to be a part of it.
H1: Continuous recognition and incentives build a sense of loyalty toward the organization and develops a strong desire to be a part of it.

Interpretation: Table 10.3 shows a significant difference between the mean and test value. Thus, rejecting the null hypothesis and proving that continuous recognition and incentives build a sense of loyalty toward the organization and develop a strong desire to be a part of it.

H0: Employees do not feel highly motivated to work when their efforts and hard work is recognized and appreciated.
H1: Employees feel highly motivated to work when their efforts and hard work is recognized and appreciated.

Interpretation: Table 10.4 shows a significant difference between the mean and test value, thus rejecting the null hypothesis and proving that employees feel highly motivated to work when their efforts and hard work is recognized and appreciated.

H0: Employees do not feel satisfied when their hard work is rewarded with incentives.
H1: Employees feel satisfied when their hard work is rewarded with incentives.

Interpretation: Table 10.5 shows a significant difference between the mean and test value, thus rejecting the null hypothesis and proving that employees feel satisfied when their hard work is rewarded with incentives.

Table 10.3. Loyalty Versus Incentives.

One-Sample Statistics

	N	**Mean**	**Std. Deviation**	**Std. Error Mean**
Continuous recognition and incentives builds' a sense of loyalty toward the organization and develops a strong desire to be a part of it	90	4.06	1.266	0.133

One-Sample Test

	Test Value = 3					
					95% Confidence Interval of the Difference	
	t	**df**	**Sig. (2-Tailed)**	**Mean Difference**	**Lower**	**Upper**
Continuous recognition and incentives builds' a sense of loyalty toward the organization and develops a strong desire to be a part of it	7.908	89	0.000	1.056	0.79	1.32

Hypothesis Testing

Section 1: Variation in Preference of Monetary incentives with Demographics.

Hypothesis

H0: Gender has no influence on preference for monetary incentive.
H1: Gender has an influence on preference for monetary incentive.

Interpretation: In Table 10.6, since "*p*" value observed is less than 0.05, we can reject null hypothesis (*H0*) with 95% confidence level. Thus, Gender has an influence on preference for monetary incentive.

Table 10.4. Motivation Level Versus Incentives.

One-Sample Statistics

	N	**Mean**	**Std. Deviation**	**Std. Error Mean**
I feel highly motivated to work when my efforts and hard work is recognized and appreciated	90	4.46	1.133	0.119

One-Sample Test

	Test Value = 3					
					95% Confidence Interval of the Difference	
	t	**df**	**Sig. (2-Tailed)**	**Mean Difference**	**Lower**	**Upper**
I feel highly motivated to work when my efforts and hard work is recognized and appreciated	12.184	89	0.000	1.456	1.22	1.69

Hypothesis

H0: Age has no influence on preference for monetary incentive.
H1: Age has an influence on preference for monetary incentive.

Interpretation: In Table 10.7, since "*p*" value observed is less than 0.05, we can reject null hypothesis (*H0*) with 95% confidence level. Thus, Age has an influence on preference for monetary incentives.

Hypothesis

H0: Marital Status has no influence on preference for monetary incentive.
H1: Marital Status has an influence on preference for monetary incentive.

Interpretation: In Table 10.8, since "*p*" value observed is higher than 0.05, we can accept null hypothesis (*H0*) with 95% confidence level. Thus, Marital Status has no influence on preference for monetary incentive.

Section 2: Relation between Loyalty and Employee Satisfaction.

Table 10.5. Satisfaction Versus Incentives.

One-Sample Statistics

	N	Mean	Std. Deviation	Std. Error Mean
I feel satisfied when the productivity achieved due to my hard work and dedication is rewarded with incentives	90	4.29	0.963	0.101

One-Sample Test

	Test Value = 3					
					95% Confidence Interval of the Difference	
	T	df	Sig. (2-Tailed)	Mean Difference	Lower	Upper
I feel satisfied when the productivity achieved due to my hard work and dedication is rewarded with incentives	12.701	89	0.000	1.289	1.09	1.49

Table 10.6. Gender Versus Monetary Incentives.

Chi-Square Tests

	Value	df	Asymp. Sig. (2-Sided)
Pearson Chi-Square	18.906	4	0.001
Likelihood Ratio	24.892	4	0.000
Linear-by-Linear Association	2.830	1	0.093
N of Valid Cases	90		

Hypothesis

H0: Loyalty built due to incentives has no influence on employee satisfaction.
H1: Loyalty built due to incentives has an influence on employee satisfaction.

Table 10.7. Age versus Monetary Incentives.

Chi-Square Tests			
	Value	**df**	**Asymp. Sig. (2-Sided)**
Pearson Chi-Square	145.208	32	0.000
Likelihood Ratio	138.308	32	0.000
Linear-by-Linear Association	12.606	1	0.000
N of Valid Cases	90		

Table 10.8. Marital Status versus Monetary Incentives.

Chi-Square Tests			
	Value	**df**	**Asymp. Sig. (2-Sided)**
Pearson Chi-Square	6.438	4	0.169
Likelihood Ratio	9.555	4	0.049
N of Valid Cases	90		

Interpretation: In Table 10.9, since "*p*" value observed is less than 0.05, we can reject null hypothesis (*H0*) with 95% confidence level. Thus, Loyalty built due to incentives has an influence on employee satisfaction.

Section 3: Employee Satisfaction and Employee Productivity.

Hypothesis

H0: The opportunity to be creative due to performance-based incentive has no influence on employee satisfaction.

H1: The opportunity to be creative due to performance-based incentive has an influence on employee satisfaction.

Table 10.9. Loyalty and Employee Satisfaction.

Chi-Square Tests			
	Value	**df**	**Asymp. Sig. (2-Sided)**
Pearson Chi-Square	79.571	9	0.000
Likelihood Ratio	69.621	9	0.000
Linear-by-Linear Association	27.721	1	0.000
N of Valid Cases	90		

Table 10.10. Employee Creativity and Employee Productivity.

Chi-Square Tests			
	Value	**df**	**Asymp. Sig. (2-Sided)**
Pearson Chi-Square	80.341	9	0.000
Likelihood Ratio	75.164	9	0.000
Linear-by-Linear Association	31.293	1	0.000
N of Valid Cases	90		

Interpretation: In Table 10.10, since "*p*" value observed is less than 0.05, we can reject null hypothesis (*H0*) with 95% confidence level. Thus, the opportunity for being creative due to performance-based incentive has an influence on employee satisfaction.

Hypothesis

H0: Employee satisfaction due to incentive plans has no influence on him/her going the extra mile with his/her efforts.
H1: Employee satisfaction due to incentive plans has an influence on him/her going the extra mile with his/her efforts.

Interpretation: In Table 10.11, since "*p*" value observed is less than 0.05, we can reject null hypothesis (*H0*) with 95% confidence level. Thus, employee satisfaction due to incentive plans has an influence on him/her going an extra mile with his/her efforts.

Findings

The study found that financial incentives, such as bonuses, profit-sharing schemes, and performance-based salary increments, positively impact employee motivation in the short term. However, non-financial incentives, such as professional

Table 10.11. Employee Satisfaction and Employee Productivity.

Chi-Square Tests			
	Value	**df**	**Asymp. Sig. (2-Sided)**
Pearson Chi-Square	60.478	9	0.000
Likelihood Ratio	48.327	9	0.000
Linear-by-Linear Association	20.631	1	0.000
N of Valid Cases	90		

development programs, flexible work schedules, and employee recognition, significantly contribute to long-term job satisfaction. The findings also indicate that employees prefer a combination of financial and non-financial incentives, as both monetary rewards and career growth opportunities play a crucial role in maintaining motivation.

Statistical analysis using SPSS 17.0 revealed a strong correlation between incentive programs and employee motivation levels. The reliability test conducted yielded a Cronbach's alpha of 0.972, indicating high internal consistency of the survey instrument. *T*-tests further confirmed that continuous recognition and incentives build a sense of loyalty toward the organization, with a significant difference ($p < 0.05$) between the mean response and test value. Employees expressed that performance incentives significantly enhance their job satisfaction, making them more committed to their roles and increasing their willingness to go beyond assigned duties.

Chi-square tests conducted on demographic variables revealed that gender and age have a significant influence on preference for monetary incentives while marital status did not show a statistically significant impact. Additionally, employees in managerial roles showed a higher inclination toward non-monetary incentives such as career growth opportunities and flexible work schedules whereas frontline healthcare workers demonstrated a preference for financial incentives.

Furthermore, the analysis identified key themes from qualitative data, including perceived fairness of incentives, alignment of rewards with individual and organizational goals, and the role of transparent communication in incentive administration. Employees emphasized that incentive structures need to be tailored to different job roles, ensuring that both financial and intrinsic motivators are adequately addressed.

The study also explored how incentives influence teamwork and collaboration. It was found that group-based incentive programs, such as team bonuses and shared recognition initiatives, fostered a more cooperative work environment. Employees participating in these schemes reported increased morale, better peer relationships, and higher job satisfaction levels.

Conclusion

Performance incentives play a crucial role in motivating healthcare employees in India. While financial incentives provide immediate motivation, non-financial incentives contribute to sustained employee engagement and job satisfaction. A balanced approach incorporating both types of incentives is essential for improving healthcare service quality and employee retention. The study suggests that a well-structured incentive program, tailored to the needs of different categories of healthcare workers, can enhance motivation and organizational commitment. Healthcare policymakers and administrators should consider implementing hybrid incentive models that incorporate financial rewards, career growth opportunities, and workplace well-being initiatives (Turner et al., 2023).

This study also highlights certain limitations, including the sample size and the scope of the research, which focuses on selected hospitals within India. Future research can expand the study to include a larger population across various healthcare institutions and incorporate longitudinal data to assess the long-term effects of performance incentives on employee motivation.

Continuous recognition and incentives build a sense of loyalty toward the organization and develops a strong desire to be a part of it. Employees feel highly motivated to work when their efforts and hard work are recognized and appreciated. Gender, age, and marital status have an influence on preference for monetary incentive. Loyalty built due to incentives has an influence on employee satisfaction. Employees tend to get actively involved in the decision-making process when their participation and performance is appreciated and rewarded. A clear understanding of the career path in turn motivates employees to work harder toward achieving them. Other non-monetary incentives help in providing work–life balance.

In conclusion, this study underscores the pivotal role of performance incentives in shaping the employee motivation. By systematically analyzing the role of monetary and non-monetary incentives our findings contribute to a deeper understanding of employee satisfaction and productivity in healthcare sector. The study highlights key insights into recognition, rewards, and opportunities and offers strategic recommendations for employers. Future research should explore new and more effective incentive structures and policies, ensuring that the evolving landscape of employee motivation continues to be examined with rigor and relevance.

References

Adams, D. (2007). *Health monitoring of structural materials and components: Methods with applications*. John Wiley & Sons.

American Express Incentive Services. (2008). How to change behavior with employee incentive programs. Downloaded from. https://www.americanexpress.com/us/business/trends-and-insights/employee-incentives-and-rewards/employee-incentive-programs/

Berger, L., Guo, L., & Presslee, A. (2003, Spring). Motivating employees with goal-based prosocial rewards. *Contemporary Accounting Research*, *40*(1), 231–256.

Chen, M., & Huang, J. (2022). The impact of team-based bonuses on collaboration and productivity in project-based environments. *Journal of Organizational Behavior*, *43*(5), 678–695.

Choi, J., Oh, J., & Kim, J. (2022). Relationship between active seniors' job change and life satisfaction: Serial multiple mediation effects of person–job fit and job satisfaction. *The Career Development Quarterly*, *70*(4), 327–341.

Condly, S. J., Clark, R. E., & Stolovitch, H. D. (2003). The effects of incentives on workplace performance: A meta-analytic review of research studies 1. *Performance Improvement Quarterly*, *16*(3), 46–63.

Deci, E., Koestner, R., & Ryan, R. (2022). Extrinsic rewards and intrinsic motivation in education: Reconsidered once again. *Review of Educational Research.* https://www.semanticscholar.org/paper/Extrinsic-Rewards-andIntrinsic-Motivation-in-Once-Deci-Koestner/ddc2022f341ccaf95a393d96e6e265c8921e28c6

Deci, E. L., & Ryan, R. M. (2000). The "what" and "why" of goal pursuits: Human needs and the self-determination of behavior. *Psychological Inquiry*, *11*(4), 227–268.

Eisenberger, R., Wen, X., Zheng, D., Yu, J., Liu, Z., Zhang, J., Wang, L., Kim, T.-Y., Krivacek, S., Zagenczyk, T. J., Joo, M.-K., Mesdaghinia, S., Lee, D.-R., & Kim, T. H. (2023). Does felt obligation or gratitude better explain the relationship between perceived organizational support and outcomes? *Group & Organization Management.* https://doi.org/10.1177/10596011231180388

Gagné, M., & Deci, E. L. (2005). Self-determination theory and work motivation. *Journal of Organizational Behavior*, *26*(4), 331–362.

Gentry, W. A., & Sparks, T. E. (2023). Hybrid incentives in the technology sector: Balancing financial rewards with career development. *Journal of Applied Psychology*, *108*(3), 410–425.

Gottlieb, J., Lopes, M., Oudeyer, P. Y., Kim, S., Reeve, J., & Bong, M. (2016). *Recent developments in neuroscience research on human motivation.* Emerald Group Publishing.

Grant, A. M., & Parker, S. K. (2009). 7 Redesigning work design theories: The rise of relational and proactive perspectives. *Academy of Management Annals*, *3*(1), 317–375.

Holcomb, T. R., & Johnson, S. G. (2023). Profit-sharing and organizational performance: The role of collaborative culture. *Academy of Management Review*, *48*(1), 96–113.

Kim, S., & Lee, J. (2023). Performance-based bonuses and employee productivity: Evidence from the sales and customer service sectors. *Journal of Business Research*, *154*, 234–249.

McShane, S. L., & Von Glinow, M. A. (2000). *Organizational behavior.* Irwin McGraw-Hill.

Mol, M. J. (2005). Does being R&D intensive still discourage outsourcing?: Evidence from Dutch manufacturing. *Research Policy*, *34*(4), 571–582.

Morris, A. (2022). Alternative view of modernity: The subaltern speaks. *American Sociological Review*, *87*(1), 1–16.

Nguyen, P. D., Nguyen, N. P., Nguyen, L. D., & Le, T. H. (2023, May). The role of organizational justice and job satisfaction in mitigating turnover intention of emotionally exhausted employees: Evidence from Vietnam. In *Evidence-based HRM: A Global Forum for Empirical Scholarship*, (Vol. 11, No. 2, pp. 215–232). Emerald Publishing Limited.

Park, S., & Lee, D. (2022). Career development opportunities and their impact on job performance and organizational commitment. *International Journal of Human Resource Management*, *34*(1), 35–55.

Robbins, S. P., & Coulter, M. (2005). *Management* (8th ed). Data status.

Ryan, R. M., & Deci, E. L. (2024). Self-determination theory. In F. Maggino (Ed.), *Encyclopedia of quality of life and well-being research* (pp. 6229–6235). Springer International Publishing.

Shilpa, R., & Patrick, H. A. (2023, October). Mediation of personality in the relationship between organizational roles & motivation: A study on ASHA workers the Indian. *Journal of Industrial Relations*, *59*(2).

Turner, M., Smith, J., & Lewis, P. (2023). The impact of hybrid incentives on job satisfaction and patient care outcomes in healthcare. *Journal of Health Economics*, *48*, 120–136.

Zhang, Y., Li, H., & Wang, Z. (2022). Long-term financial incentives and their effect on employee loyalty and performance in knowledge-based industries. *Journal of Management Studies*, *59*(6), 1023–1042.

Chapter 11

Intellectual Property Challenges in AI-Powered Digital Healthcare

Partha Protim Bora

ICFAI University, India

Abstract

This is a big improvement in diagnosis, personalised medicine and telemedicine, thanks to the use of artificial intelligence (AI). It's also led to better results for patients and better operations. However, these technologies also bring about a lot of new chances and risks for intellectual property (IP) rights. The goal of this chapter is to show why IP is important for safeguarding AI-based medical progress. To do this, it looks at the business of digital healthcare and various types of IP, including trade secrets, brands, patents and copyrights. It talks about things like patent eligibility, data ownership, privacy issues and global IP enforcement as it looks into how hard it is to protect and maintain IP rights for AI systems. Using AI to handle IP and embracing collaborative innovation models are some of the things that this chapter talks about. It also talks about how to treat IP in healthcare that is powered by AI in a smart way. Medical companies can protect ideas, lower risks and grow in a way that lasts if they link their IP strategy to their business goals and keep an eye on what's coming up. There are some ideas at the end of the chapter to help people in the field, such as healthcare organisations, lawmakers and IP experts, get around the problems and make the most of the opportunities.

Keywords: Digital healthcare; artificial intelligence (AI); intellectual property (IP); electronic health records (EHR); stakeholders

Digital Transformation and Artificial Intelligence for Operational Excellence in Healthcare, 211–225

doi:10.1108/978-1-83662-314-420251030

Introduction

Background of Digital Healthcare

Due to rapid digital technology development, healthcare is in turmoil. According to researchers, digital health technologies such as electronic health records (EHRs), telemedicine and artificial intelligence (AI)-powered applications (Fig. 11.1) have transformed healthcare by improving efficiency and patient outcomes. AI could transform healthcare, including diagnosis, treatment planning, patient monitoring and administration (Cohen et al., 2020). AI has revolutionised internet healthcare. Medical professionals are using AI techniques, like computer vision, machine learning, and natural language processing, to automate administrative tasks, customise treatments, assess enormous amounts of data and predict disease outbreaks. These advancements make healthcare systems more efficient and cost-effective, improving patient outcomes. AI-powered chatbots and virtual assistants simplify patient interactions and reduce healthcare professional workload (Thakare et al., 2022). AI-driven diagnostics can analyse medical images faster and more accurately than clinicians. AI's ongoing growth could transform healthcare by eliminating key issues like rising costs, a shortage of skilled professionals and poor areas' lack of treatment. The widespread use of AI in digital healthcare raises various legal, ethical and regulatory issues, including intellectual property (IP) rights.

Importance of IP in Digital Healthcare

IP drives innovation and finance in the digital healthcare sector. New technology developers must safeguard their ideas with IP rights. Patents, copyrights, trademarks and trade secrets protect digital healthcare's exclusive technologies and

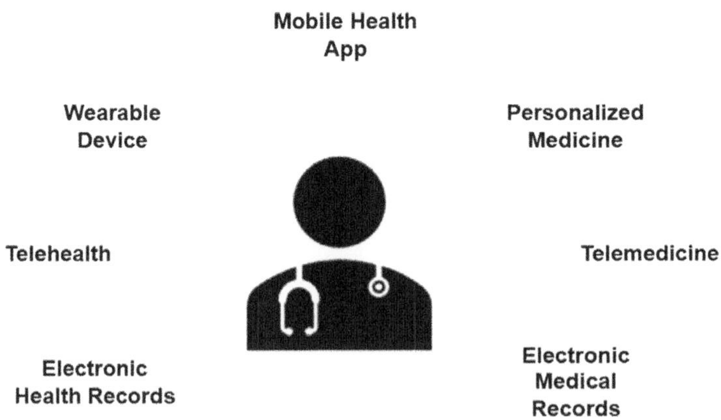

Fig. 11.1. Digital Health Technologies. *Source:* Author's own work, adapted from Gerke et al. (2020).

breakthroughs (Lee et al., 2021). IP protection for AI-driven healthcare solutions is crucial. AI algorithms, software platforms and digital tools require significant R&D. Patents allow innovators and companies to protect their ideas from copycats. Businesses maintain investing in new technology because they can get a competitive edge and make money by licensing, collaborating or selling their IP. In addition to ethical technology use, preserving IP in digital healthcare is essential for competitiveness (Apell & Eriksson, 2023). IP laws restrict who can use, edit or disseminate AI in healthcare, limiting abuse. Avoids biassed algorithm deployment and illegal data mining. Thus, IP protects business interests and maintains public trust in digital healthcare solutions.

Purpose and Scope of the Chapter

This chapter examines the complex relationship between digital healthcare AI, IP rights and AI's rapid growth. As AI transforms healthcare, IT developers, providers, lawmakers and attorneys must understand IP protection's opportunities and risks. The chapter begins with a comprehensive analysis of digital healthcare's multiple kinds of IP and their regulatory mechanisms. The essay will highlight AI's revolutionary potential in healthcare and how AI-driven improvements are increasing operational excellence in the field. The chapter will then talk about the problems that come up when trying to protect IP in healthcare solutions that use AI. These include problems with who owns data, getting patents for AI, and enforcing IP around the world. Lastly, the chapter will talk about ways to make IP laws better so that AI-powered healthcare innovations can happen faster. This covers the constantly changing laws, how to use AI tools to safeguard IP and how to make sure that IP management fits with the goals of the organisation. Finally, readers will understand how IP leads to new ideas and better operations in digital healthcare.

Overview of Intellectual Property Rights in Digital Healthcare

Types of IP Relevant to Digital Healthcare

In the rapidly evolving field of digital healthcare, IP rights are essential for protecting the innovations that drive the industry forward (Fig. 11.2). Several forms of particularly relevant to this sector:

Patents: For a certain amount of time, usually 20 years from the date of filing, only the person who invented the thing can make, use or sell it. Patents are very important in digital healthcare for protecting new ideas like AI algorithms, medical devices and software tools that help with diagnosis, treatment or operations. Patents encourage companies to come up with new ideas by giving them exclusive rights to their inventions. This stops competitors from stealing their technology (Trenfield et al., 2022). People often patent AI-based diagnostic tools, like algorithms that can find diseases in medical pictures, to protect the technology behind them and make sure the company can get a return on its investment.

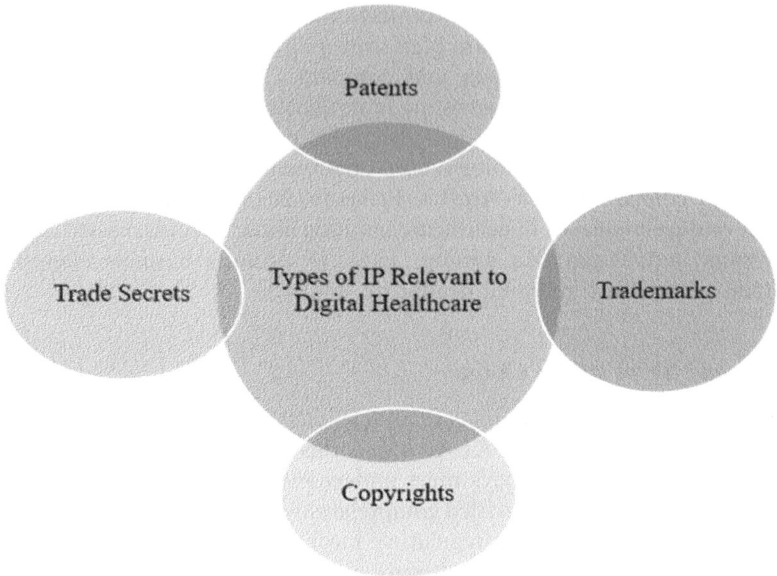

Fig. 11.2. Types of IP Relevant to Digital Healthcare. *Source:* Self-Created.

Trademarks: It is allowed to register or use a symbol, word or phrase as a trademark to show that it belongs to a certain company or product. In digital healthcare, trademarks protect the naming of goods and services so that customers can tell where they came from and tell them apart from similar products and services from other companies. Trademarks are very important for keeping a brand's personality and building trust, especially in fields where reputation and dependability are very important (Paul et al., 2021). For example, a healthcare app or AI platform could build a strong brand that people connect with quality and usefulness. Using trademarks on these names keeps other people from copying them, so customers know they are getting the real thing.

Copyrights: Copyright gives creators exclusive rights to reproduce, distribute and display original works including software code, databases and educational content. In digital healthcare, copyrights safeguard software and digital content that power numerous solutions (Gerke et al., 2020). Copyrights protect software, digital health records, AI training datasets and other IP. Copyright protection may restrict unauthorised use or distribution of code and material on an AI-driven healthcare platform with proprietary software and databases.

Trade Secrets: A trade secret is a type of IP that includes formulas, practices, processes, designs or instruments that most people don't know or can't easily find. This information gives one business an economic edge over rivals. The public does not have to know about trade secrets like they do with patents (Pantanowitz et al., 2022). People often keep trade secrets to protect their own formulas, data analysis methods and other secret business processes that give their company an edge over their competitors. Because it wants to stay ahead of the competition, an AI-based diagnostic tool might use a secret formula that is only known to members of the company.

Legal Framework and Regulations

The protection of IP in digital healthcare is governed by a complex web of global and regional legal frameworks. These frameworks are designed to balance the interests of innovators, consumers and the public, ensuring that IP rights are adequately protected while also promoting innovation and access to healthcare.

Global Legal Framework: The World Intellectual Property Organisation (WIPO) is very important for making sure that IP rules in different places are the same. Treaties between countries, like TRIPS (the Agreement on Trade-Related Aspects of Intellectual Property Rights), set basic standards for protecting IP that all member states must follow. Aldoseri et al. (2024) say that TRIPS needs member states to protect inventions with patents in all areas of technology. This includes digital healthcare. The PCT makes it easier to get patents in more than one country by letting inventors file a single international application that can be followed in different places. This helps a lot for digital healthcare innovations that need to be safe in many areas.

India Legal Framework: In India, the legal framework governing IP rights in digital healthcare includes the Patents Act, 1970, which protects healthcare innovations, and the Copyright Act, 1957, which covers AI-driven healthcare software. The Drugs and Cosmetics Act also plays a crucial role in regulating medical technology innovations. Additionally, the Personal Data Protection Bill, 2019, aims to regulate the handling of sensitive healthcare data in AI applications

Regional Legal Frameworks: In the United States, the US Patent and Trademark Office (USPTO) governs patent and trademark registrations while copyright protection is managed by the US Copyright Office. The United States has a well-established legal framework for IP protection, with significant case law addressing the patentability of software and AI inventions. The European Patent Office (EPO) oversees patent protection across EU member states. The European Union (EU) also has comprehensive trademark and copyright regulations that provide robust protection for digital healthcare innovations (Alrahbi et al., 2022). The General Data Protection Regulation (GDPR) also plays a crucial role in regulating the use of personal data in AI-driven healthcare solutions, impacting how IP is managed. Countries like Japan, South Korea and China have rapidly evolving IP laws that are increasingly aligned with international standards. However, challenges remain, particularly in enforcement and the protection of trade secrets.

Key Stakeholders

Technology companies innovate digital healthcare via AI algorithms, software platforms, and gadgets. Many businesses value IP protection to secure their ideas and commercial advantage. Tech companies must spend time and money to acquire and enforce IP rights in several jurisdictions. Since abstract notions and patentable inventions are sometimes indistinguishable, AI-related IP management is problematic. Healthcare providers including hospitals and clinics use and produce digital technologies (Ashiwaju et al., 2024). They may seek IP protection for in-house AI-powered diagnosis or treatment methods. Healthcare practitioners struggle to balance IP protection and patient care. They also struggle with IP compliance while adopting digital healthcare technologies. US and European regulatory organisations, like the FDA and EMA, are essential for safe and effective digital healthcare technologies. These organisations determine which innovations are patentable and copyrightable, affecting IP. For their regulations to not impede inventiveness, regulatory authorities must keep up with new advances. They must also ensure that everyone may use critical healthcare technologies while protecting IP.

Legal professionals and IP attorneys can help inventors navigate IP law. The publication describes IP protection, portfolio management and IP rights best practices. Legal practitioners must stay abreast of changing IP laws, especially in digital healthcare (Dal Mas et al., 2023). They also face the difficulty and cost of IP lawsuits. The public and patients benefit most from digital healthcare advances. By questioning IP morality and advocating for healthcare technology access, they advance IP law. It is difficult to guarantee that IP regulations would not prevent access to vital healthcare services. The public's right to profit from medical discoveries while respecting IP is another difficult subject. In conclusion, digital healthcare IP management involves various types of IP rights, complicated legal frameworks and many players (Stahl, 2021). Understanding these interactions is essential to promoting innovation, protecting investments and ensuring ethical and effective digital healthcare technology use.

AI in Digital Healthcare: Transformative Potential

Applications of AI in Digital Healthcare

AI has revolutionised several aspects of digital healthcare due to its better capabilities. Telemedicine, personalised medicine and diagnostics employ AI to improve patient care and expedite operations.

AI-powered diagnostic technologies have substantially increased medical diagnosis precision and efficiency. Machine learning algorithms can analyse X-rays, MRIs and CT scans with high accuracy (Wanjale et al., 2023), especially for image identification algorithms. In some cases, AI algorithms can detect tumors or fractures faster and more accurately than people. Thus, healthcare providers can focus more on complex cases, improving patient outcomes through earlier intervention.

AI is pioneering personalised medicine, which considers genetics, lifestyle and environment to create individualised treatment programs. AI algorithms can analyse a patient's genetics, medical history and real-time wearable device data to predict treatment outcomes. This lets doctors give more tailored and effective treatment by eliminating guesswork and ineffectiveness (Qvist-Sørensen, 2020). AI-powered technologies can recommend the best cancer treatment for a patient's genetics to enhance outcomes and reduce adverse effects.

AI helped telemedicine expand during and after the COVID-19 pandemic. For preliminary evaluations, arranging appointments and personalised health advice, virtual assistants and chatbots powered by AI are becoming more popular. Through wearable gadget data, AI can improve remote patient monitoring and alert healthcare providers to potential health risks before they become critical. Real-time monitoring is essential for managing long-term health concerns like diabetes and heart disease, which require ongoing attention.

Impact on Operational Excellence

AI-driven advances are essential to operational excellence and clinical revolutionisation. Healthcare systems are using AI to improve patient outcomes, streamline operations and cut costs. AI speeds up healthcare delivery by automating routine tasks and streamlines decision-making. AI-driven scheduling solutions can maximise operating room and medical staff distribution by anticipating patient demand and adjusting timetables (Compagnucci et al., 2022). Thus, patients wait less and healthcare providers deliver better service. AI-powered EHR systems automatically organise and update patient data, reducing administrative tasks and errors.

AI's ability to find patterns in massive data sets could improve patient health. We can use predictive analytics to identify patients at risk of problems or readmissions and intervene to lower their risk. AI-driven clinical decision-making systems help doctors choose the best therapies and prevent medical errors. By delivering tests and treatments quickly and accurately, AI can enhance health outcomes and patient happiness.

AI can cut healthcare costs by a large amount. AI automates tasks like data entry and billing, which cuts down on running costs and the need for high-paid administrative staff. AI treatment planning and diagnostics cut down on tests and processes that aren't needed, which lowers the cost of healthcare. AI systems that can guess how a patient will do could save money in healthcare by cutting down on hospital readmissions and costs (Rana et al., 2022). So, AI helps healthcare systems stay financially stable, which lets them focus on providing good care and better allocating their resources.

Case Studies

Mayo Clinic's Use of AI for Predicting Patient Deterioration

The Mayo Clinic has set up an AI system that looks at real-time data about patients to figure out which ones are most likely to get worse. The Early Warning System (EWS) constantly checks vital signs and other health indicators using machine learning algorithms. This lets healthcare workers know about possible problems before they get too bad (Bhavnani et al., 2017). Because of this, the Mayo Clinic has been able to lower the number of unplanned admissions to the intensive care unit (ICU) and improve patient outcomes. This shows that AI has the ability to improve both patient safety and operational efficiency.

IBM Watson for Oncology

Intelligence-powered IBM Watson for Oncology helps oncologists choose treatments based on solid proof. The platform looks at a huge amount of clinical data, study studies and patient information to give cancer patients personalised advice on how to treat their illness. IBM Watson for Oncology uses AI to help doctors find the best treatment choices faster. This improves patient outcomes and cuts down on the time doctors have to spend doing research and making decisions by hand. This example shows how AI can help doctors make choices and improve the way healthcare works (Li et al., 2021).

AI in Radiology at Stanford Medicine

Stanford Medicine was one of the first to use AI to improve imaging services. AI programs look at medical pictures like X-rays and MRIs to find COVID-19, pneumonia and broken bones. There is evidence that these AI tools can diagnose problems as well as or better than human doctors, especially when time is of the essence. Stanford Medicine has been able to speed up diagnosis by automating the analysis of medical images. This has led to faster treatment and better results for patients. This use of AI in imaging shows how AI could improve both the speed and accuracy of healthcare.

Challenges in IP Rights for AI Innovations in Digital Healthcare

IP rights issues are one of many barriers to AI in digital healthcare (Fig. 11.3). The ever-changing world of AI makes safeguarding, administering and enforcing IP rights difficult. AI's ethical and legal implications, data ownership and privacy issues, IP enforcement issues and patent protection difficulties are all major obstacles. Digital healthcare innovations based on AI are difficult to patent. Patenting new ideas is important, but AI's unique traits make patent applications more difficult. Patenting AI innovations is a major challenge (Rasheed, 2024). AI was not a main focus while creating traditional patent laws; hence, its patentability is dubious. Even mathematical models of AI systems may not be patentable in some countries. The Alice Corp. v. CLS Bank International verdict makes patenting AI algorithms and other software-based breakthroughs harder in the United States. This is a major challenge for AI-powered medical solution pioneers. Novelty and non-obviousness also challenge AI. Proving that an AI-based innovation is unique and non-obvious is difficult because AI systems often employ prior data and technology (Chikhaoui et al., 2022). An AI model that

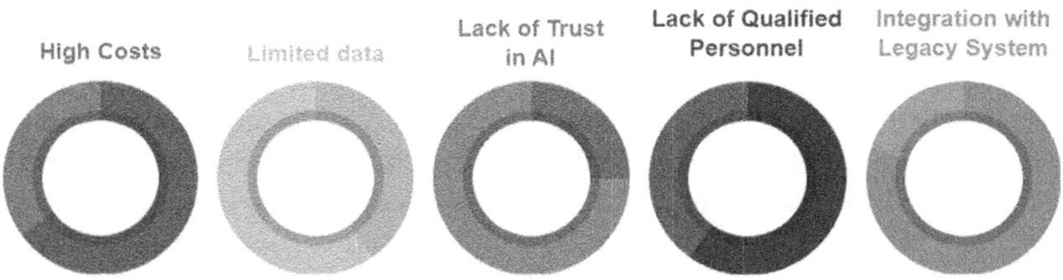

Fig. 11.3. Challenges in IP Rights for AI Innovations in Digital Healthcare. *Source:* Author's own source, adapted from Chikhaoui et al. (2022).

incorporates public medical data may not be novel but rather a natural extension of present technologies. Due to the rapid growth of AI, patent protection is becoming harder, making today's original ideas obsolete tomorrow. Drafting patent claims for AI inventions might be difficult. Claims should be clear to boost approval odds and broad to encompass the full innovation. Claims that are overly broad or general may not provide enough infringement protection. Due to AI's constant learning and adaptation, patent applications may struggle to define the breakthrough. This may confuse the law and lead to AI patent interpretation disputes.

Data Ownership and Privacy Concerns

Data is the foundation of AI systems in healthcare, as algorithms use massive patient data to diagnose and cure patients. AI data use presents significant ownership, privacy and regulatory compliance issues. AI systems struggle to establish data ownership since healthcare data comes from patients, providers and third parties. After aggregation or anonymisation, competing data ownership claims can lead to disagreements. If an AI company uses hospital patient data to produce a new diagnostic tool, ownership and IP issues may arise (Flynn et al., 2020). This might happen to the hospital, patients or AI company. These disputes could delay healthcare AI research and development. Healthcare privacy is crucial since patient data is so intimate. Healthcare AI applications must comply with Europe's GDPR on data collection, processing and storage. Such criteria are especially difficult to meet for real-time AI systems that process and evaluate data. Due to AI's dependence on vast datasets, data breaches and re-identification of anonymised data may harm healthcare providers and IT companies' legal and reputational standing (Lal et al., 2022). Effective healthcare AI requires data exchange across systems and enterprises. Interoperability, data standards and regulations hinder data exchange. If healthcare organisations use multiple data formats or have varying data protection levels, integrating data for AI research may be difficult. In the EU, strict data protection laws might hinder foreign data transfers and AI projects.

IP Enforcement Issues

The lack of international IP law makes IP enforcement of AI inventions difficult. Some jurisdictions may not acknowledge patented or protectable items. Asia, Europe, and the United States have different patentability laws for AI algorithms and other software-based inventions. Inconsistency makes the legal landscape fragmented, making it hard and expensive for inventors to secure their IP across systems. Even inside a jurisdiction, AI IP rights are hard to enforce (Mithas et al., 2022). AI systems' technological complexity makes it difficult for courts and regulatory authorities to determine violation. Proving that an AI system stole or plagiarised a patent-protected algorithm may entail time and money, as well as expert testimony. AI advancements are often intangible and hidden in software code or cloud-based services, making it harder to defend IP rights against infringing conduct. International AI adoption in digital healthcare increases IP infringement risk. Unauthorised parties in countries with inadequate IP protection may replicate and distribute US-developed AI-powered healthcare software (Aldoseri et al., 2023). Due to its global reach, innovators may lose money and market share if they can't monitor and enforce their IP rights. Reverse engineering and code de-obfuscation techniques powered by AI increase the risk of IP theft and illicit use.

Ethical and Legal Implications

AI that independently evaluates patient data and makes decisions raises patient rights and informed consent concerns. For instance, should the patient know that an AI system, not a clinician, recommended a treatment? Data used to train AI systems may have major effects that patients may not understand, compromising informed consent. AI systems making medical choices like diagnoses or therapy suggestions exacerbate these issues. An issue with bias in data can cause AI to produce biassed results (Yang et al., 2022). Making decisions about patient care based on AI raises a lot of ethical questions in healthcare. Health disparities can get worse when AI uses under-represented data during training to make less accurate diagnoses or treatment ideas for certain groups of people. Keeping AI systems fair and unbiased takes constant checking and making sure they are working right. Using AI in healthcare makes it harder to be responsible and accountable. Who is responsible if an AI system gives the wrong diagnosis or medication? Who made AI? The patient, the doctor or the AI creator? Traditional legal systems aren't ready for AI-based job assignments, so they're not certain. Without clear rules on who is responsible for what, healthcare professionals might not want to use AI systems, which would slow the growth of AI. Finally, it's hard to regulate AI in healthcare while also encouraging growth (Lhotska, 2020). Too many rules could stop people from coming up with new ideas and stop the creation and use of AI devices that could save lives. Without oversight, using AI in the wrong way could hurt people. To ensure ethical AI use, regulators, healthcare providers and AI makers must work together to find a balance between regulation and new ideas. In conclusion, rules about IP make it harder for digital healthcare

AI to grow. It is important for lawmakers, healthcare professionals and AI developers to work together to make, protect and use AI technologies in a way that maximises their potential while minimising the risks they pose to patients and society. To solve these problems, we need to do this.

Opportunities for Enhancing IP Strategy in Digital Healthcare

The ever-changing digital healthcare business, especially with AI, requires a solid IP strategy to protect inventions and drive growth. Despite IP challenges in AI-driven healthcare, IP management, IP enforcement and collaborative innovation models that balance protection and advancement are viable. To protect their innovations globally, businesses should consider registering patents in many countries (Schönberger, 2019). This is crucial in digital healthcare due to the global deployment of AI technologies. Patents can protect global cash streams and prevent competitors from accessing strategic markets.

IP management in AI-driven healthcare requires licensing. In industries where they don't have a physical presence, companies can license their AI technologies to other companies to monetise their IP. Strategic license agreements let companies from diverse industries collaborate faster on AI developments. Businesses could consider licensing AI models or data sets alongside traditional licensing. AI systems are data-intensive, making proprietary data set licensing valuable (Bernal & Mazo, 2022). Well-structured agreements allow businesses to retain IP and generate additional revenue. Strategic relationships are essential for AI-driven healthcare innovation. These relationships might be joint ventures, research collaborations or public–private partnerships. Sharing resources and knowledge with other businesses can help them achieve AI goals that would be difficult to achieve alone. Partnerships are another way to navigate international IP rules. A corporation may partner with a local company in a foreign market to better understand and follow local IP laws. These collaborations can also help businesses reach more customers and commercialise AI faster.

Best Practices for Achieving Operational Excellence Through IP Protection

When working with new technologies like AI, it's important to protect your IP in a smart way in order to be the best at digital healthcare practice. By making sure their IP strategy is in line with their company goals, managing risk and spotting trends, healthcare organisations can protect their innovations and make sure they will be successful in the long run. For AI to improve healthcare operations, it's important to connect IP strategy to business goals (Sriram & Subrahmanian, 2020). A well-thought-out IP plan can help your business be more innovative, competitive and long-lasting. Before healthcare companies can align their IP strategy with their business goals, they need to know what their long-term goals are. This could mean going into new markets, making healthcare solutions that use AI or improving the ones that are already out there. Once you have goals, you need to make an IP plan to reach them and keep them safe. Mozumder et al. (2023) say that a healthcare provider that wants to be a leader in AI-powered diagnostics should focus on patenting their own AI algorithms and data processing technologies as part of their IP plan. The company can buy or lease IP from other businesses in order to grow technically.

Including IP problems early in the product development process is another good method. Protect ideas before they hit the market by hiring IP experts early on to find IP assets and risks. Shortening the time it takes to get a product to market, making operations more efficient and making marketing easier all while protecting IP. Putting IP planning and R&D together helps make the company culture more creative. Getting teams to think about IP security while they're coming up with ideas can help them create more valuable and defendable IP assets.

For protecting IP in the AI-driven healthcare field, where new holes appear at a scary rate, risk management is a must. To protect their IP holdings and keep damage to a minimum, businesses should follow best practices for IP risk management. A good idea is to do regular IP audits to find and evaluate IP assets, liabilities and threats. IP audits look at trade secrets, patents, trademarks and copyrights (Paul et al., 2021). This method helps companies find IP assets that aren't being used enough, find violations and look at how well their IP protection tactics are working. Before you buy or license IP, make sure it's legal, enforceable and free of any encumbrances. A company can avoid unintentional IP infringement and expensive legal battles by doing their research.

Another way to deal with IP problems in AI-powered healthcare is through IP insurance. Insurance can help pay for IP litigation, like fighting charges of infringement or going to court against people who do this. A company can protect its business and bottom line by giving the cost of IP disputes to an insurance company. Healthcare companies that use AI can also tailor their IP insurance coverage to each patient. One can make rules to handle AI system risks like disagreements over who owns data and problems with AI algorithms being able to be patented.

Future research in AI-driven healthcare IP should focus on improving patent frameworks for AI-generated innovations, enhancing cross-border IP enforcement strategies and developing AI-based solutions for detecting and managing IP infringements. Additionally, further studies are needed on the ethical implications of AI ownership in healthcare to ensure fair innovation distribution.

Conclusion

Our chapter looked at the difficult connection between digital healthcare driven by AI and IP rights. After talking about copyrights, patents, logos and trade secrets, we moved on to IP in digital healthcare and how important they are for keeping discoveries safe. Later, we looked at the IP rules that apply to this business and named some of the most important players, such as tech companies, healthcare providers and government agencies. Within digital healthcare, AI has improved organisational excellence and patient outcomes, especially in diagnostics, personalised medicine and telemedicine. Investing in these areas could change the business. This part also talked about who owns data, privacy issues, who can get a patent, and how IP is enforced in different countries to protect AI breakthroughs. In healthcare, these problems are made worse by AI ethics and legal issues, such as finding a balance between patient rights and new ideas. Despite these problems, digital healthcare can make IP strategy better by connecting IP to business goals, using collaborative innovation techniques and using AI to handle IP. To fully use AI in digital healthcare, the industry needs strong IP plans. As AI speeds up growth and innovation in this field, it becomes more important to protect IP as a result. In addition to keeping findings safe, good IP management encourages growth, high-quality operations, and constant improvement. With AI driving the healthcare sector, companies can get ahead by planning for IP issues. Advocates for healthcare, lawmakers and IP experts must all work together to resolve these issues and seize these chances. Protecting healthcare businesses' ideas from the start should include IP problems in strategy planning and product development. Authorities must, on the other hand, make laws that encourage new ideas while protecting patients' rights and privacy. Patent laws and data privacy rules might need to be changed to keep up with AI progress in order to do this. Furthermore, IP experts should use AI-powered tools and technologies to improve IP management, such as finding assets, keeping an eye on rights, and enforcing them. Digital healthcare ecosystem players can protect IP and make the most of AI's transformative potential by following these rules. Overcoming problems and making the most of AI's potential are key to the future of healthcare.

References

Aldoseri, A., Al-Khalifa, K. N., & Hamouda, A. M. (2023). Re-thinking data strategy and integration for artificial intelligence: Concepts, opportunities, and challenges. *Applied Sciences*, *13*(12), 7082.

Aldoseri, A., Al-Khalifa, K. N., & Hamouda, A. M. (2024). AI-powered innovation in digital transformation: Key pillars and industry impact. *Sustainability*, *16*(5), 1790.

Alrahbi, D. A., Khan, M., Gupta, S., Modgil, S., & Chiappetta Jabbour, C. J. (2022). Challenges for developing health-care knowledge in the digital age. *Journal of Knowledge Management*, *26*(4), 824–853.

Apell, P., & Eriksson, H. (2023). Artificial intelligence (AI) healthcare technology innovations: The current state and challenges from a life science industry perspective. *Technology Analysis & Strategic Management*, *35*(2), 179–193.

Ashiwaju, B. I., Agho, M. O., Okogwu, C., Orikpete, O. F., & Daraojimba, C. (2024). Digital transformation in pharmaceutical supply chain: An African case. *Matrix Science Pharma*, *7*(3), 95–102.

Bernal, J., & Mazo, C. (2022). Transparency of artificial intelligence in healthcare: Insights from professionals in computing and healthcare worldwide. *Applied Sciences*, *12*(20), 10228.

Bhavnani, S. P., Parakh, K., Atreja, A., Druz, R., Graham, G. N., Hayek, S. S., . . . & Shah, B. R. (2017). 2017 Roadmap for innovation—ACC health policy statement on healthcare transformation in the era of digital health, big data, and precision health: A report of the American college of cardiology task force on health policy statements and systems of care. *Journal of the American College of Cardiology*, *70*(21), 2696–2718.

Chikhaoui, E., Alajmi, A., & Larabi-Marie-Sainte, S. (2022). Artificial intelligence applications in healthcare sector: Ethical and legal challenges. *Emerging Science Journal*, *6*(4), 717–738.

Cohen, I. G., Evgeniou, T., Gerke, S., & Minssen, T. (2020). The European artificial intelligence strategy: Implications and challenges for digital health. *The Lancet Digital Health*, *2*(7), e376–e379.

Compagnucci, M. C., Wilson, M. L., Fenwick, M., Forgó, N., & Bärnighausen, T. (Eds.). (2022). *AI in EHealth: Human autonomy, data governance and privacy in healthcare*. Cambridge University Press.

Dal Mas, F., Massaro, M., Rippa, P., & Secundo, G. (2023). The challenges of digital transformation in healthcare: An interdisciplinary literature review, framework, and future research agenda. *Technovation*, *123*, 102716.

Flynn, S., Geiger, C., Quintais, J. P., Margoni, T., Sag, M., Guibault, L., & Carroll, M. W. (2020). Implementing user rights for research in the field of artificial intelligence: A call for international action. In *Joint PIJIP/TLS research paper series*, (Vol. 48).

Gerke, S., Minssen, T., & Cohen, G. (2020). Ethical and legal challenges of artificial intelligence-driven healthcare. In *Artificial intelligence in healthcare* (pp. 295–336). Academic Press.

Lal, A., Dang, J., Nabzdyk, C., Gajic, O., & Herasevich, V. (2022). Regulatory oversight and ethical concerns surrounding software as medical device (SaMD) and digital twin technology in healthcare. *Annals of Translational Medicine*, *10*(18).

Lee, J. A., Hilty, R., & Liu, K. C. (Eds.). (2021). *Artificial intelligence and intellectual property*. Oxford University Press.

Lhotska, L. (2020). Application of industry 4.0 concept to health care. In *pHealth 2020* (pp. 23–37). iOS Press.

Li, J. P. O., Liu, H., Ting, D. S., Jeon, S., Chan, R. P., Kim, J. E., . . . & Ting, D. S. (2021). Digital technology, tele-medicine and artificial intelligence in ophthalmology: A global perspective. *Progress in Retinal and Eye Research*, *82*, 100900.

Mithas, S., Chen, Z. L., Saldanha, T. J., & De Oliveira Silveira, A. (2022). How will artificial intelligence and Industry 4.0 emerging technologies transform operations management? *Production and Operations Management*, *31*(12), 4475–4487.

Mozumder, M. A. I., Armand, T. P. T., Imtiyaj Uddin, S. M., Athar, A., Sumon, R. I. , Hussain, A., & Kim, H. C. (2023). Metaverse for digital anti-aging healthcare: An overview of potential use cases based on artificial intelligence, blockchain, IoT technologies, its challenges, and future directions. *Applied Sciences*, *13*(8), 5127.

Pantanowitz, L., Bui, M. M., Chauhan, C., ElGabry, E., Hassell, L., Li, Z., Parwani, A. V., Salama, M. E., Sebastian, M. M., Tulman, D., Vepa, S., & Becich, M. J. (2022). Rules of engagement: Promoting academic-industry partnership in the era of digital pathology and artificial intelligence. *Academic Pathology*, *9*(1), 100026.

Paul, S., Riffat, M., Yasir, A., Mahim, M. N., Sharnali, B. Y., Naheen, I. T., Rahman, A., & Kulkarni, A. (2021). Industry 4.0 applications for medical/healthcare services. *Journal of Sensor and Actuator Networks*, *10*(3), 43.

Qvist-Sørensen, P. (2020). Applying IIoT and AI–Opportunities, requirements and challenges for industrial machine and equipment manufacturers to expand their services. *Central European Business Review*, *9*(2), 46-77.

Rana, S. K., Rana, S. K., Nisar, K., Ag Ibrahim, A. A., Rana, A. K., Goyal, N., & Chawla, P. (2022). Blockchain technology and artificial intelligence based decentralized access control model to enable secure interoperability for healthcare. *Sustainability*, *14*(15), 9471.

Rasheed, H. (2024). Consideration of cloud-web-concepts for standardization and interoperability: A comprehensive review for sustainable enterprise systems, AI, and IoT integration. *Journal of Information Technology and Informatics*, *3*(2).

Schönberger, D. (2019). Artificial intelligence in healthcare: A critical analysis of the legal and ethical implications. *International Journal of Law and Info Technology*, *27*(2), 171–203.

Sriram, R. D., & Subrahmanian, E. (2020). Transforming health care through digital revolutions. *Journal of the Indian Institute of Science*, *100*(4), 753–772.

Stahl, B. C. (2021). *Artificial intelligence for a better future: An ecosystem perspective on the ethics of AI and emerging digital technologies* (p. 124). Springer Nature.

Thakare, V., Khire, G., & Kumbhar, M. (2022). Artificial intelligence (AI) and internet of things (IoT) in healthcare: Opportunities and challenges. *ECS Transactions*, *107*(1), 7941.

Trenfield, S. J., Awad, A., McCoubrey, L. E., Elbadawi, M., Goyanes, A., Gaisford, S., & Basit, A. W. (2022). Advancing pharmacy and healthcare with virtual digital technologies. *Advanced Drug Delivery Reviews*, *182*, 114098.

Wanjale, K., Chitre, A. V., & Doshi, R. (2023). Opting for Industry 4.0: Challenge or opportunity. In *AI, IoT, big data and cloud computing for industry 4.0* (pp. 3–20). Springer International Publishing.

Yang, J., Luo, B., Zhao, C., & Zhang, H. (2022). Artificial intelligence healthcare service resources adoption by medical institutions based on TOE framework. *Digital Health*, *8*, https://doi.org/10.1177/20552076221126034

Chapter 12

AI-Driven Precision Nutrition Marketing: A Catalyst for Improved Public Health

Angad Munshi[a], *Sarita Nagvanshi*[b], *Ashim Raj Singla*[a] *and Teena Singh*[b]

[a]Indian Institute of Foreign Trade, India
[b]New Delhi Institute of Management, India

Abstract

The convergence of food, healthcare, and artificial intelligence (AI) presents a transformative opportunity to revolutionize health and wellness. Food, as a cornerstone of disease prevention and management, faces challenges due to the complexity of dietary needs and behavior change. AI, with its ability to analyze vast datasets and identify patterns, offers innovative solutions by enabling targeted interventions and personalized marketing strategies that promote healthier lifestyles. This chapter explores AI's role in advancing nutrition, healthcare, and marketing through a holistic and data-driven approach. AI empowers the development of personalized health recommendations, optimizes consumer segmentation, and refines marketing strategies to resonate with individual preferences. By integrating AI, healthcare systems can address global challenges, such as rising costs and aging populations, while enhancing the effectiveness of nutrition-based interventions. The study critically examines existing literature and case studies, emphasizing real-world applications over technical complexities. It highlights ethical considerations, including algorithmic biases and privacy concerns, to ensure the responsible use of AI in influencing behavior change. Furthermore, the chapter delves into AI's ability to bridge the gap between dietary knowledge and behavior change, offering insights into its potential to improve health outcomes.

Keywords: Artificial intelligence (AI); precision nutrition; public health; personalized marketing; health interventions

Digital Transformation and Artificial Intelligence for Operational Excellence in Healthcare, 227–252

doi:10.1108/978-1-83662-314-420251034

Introduction

The convergence of food, healthcare, and artificial intelligence (AI) presents a transformative opportunity to revolutionize health and wellness. While food is increasingly recognized as a cornerstone of disease prevention and management, the complexity of dietary needs and the challenges of behavior change have hindered progress. AI, with its ability to analyze vast datasets and identify patterns, offers a powerful tool to address these challenges. By understanding the intricate interplay between nutrition, health, and consumer behavior, we can leverage AI to develop targeted interventions and personalized marketing strategies that promote healthier lifestyles.

Advancements in AI offer unprecedented capabilities to analyze vast datasets, uncover patterns, and deliver personalized health recommendations. These innovations even enhance clinical effectiveness in telemedicine adoption (Mishra & Singh, 2022) and help overcome vaccination barriers in resource-limited settings (Mishra, 2022).

By integrating AI into the domain of food and healthcare, we can move beyond traditional approaches, enabling a more holistic and data-driven understanding of how diet impacts health outcomes. This integration is particularly relevant today as healthcare systems worldwide grapple with the dual challenges of rising healthcare costs and an aging population. Furthermore, AI's ability to drive targeted marketing strategies enhances the reach and effectiveness of nutrition-based interventions, ensuring that individuals receive personalized recommendations that resonate with their unique needs and preferences.

This chapter aims to explore the transformative role of AI in advancing the intersection of nutrition, healthcare, and marketing. By leveraging AI's ability to analyze dietary data, predict health risks, and deliver personalized dietary recommendations, this study will demonstrate AI's significant role in enhancing health outcomes and promoting healthier lifestyles. It will also examine how AI-driven precision marketing can optimize consumer segmentation and develop personalized strategies that resonate with individual needs. Ethical considerations will be addressed, highlighting how AI can be used responsibly to influence behavior change. Through a critical review of existing literature and case studies, this research study will delve into the challenges and opportunities of integrating AI in nutrition and healthcare. Rather than focusing on the technical complexities of AI, the study emphasizes its real-world applications, providing insights into how AI can bridge the gap between dietary knowledge and behavior change. Ultimately, this chapter seeks to contribute to the growing body of knowledge supporting the integration of AI in healthcare and marketing, offering a pathway to more personalized, efficient, and ethical food-related health interventions.

The Intersection of Food, Healthcare, and AI in Marketing

Before diving into specific strategies, it is crucial to understand the broader landscape where food, healthcare, and AI converge. This intersection offers a dynamic environment where personalized nutrition can drive better health outcomes, and AI-powered marketing strategies can effectively influence consumer behavior. By recognizing the complexity and interdependence of these fields, we can better explore how AI enables more targeted interventions, tailored recommendations, and precision marketing efforts that resonate with individual needs.

Impact of Diet on Health Outcomes

Diet significantly influences health outcomes, particularly in preventing and managing chronic diseases like cardiovascular disease, diabetes, obesity, and cancer (Lorenzo et al., 2022; Pascual et al., 2021; Tomé-Carneiro & Visioli, 2023; Wang et al., 2023). Diets rich in fruits, vegetables, whole grains, and lean proteins – such as the Mediterranean diet – offer protective effects due to their antioxidants, fiber, and healthy fats (FENS, 2015; Jenna, 2020; Trichopoulou et al., 2014). Conversely, high saturated fat and sugar intake are linked to obesity and cancer progression (Australian Government, 2013; Australian Government Department of Health and Aged Care, 2023). Specific interventions like the DASH diet reduce blood pressure and cardiovascular risk while plant-based diets lower cholesterol and BMI (Ley et al., 2014; Pallazola et al., 2019). Omega-3s reduce inflammation, and vitamin D and calcium support bone health (Reynolds & Mitri, 2024; Zupo et al., 2023). Thus, dietary choices are vital for long-term health (Jenna, 2020).

Diet as a Preventive Healthcare Tool

Nutrition and immunity are deeply interconnected, with vitamins, minerals, and antioxidants boosting immune function and reducing inflammation (Cassotta et al., 2023; Harvard & Chan School of Public Health, 2023). Plant-based diets rich in fiber and phytochemicals lower cancer risk, while high-fat, processed foods increase susceptibility. Cohort studies and trials confirm the role of healthy diets in cancer prevention and reducing chronic inflammation, infections, and long-term health risks (Golonko et al., 2024; Hinduja et al., 2023; Mittelman, 2020; Narimatsu & Yaguchi, 2022).

Diet and Chronic Disease Management

Balanced diets are vital for chronic disease management, with low-carb and anti-inflammatory diets improving glycemic control in diabetes (Narimatsu & Yaguchi, 2022; Rosenfeld et al., 2022). Mediterranean and DASH diets reduce cardiovascular risks by lowering saturated fats and promoting heart-healthy foods (Sacks et al., 2017). Whole-food, minimally processed diets aid sustainable weight management and obesity risk reduction (Harvard & Chan School of Public Health, 2023). Meta-analyses highlight the efficacy of plant-based, low-carb, and Mediterranean diets in managing diabetes, heart disease, and obesity (Rosenfeld et al., 2022; Sacks et al., 2017).

AI's Role in Marketing

AI is transforming marketing by enabling hyper-personalization, predictive analytics, and automation. It is a tool to understand consumers deeply, predict their needs, and deliver tailored experiences. Several instances where company uses AI to deliver personalized marketing to individual customers at scale. By leveraging AI and large datasets, a company (for instance, Blueshift) uses hyper-personalization using AI-powered marketing to make customized decisions for each customer's unique journey.[1]

AI-Powered Customer Experience (CX): AI is redefining customer engagement, seamlessly orchestrating personalized experiences through machine learning, behavioral analytics, and real-time adaptability. Beyond mere automation, AI curates dynamic, intuitive interactions, transforming CX into a strategic differentiator. As 65% of CX leaders acknowledge AI's pivotal role, the future of engagement is inextricably AI-driven.[2] Generative AI amplifies this evolution, enabling profound customer insights, refining usability, streamlining journeys, cutting costs and fortifying loyalty.

AI in Personalized Nutrition: A Market in Motion: Personalized nutrition, powered by AI, is witnessing unprecedented growth, fueled by the demand for tailored health solutions. AI-driven systems synthesize vast datasets to refine dietary recommendations, optimize meal planning, and bridge nutritional gaps. Despite concerns over privacy and cost, innovation drives expansion. The global AI in Personalized Nutrition market, valued at $1.6 billion in 2022, is projected to reach $10.5 billion by 2030, growing at a 21.9% CAGR – propelled by AI advancements and the increasing prioritization of precision nutrition (futuredatastats.com) – though challenges like data privacy concerns remain.

Key Market Segments

The landscape of AI-driven nutrition unfolds across type, application, end-user, and provider categories, with significant growth observed across North America, Europe, and Asia Pacific (See Fig. 12.1).

AI Techniques in Personalized Nutrition: AI offers a comprehensive suite of tools for optimizing nutrition. AI leverages machine learning, deep learning, and natural language processing (NLP) to reimagine dietary intelligence. Machine learning models refine over time, predicting deficiencies, tailoring diets, and detecting allergens. Deep learning deciphers intricate nutritional patterns, processing visual data to assess dietary intake. NLP enhances human–AI interactions, facilitating intuitive, conversational guidance. Meanwhile, computer vision classifies food items, estimates portion sizes, and enables real-time dietary tracking.

---

[1]https://blueshift.com/

[2]https://www.fullstory.com/blog/ai-in-customer-experience/#ai-cx-understanding-ai-in-customer-experience

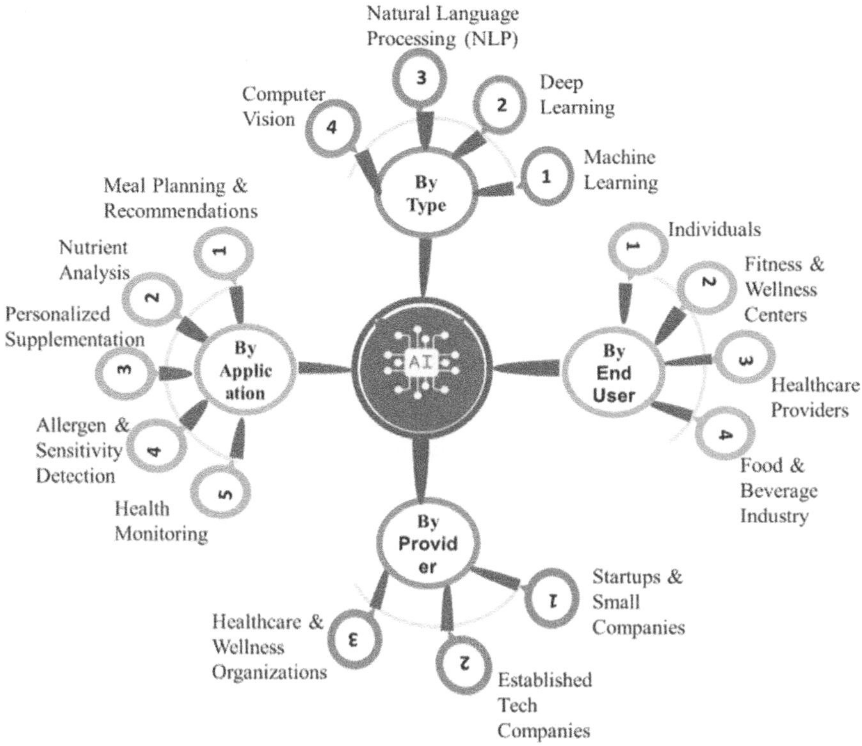

Fig. 12.1. AI in Personalized Nutrition Market Segmental Analysis. *Source:* Author's Own Source.

Applications of AI in Personalized Nutrition: AI tailors meal plans to align with dietary preferences, restrictions, and health objectives. Advanced analytics pinpoint nutritional imbalances, refine supplementation strategies, and detect allergens, ensuring dietary compliance. AI-powered health monitors track physiological markers (like blood pressure and glucose levels), providing continuous, real-time nutrition insights. The convergence of these capabilities is redefining nutritional science, making it predictive, personalized and adaptive.

End-Users of AI-Powered Nutrition Solutions: AI-driven nutrition solutions cater to diverse stakeholders. Individuals leverage AI for self-optimized health while fitness and wellness centers integrate AI to craft hyper-personalized regimens. Healthcare providers deploy AI-enhanced nutrition plans to manage medical conditions effectively. The food and beverage industry, in parallel, utilizes AI to engineer customized products, meeting evolving consumer expectations with precision.

Providers of AI-Powered Nutrition Solutions: AI-powered nutrition solutions come from diverse sectors. Startups and small companies lead innovation, developing cutting-edge technologies that push the boundaries of AI in nutrition. Large tech firms leverage their resources to create scalable AI platforms while healthcare and wellness organizations integrate AI to enhance patient care through personalized nutrition. Key players include Nutrino Health, DayTwo, Lumen, Nutrigenomix and Viome, collectively shaping the future of AI-driven nutrition.

Regional Market Growth

The market for AI in personalized nutrition is experiencing significant regional growth, with North America leading the way. This region's prominence is fueled by the presence of key technology players, a growing adoption of AI technologies, and increasing consumer awareness about the benefits of personalized nutrition. Europe also plays a crucial role, with countries like the United Kingdom, Germany, and France seeing substantial growth due to the rising demand for personalized health and wellness solutions. In the Asia–Pacific region, rapid market expansion is evident in countries such as China, Japan, and India, driven by a growing population, rising disposable incomes, and a shift toward a more health-conscious lifestyle. Latin America shows promising potential for market expansion, supported by a growing focus on preventive healthcare and the adoption of advanced technologies in the food and nutrition industry. Meanwhile, the Middle East and Africa are emerging as key players, with countries like the United Arab Emirates and Saudi Arabia increasingly embracing technological advancements in healthcare and wellness.

Marketing Strategies/Tactics

AI has the potential to revolutionize marketing strategies by offering a level of precision and insight beyond human capability. As illustrated in the accompanying Fig. 12.2 (a&b), AI can optimize multiple aspects of marketing, from data-driven decision-making to personalized customer interactions. For example, AI enables the creation of hyper-targeted influencer marketing campaigns and the development of innovative loyalty programs, unlocking new dimensions of engagement. While this section provides a brief overview of adaptable strategies, it's important to recognize that advancements in AI will continue to enhance and expand these approaches, introducing even more sophisticated and impactful marketing innovations.

Leveraging AI for Precision ICP Development

Accurate identification of an Ideal Customer Profile (ICP) is essential for businesses leveraging AI, which revolutionizes customer profiling by automating data collection, analysis, and segmentation. AI-powered tools analyze vast datasets to uncover patterns, hidden characteristics, and preferences, enabling highly tailored marketing strategies. Predictive analytics further enhance ICP development by

(a)

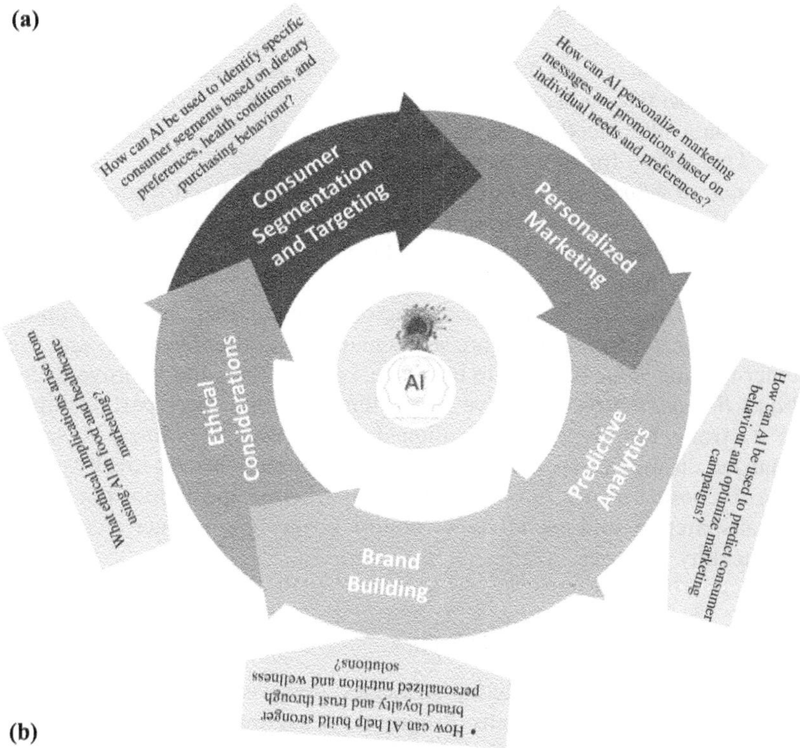

(b)

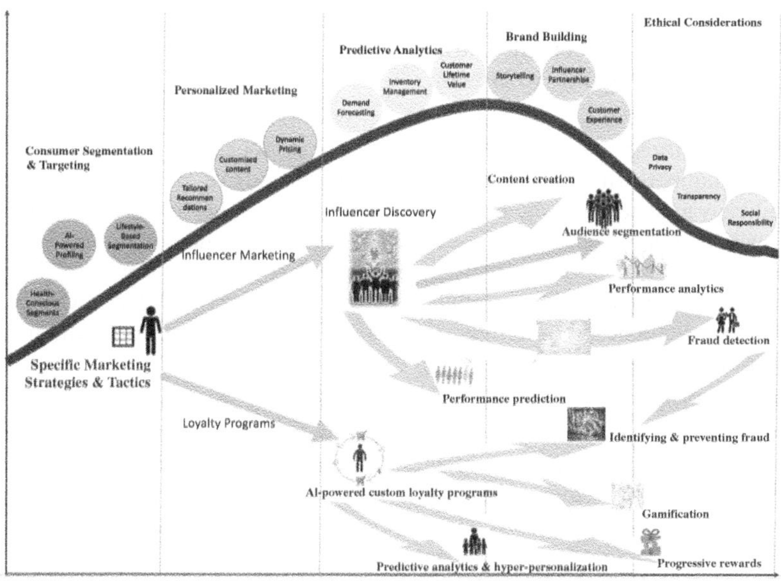

Fig. 12.2. AI-Driven Innovations in Marketing Strategies. *Source:* Author's Own Source.

anticipating customer behavior and preferences in real-time, improving customer satisfaction and loyalty.

Consumer Segmentation and Targeting (CST): AI enables precise segmentation, such as identifying health-conscious consumers or lifestyle-based groups, by analyzing data like social media behavior, purchase history, and website interactions. This allows for more personalized targeting.

Personalized Marketing: AI-driven strategies offer tailored recommendations, customized content, and dynamic pricing based on individual customer data, enhancing engagement and satisfaction. Dynamic pricing optimizes revenue by adjusting prices in real-time.

Predictive Analytics: By analyzing factors like weather, holidays, and consumer behavior, businesses can forecast demand, optimize inventory, and predict customer lifetime value (CLTV) to tailor marketing efforts and improve retention.

Brand Building (BB): Effective storytelling and influencer partnerships help create a strong brand perception aligned with consumer values. A seamless, personalized customer experience across all touchpoints fosters loyalty.

Ethical Considerations (EC): AI-driven marketing must prioritize data privacy, transparency, and social responsibility, ensuring consumer trust and promoting healthy lifestyles.

Specific Marketing Strategies and Tactics

There are several specific marketing strategies; however, we are focusing on two Influencer Marketing and Loyalty Programs. A survey by The Financial Brand (Marous, 2024) revealed that 29% of marketers expect a significant shift toward consumer personalization while 26% anticipate a rise in AI adoption. Notably, 47% plan to use AI in content marketing. By embracing AI, businesses can stay ahead of the curve and drive growth.

Influencer Marketing. AI has emerged as a pivotal force in the influencer marketing landscape. Influencer marketing has skyrocketed, transforming from niche to mainstream. Influencers shape opinions, drive purchases, and their credibility is gold for brands. But finding the right fit takes time. By automating tasks such as influencer discovery, campaign prediction, and content creation, AI empowers brands to optimize their strategies and achieve maximum ROI. From identifying the most suitable influencers to detecting fraudulent activity, AI ensures that influencer marketing remains an effective and ethical channel for reaching target audiences.

Loyalty Programs. AI is reshaping customer loyalty programs, providing businesses with the ability to enhance engagement and foster long-term loyalty through advanced data-driven strategies. *The Role of AI in Loyalty Programs can be viewed from many ways:*

Data-Driven Personalization: AI enables businesses to analyze large volumes of customer data, generating deep insights into individual preferences, behaviors, and purchasing patterns. Research shows that such data-driven analysis allows for the creation of hyper-personalized experiences within loyalty programs, improving customer satisfaction and retention (Arora et al., 2021; Babatunde et al., 2024; Deloitte, n.d.; Rosário & Dias, 2023).

Optimized Customer Journeys: AI-powered recommendation engines help personalize the delivery of targeted offers, rewards, and incentives. By leveraging predictive analytics, businesses can anticipate customer needs and provide tailored incentives, ensuring that loyalty programs resonate more deeply with each consumer (Bhalla, 2020; Kumar et al., 2024).

Enhanced Customer Experience: AI also contributes to seamless customer experiences by streamlining interactions within loyalty programs. This includes real-time adjustments to offers based on changing customer behaviors, ultimately leading to increased satisfaction and stronger brand loyalty (Ameen et al., 2021; Aw et al., 2022), however the challenges remain (Chamorro-Premuzic, 2023).

Connecting AI Advances to Key Research Areas: Transformative Impacts on Food Marketing and Consumer Well-Being

AI's profound ability to analyze and interpret vast datasets provides a powerful foundation for addressing pressing issues in food marketing and public health. By leveraging AI to optimize food distribution, personalize nutrition, and measure the effectiveness of campaigns, we can tackle food deserts, promote healthier eating habits, and ensure more equitable access to nutrition. However, as we harness AI's potential, it is crucial to consider the ethical implications of its use, ensuring that our strategies respect consumer rights and promote well-being. The research questions outlined provide a roadmap for exploring these critical areas and identifying emerging opportunities to refine and enhance AI applications in food marketing.

> *RQ1*: How can AI optimize food distribution and accessibility to alleviate food deserts and promote healthier diets?

In order to understand and address this question, it is important to know what actually 'Food Desert' means. Food desert is a geographic area, particularly lower income neighborhoods and communities, where access to affordable, quality, and nutritious foods is limited. Research into the health implications of food deserts began in the United Kingdom in the 1990s although economists and geographers had been studying spatial determinants of firm location, transaction costs, and differential prices of food for the poor since at least the 1960s (National Library of Medicine). Researchers are looking at the effect of food deserts on health outcomes, as well as examining which interventions have the greatest potential to improve conditions.

The congressional mandate in the USA came around and the 2008 Farm Bill directed the US Department of Agriculture (USDA) to undertake a study of food deserts in the United States to assess their incidence and prevalence, to identify characteristics and factors causing and influencing food deserts and their effect on local populations, and to provide recommendations for addressing the causes and effects. The Economic Research Service (ERS), in collaboration with the Institute of Medicine (IOM) and the National Research Council (NRC), convened a workshop on January 26–27, 2009, in Washington, DC, where experts discussed multidisciplinary approaches to measuring and mitigating the public health impacts of food deserts (Institute of Medicine and National Research Council, 2009).

The applications of AI in public health nutrition hold immense potential and can be a Game-Changer, with current research merely scratching the surface of what can be achieved. The wealth of data and AI's advancing capabilities present endless possibilities for innovation. AI's ability to analyze vast datasets and identify patterns opens up transformative possibilities:

- *Predict regional nutritional* needs based on environmental and socio-economic factors, guiding policymakers in targeted food production.
- *Track global food trends*, enabling proactive interventions to address emerging nutritional challenges.
- *Standardize nutritional guidelines* through international collaboration, ensuring consistent and healthier outcomes for populations worldwide.

Imagine a future where AI-driven models optimize food supply chains, create personalized nutrition plans, and detect diseases early. As AI advances, it stands at the forefront of reshaping public health nutrition, offering innovative solutions to improve global nutritional health (An & Wang, 2023).

Initiatives like the NOURISH platform, developed by an interdisciplinary team from UC San Francisco and UC San Diego, address health disparities in food deserts by equipping small business owners with tools to provide fresh food to underserved communities. Supported by NSF and USDA, the platform leverages AI and data science to create dynamic maps, offer business guidance, and promote culturally appropriate food, fostering local entrepreneurship and healthier food options (Dillon, 2024). It has been further developed to support the 24 million Americans living in food deserts, where fresh food is scarce, and ultra-processed options dominate, exacerbating diabetes and other cardiometabolic diseases (Dillon, 2024).

The United Nations' 2030 Agenda for Sustainable Development (United Nation) identifies 17 global goals, with the second focusing on eliminating hunger. Experts highlight the role of data analytics in achieving these goals, particularly in tackling food insecurity. According to Business Insider (2021), precision agriculture – leveraging AI, drones, and sensors – is significantly improving global food security by helping small-scale farmers optimize yields, reduce waste, and enhance productivity. The UN Development Program (UNDP, 2021) reports that nearly half of global freshwater used in agriculture and about one-third of food produced is wasted. Precision agriculture offers a solution by helping small-scale farmers maximize crop yields, reduce waste, and improve productivity through data-driven insights.

Inefficiencies in the global food supply chain contribute to substantial food waste and economic losses, amounting to $680 billion in industrialized countries and $310 billion in developing ones. Addressing these challenges requires improved storage, distribution, and localized sourcing. As the global population grows, doubling food production by 2050 will necessitate resilient supply chains, data-driven decision-making, and efficiency, particularly in developing nations (Business Insider, 2021). Additionally, alternative foods can enhance food security and contribute to the 2030 Agenda goals by diversifying nutrient sources, including protein, and improving overall diet quality (Mariutti et al., 2021).

Promoting sustainability in food and nutrition systems is essential for overcoming industry challenges. This requires boosting productivity, reducing waste, adopting sustainable practices, and strengthening resilience. However, transforming food consumption patterns and enhancing production efficiency will depend on integrating advancements from fields such as AI. By leveraging AI, we can:

- *Revolutionize production:* Optimize crop yields, improve resource efficiency, and predict disease outbreaks.
- *Streamline processing:* Enhance food safety, reduce waste, and improve quality.
- *Optimize distribution:* Improve supply chain efficiency, minimize food loss, and ensure equitable access.
- *Influence consumer behavior:* Develop personalized nutrition plans, promote sustainable food choices, and reduce food waste.

This narrative review highlights how AI can revolutionize the food system – from production and processing to distribution and consumption – by increasing efficiency and sustainability. AI-driven insights can optimize every aspect, including marketing strategies, supply chains, and consumer behavior, making AI an invaluable asset in achieving sustainable food security (Namkhah et al., 2023).

Given the discussed insights, what are the potential future research directions? Fig. 12.3 illustrates potential areas for future research.

RQ2: What AI-driven strategies can most effectively encourage healthy food consumption and behavior change?

Several research studies examine food consumption and behavioral changes. Despite the availability of numerous weight management apps, many struggle to lose weight effectively. This study explores an AI-driven app (eTRIP) designed to curb momentary eating impulses and improve eating behaviors. Real-time, personalized interventions recalibrate unhealthy habits using chatbots, image recognition, and nudges to provide tailored support (Chew et al., 2024).

AI's role in nutrition is shaping a transformative landscape. For instance, research (Theodore Armand, 2024) underscores AI's potential to revolutionize nutrition science, shifting dietary research and personalized interventions. From dietary assessment to customized nutrition plans, AI offers innovative solutions to

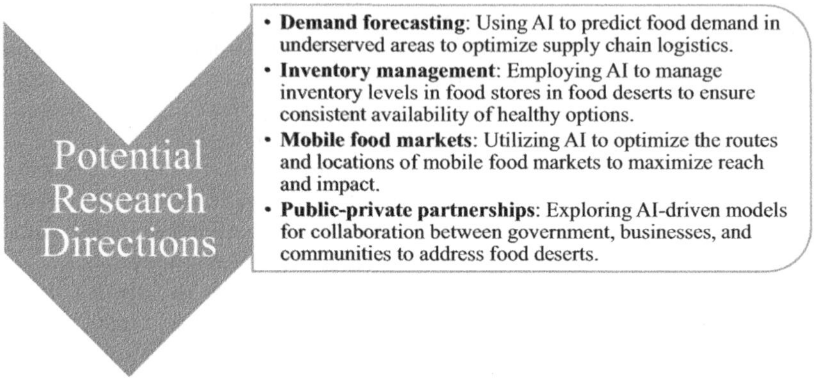

Fig. 12.3. Potential Areas for Future Research Regarding Role of AI in Optimizing Food Distribution and Accessibility to Alleviate Food Deserts and Promote Healthier Diets. *Source:* Author's Own Source.

improve health outcomes. While still emerging, AI-driven technologies present transformative tools for enhancing health strategies, requiring ethical considerations and collaborative efforts. With rising mobile penetration, app-based interventions must integrate AI strategies rapidly. Evaluating food tracking apps may yield deeper insights.

Studies highlight pervasive shortcomings in food tracking and recommendation apps, revealing limited AI-driven functionalities and subpar software quality. Findings of Samad (2022) identify gaps between user expectations and current capabilities, providing a framework for evaluating these apps and guiding developers toward more effective, user-friendly solutions. AI nutritionists are poised to personalize dietary management by offering tailored, accessible guidance. As AI capabilities advance and behavioural insights are incorporated, these tools will revolutionize nutrition, making personalized health strategies scalable and driving broader market adoption (Guo, 2024).

AI is also transforming the food service sector, enhancing customer service, optimizing inventory, automating processes, and enabling personalized marketing. Businesses leveraging AI can boost efficiency, reduce waste, and ensure food safety (Srivastava, 2024). From data-driven insights to robotic precision, AI is a culinary catalyst, optimizing production, streamlining supply chains, and revolutionizing customer experiences. From farm to fork, AI is driving efficiency, sustainability, and innovation. Research should focus on optimizing AI-driven marketing strategies to foster exceptional customer experiences (Fig. 12.4).

RQ3: How can AI be leveraged to create highly personalized nutrition plans that align with individual preferences and health goals?

Fig. 12.4. Research Avenues for Optimizing Marketing Strategies and Enhancing Customer Experiences. *Source:* Author's Own Source.

The global AI in personalized nutrition market is on a rapid rise, valued at $1.6 billion in 2022 and projected to reach $10.5 billion by 2030, growing at a CAGR of 21.9%. This significant growth reflects the increasing demand for tailored nutrition solutions (Futuredatastats, 2024).

AI is being used to create highly personalized nutrition plans by combining deep generative networks with LLMs (Large Language Models) like ChatGPT, tailoring them to individual preferences and health goals. AI-powered programs can track your dietary intake, analyze food data, and offer personalized recommendations to ensure you're getting the nutrients you need (Microsoft, July 16, 2024). By identifying beneficial and hindering foods, AI helps you stay on track toward your health goals. The study of Papastratis et al. (2024) introduces a novel AI-based nutrition method that leverages deep learning and nutritional guidelines to provide highly accurate, personalized weekly meal plans. By combining advanced modeling techniques and a vast culinary database, this method offers a reliable and versatile solution for dietary recommendations. Similarly, Amiri et al. (2023) have introduced a novel AI-powered meal planner that generates personalized, healthy meal plans tailored to individual needs. By combining semantic reasoning, fuzzy logic, and heuristic search, the system offers flexible and optimized meal options that consider health concerns, nutrition requirements, and personal preferences. Evaluation results demonstrate the system's effectiveness in providing valuable dietary guidance. AI has been assisting in being an individual's personalized health coach. AI-powered nutrition and fitness plans offer tailored solutions to help you achieve your health goals. By analyzing data and preferences, these apps provide personalized meal plans, workout routines, and real-time feedback. Success stories demonstrate the effectiveness of AI in improving health outcomes and motivation (Avinash, 2024). Another interesting new frontier goes beyond just the meal preferences recommendations. The research study of Yaiprasert and Hidayanto (2024) presents a novel ensemble machine learning approach for personalized meal services, bridging a gap in the food delivery industry. The innovative framework combines diverse algorithms to accurately classify and assign tasks, demonstrating the power of AI-driven decision-making. Beyond technical success, this technology holds immense potential for enhancing accessibility, promoting healthier lifestyles, and creating new job opportunities. As AI continues to evolve, we can expect even more sophisticated and personalized health solutions that empower individuals to take control of their well-being. By pursuing the following research directions (Fig. 12.5) and leveraging effective marketing strategies, we can further advance the field of AI-powered personalized meal planning and contribute to improving public health and well-being while also achieving commercial success.

RQ4: What are the ethical implications of using AI in food marketing, and how can these be mitigated to ensure consumer well-being?

AI is revolutionizing food manufacturing by leveraging advanced algorithms (by integrating machine learning, computer vision, and predictive algorithms) to optimize processes, enhance quality, and ensure safety. From quality control and predictive maintenance to supply chain optimization and product development, AI enables real-time monitoring, risk assessment, and innovation. This technology is

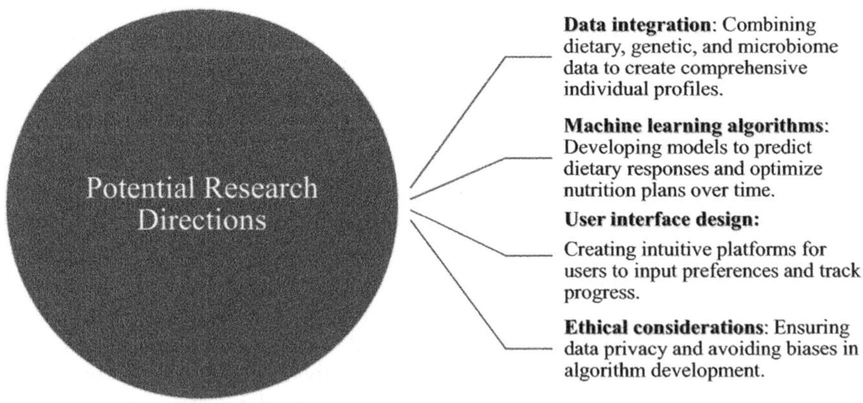

Fig. 12.5. Strategic Research Trajectories in AI-Enhanced Meal Planning: Bridging Public Health, Well-Being, and Market Success. *Source:* Author's Own Source.

driving efficiency, sustainability, and consumer satisfaction, making it an indispensable tool for the modern food industry. AI and robotics are revolutionizing food production by optimizing processes, improving sustainability, and enabling personalized nutrition. Advanced algorithms analyze data to minimize environmental impact while smart manufacturing processes enhance efficiency and quality control. This technology is shaping the future of food supply chain automation, promising a more sustainable and personalized food industry.

AI is revolutionizing the food industry by driving unparalleled efficiency, quality, and sustainability. Through real-time quality control, predictive maintenance, and optimized supply chain operations and delivery routes, AI ensures consistent product safety, minimizes downtime, and significantly reduces food waste, and reduces costs. These multivariate transformative advancements not only deliver substantial cost savings, boost customer satisfaction but also foster innovation and secure a competitive edge in the modern marketplace. These improvements have many benefits as depicted in Fig. 12.6. Overall, these improvements are crucial for businesses to succeed in today's competitive food industry.

Coupled with the transformative advancements of AI in food industry, AI implementation in the food industry presents challenges like data security, workforce training, and integration. Despite these obstacles, AI offers significant potential for optimizing resource usage, enhancing quality, and improving sustainability. Addressing these challenges through robust security measures, targeted training, and careful integration will enable food businesses to harness the power of AI and drive innovation.

The transformative potential of AI in food supply chains is undeniable, from optimizing decision-making to enhancing efficiency. However, the ethical implications of AI's widespread adoption cannot be overlooked. Transparency, traceability, and accountability are essential components of AI development and

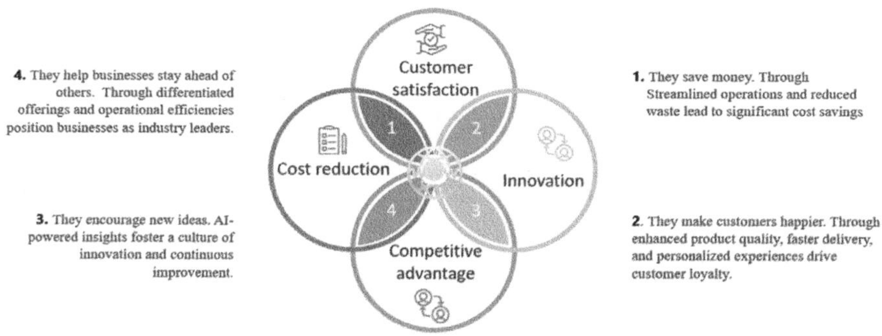

Fig. 12.6. Transformative Advancements and Their Multivariate Benefits of AI in the Food Industry. *Source:* Author's Own Source.

deployment to ensure responsible and trustworthy use. The ethical framing of AI by stakeholders significantly influences technology adoption, impacting both trust and the realization of AI's full benefits. The research study of Manning et al. (2022) underscores the urgent need for governance structures that balance AI's advantages with ethical imperatives, ultimately fostering greater engagement and performance outcomes within the food sector.

Algorithms, ranging from simple rule-sets to complex self-learning processes also called black box algorithms (Durán & Jongsma, 2021; Setzu et al., 2021), can introduce ethical concerns due to their opacity and potential for bias (Jacobs et al., 2021; Kowalska & Manning, 2021). These concerns, centered on transparency, accountability, and responsibility, are particularly relevant in the context of personal data usage (Durán & Jongsma, 2021). While questions can also arise around aspects of auditability, trustworthiness, culpability, reliability, explainability, interpretability and accessibility (Durán & Jongsma, 2021; Martin, 2019; Setzu et al., 2021), particularly for the service sector industry with special reference to diet and health. The study of Manning et al. (2022) aims to explore the ethical narrative surrounding AI adoption in food supply chains, fostering a common discourse to build trust and enable more considered AI utilization.

Prioritizing ethical research directions in AI-driven marketing is inevitable. Thus, building upon the identified ethical challenges in AI-driven marketing, the following potential research directions (Fig. 12.7) are proposed for future investigation:

By prioritizing these research directions, we can contribute to the development of AI-driven marketing practices that are both innovative and ethical, benefiting both consumers and businesses alike.

RQ5: How can AI be employed to accurately measure the influence of marketing campaigns on consumer behavior and subsequent health outcomes?

Fig. 12.7. Research Directions for Navigating the Ethical Landscape of AI in Marketing. *Source:* Author's Own Source.

The digital age has reshaped consumer dynamics, where the advent of e-commerce platforms and online shopping has revolutionized purchasing patterns globally, enabling seamless price comparisons, reviews, and broader product access from home (Katsikeas et al., 2020; Ngarmwongnoi et al., 2020; Thaichon et al., 2022). Social media's rise has amplified brand-consumer interactions (Mogaji et al., 2021; Voramontri & Klieb, 2019), while voice technology redefines engagement, integrating voice commands into shopping and service interactions (Ford et al., 2023; Sattarapu et al., 2023). Consumers continuously adapt, weaving technology into brand behavior (Eastman et al., 2023; Kaur et al., 2023; Lim et al., 2023).

Emerging generative AI tools, such as ChatGPT, Gemini, and Co-Pilot, are pivotal in transforming consumer engagement, offering personalized recommendations, and enhancing decision-making processes (Dwivedi et al., 2023). Early multidisciplinary studies reveal significant shifts in consumer behavior across education, retail, and banking (Dwivedi et al., 2023). As this transformation unfolds, a deepened theoretical framework and adaptive strategies are essential for leveraging AI's potential to optimize consumer behavior and maintain competitive advantage in a rapidly evolving marketplace (Amankwah-Amoah et al., 2024; Jain et al., 2023; Peres et al., 2023).

AI is a powerful tool for assessing the impact of marketing campaigns on consumer behavior and health outcomes (Bohr & Memarzadeh, 2020). However, ethical considerations are crucial in AI-driven marketing to prevent manipulative or discriminatory practices. Addressing biases in AI models – often stemming from non-representative datasets – is essential for fairness and inclusivity. By analyzing online activity, personalizing content, and predicting behavior, AI enhances campaign effectiveness. Furthermore, integrating marketing data with healthcare records and wearable device data enables the tracking of health metrics and correlations between marketing exposure and health outcomes.

While AI offers advantages such as cost reduction, accuracy, and precise targeting, challenges related to data privacy, ethics, and model bias must be addressed. Responsible and transparent AI implementation allows marketers to gain valuable insights while ensuring ethical marketing strategies. Utilizing diverse data and prioritizing transparency can help maximize AI's potential in understanding consumer behavior and health outcomes.

Previous research highlights AI's transformative role in digital marketing (Haleem et al., 2022; Mogaji & Jain, 2024), particularly in real-time customer engagement and competitive analysis. Building on this, Gupta et al. (2024) examined the chatbot "Genie" in restaurant customer service, demonstrating its effectiveness in streamlining operations, enhancing experiences, and driving financial growth. Similarly, AI is revolutionizing e-commerce by enabling precise consumer behavior prediction, allowing marketers to personalize strategies and optimize sales (Gkikas & Theodoridis, 2022). Machine learning and predictive analytics help businesses remain competitive though AI also raises ethical concerns related to consumer prioritization, market concentration, and manipulation. Naz and Kashif (2024) provide a framework for understanding these ethical implications through industry expert perspectives.

Generative AI is reshaping consumer behavior and marketing, opening new research avenues crucial for advancing AI's role in consumer engagement. The following schematic (Fig. 12.8) illustrates four key areas for exploration.

However, AI's potential comes with significant responsibilities. Data privacy must be safeguarded to ensure public health initiatives respect individual and community rights. Bias is another critical issue – AI models reflect the quality of their training data, and biased datasets can exacerbate health disparities. To fully leverage AI's strengths, it is imperative to develop strategies to mitigate its potential harms. Collaboration between technology and public health can ensure AI serves as a force for good in promoting global nutritional health (An & Wang, 2023).

Discussion and Conclusion

AI stands as the vanguard of marketing transformation, reshaping strategies with unprecedented precision. Automating tasks, driving hyper-personalization, and empowering content creation, it refines targeting and amplifies campaign efficiency. Predictive analytics enable real-time calibration of marketing approaches, while AI-driven chatbots and recommendation systems forge deeper customer bonds, cultivating brand loyalty.

In parallel, AI extends its influence to health and wellness, crafting individualized meal plans, analyzing vast nutrition data, and offering tailored recommendations based on unique health profiles. Integrating biometric data, AI refines dietary suggestions, fostering sustained health improvements. Wearables, linked to AI, provide continuous feedback, motivating individuals to track progress and maintain long-term wellness goals. This dual thrust, in both marketing and health, underscores AI's vast potential to redefine consumer experiences.

Yet, this integration is far from seamless. Ethical quandaries emerge, from privacy violations to algorithmic biases, shaping the discourse on AI's role in marketing. The systematic review by Su et al. (2023) dissects these challenges into algorithmic, societal, and existential domains. Algorithmic biases – often birthed from skewed datasets – threaten to perpetuate systemic inequalities through discriminatory practices. Societal concerns spotlight privacy encroachments, erosion of autonomy, and AI-driven misinformation that risks undermining consumer trust. Existentially, AI's potential to displace human labor and erode decision-making autonomy looms large.

These concerns transcend theoretical boundaries; their real-world implications are profound. As AI's reach expands across marketing and healthcare, ethical stewardship becomes imperative. Without such oversight, AI risks exacerbating social disparities, undermining its potential to benefit society equitably. Su et al. (2023) advocate for an urgent ethical framework grounded in transparency, fairness, and accountability – cornerstones to guide AI's responsible deployment.

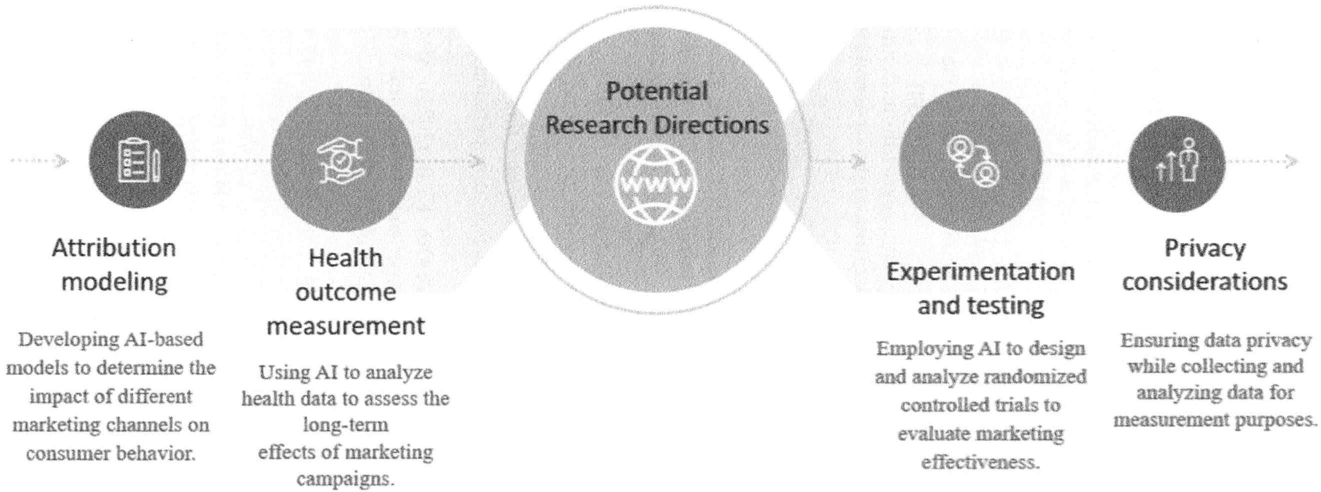

Fig. 12.8. AI-Driven Insights Into Marketing Effects: Research Frontiers in Consumer Behavior and Health Outcomes. *Source:* Author's Own Source.

References

Amankwah-Amoah, J., Abdalla, S., Mogaji, E., Elbanna, A., & Dwivedi, Y. K. (2024). The impending disruption of creative industries by generative AI: Opportunities, challenges, and research agenda. *International Journal of Information Management*, 102759. https://doi.org/10.1016/j.ijinfomgt.2024.102759

Ameen, N., Tarhini, A., Reppel, A., & Anand, A. (2021). Customer experiences in the age of artificial intelligence. *Computers in Human Behavior*, *114*, 106548. https://doi.org/10.1016/j.chb.2020.106548

Amiri, M., Li, J., & Hasan, W. (2023). Personalized flexible meal planning for individuals with diet-related health concerns: System design and feasibility validation study. *JMIR Formative Research*, *7*. https://doi.org/10.2196/46434

An, R., & Wang, X. (2023). Artificial intelligence applications to public health nutrition. *Nutrients*, *15*(19). https://doi.org/10.3390/nu15194285

Arora, N., Ensslen, D., Fiedler, L., Liu, W. W., Robinson, K., Stein, E., & Schüler, G. (2021). *The value of getting personalization right-or wrong-is multiplying* (pp. 1–12). McKinsey & Company. https://www.mckinsey.com/capabilities/growth-marketing-and-sales/our-insights/the-value-of-getting-personalization-right-or-wrong-is-multiplying

Australian Government Department of Health and Aged Care. (2023, June 2). *Healthy food partnership*. https://www.health.gov.au/our-work/healthy-food-partnership

Australian Government, National Health and Medical Research Council, Department of Health and Aging. (2013). *East for health: Australian dietary guidelines 1–5*. Eat For Health. https://www.eatforhealth.gov.au/guidelines/australian-dietary-guidelines-1-5. Accessed on August 31, 2025.

Australian Government Department of Health, Disability and Ageing. (2024, August 16). *Partnership reformulation program*. https://www.health.gov.au/our-work/healthy-food-partnership/partnership-reformulation-program

Avinash. (2024, July 16). *The role of AI in personalized nutrition and fitness plans*. Roars Inc. https://www.roarsinc.com/our-journal/the-role-of-ai-in-personalized-nutrition-and-fitness-plans/

Aw, E. C. X., Tan, G. W. H., Cham, T. H., Raman, R., & Ooi, K. B. (2022). Alexa, what's on my shopping list? Transforming customer experience with digital voice assistants. *Technological Forecasting and Social Change*, *180*, 121711. https://doi.org/10.1016/j.techfore.2022.121711

Babatunde, S. O., Odejide, O. A., Tolulope Esther Edunjobi, T. E., & Ogundipe, D. O. (2024, March). The role of AI in marketing personalization: A theoretical exploration of consumer engagement strategies. *International Journal of Management & Entrepreneurship Research*, *6*(3), 936–949. https://doi.org/10.51594/ijmer.v6i3.964

Bhalla, A. (2020). *Why building consumer trust is the key to unlocking AI's true potential*. World Economic Forum. https://www.weforum.org/stories/2020/08/consumer-trust-ai-potential/

Bohr, A., & Memarzadeh, K. (2020). The rise of artificial intelligence in healthcare applications. *Artificial Intelligence in Healthcare*, 25–60. https://doi.org/10.1016/B978-0-12-818438-7.00002-2

Business Insider. (2021). *Feeding the world with precision*. https://www.businessinsider.com/sc/data-analytics-helps-solve-food-insecurity-2021-3?IR=T

Cassotta, M., Cianciosi, D., Giuseppe, R. D., Navarro-Hortal, M. D., Diaz, Y. A., Forbes-Hernández, T. A., Pifarre, K. T., Barrera, A. E. P., Grosso, G., Xiao, J., Battino, M., & Giampieri, F. (2023). Possible role of nutrition in the prevention of inflammatory bowel disease–related colorectal cancer: A focus on human studies. *Nutrition*, *110*, 111980. https://doi.org/10.1016/j.nut.2023.111980

Chamorro-Premuzic, T. (2023, March 23). Should you share AI-driven customer insights with your customers? *Harvard Business Review*. https://hbr.org/2023/03/should-you-share-ai-driven-customer-insights-with-your-customers

Chew, H., Chew, N., Loong, S., Lim, S., Tam, W., Chin, Y., Chao, A., Dimitriadis, G., Gao, Y., So, J., Shabbir, A., & Ngiam, K. (2024). Effectiveness of an artificial intelligence-assisted app for improving eating behaviors: Mixed methods evaluation. *Journal of Medical Internet Research*, *26*, e46036. https://doi.org/10.2196/46036

Colchero, M. A., Molina, M., & Guerrero-López, C. M. (2017). After Mexico implemented a tax, purchases of sugar-sweetened beverages decreased and water increased: Difference by place of Residence, Household Composition, and income level. *The Journal of Nutrition*, *147*(8), 1552–1557. https://doi.org/10.3945/jn.117.251892

Deloitte. (n.d.). *Connecting with meaning: Hyper-personalizing the customer experience using data, analytics, and AI*. Deloitte Canada. https://www.deloitte.com/ca/en/services/consulting/perspectives/connecting-with-meaning.html

Department of Health and Social Care, Department of Health (Northern Ireland), The Scottish Government and Welsh Government. (2020, July 30). *Front-of-pack nutrition labelling in the UK: Building on success*. https://www.gov.uk/government/consultations/front-of-pack-nutrition-labelling-in-the-uk-building-on-success

Diabetes. (2024, April 28). In K. R. Feingold, B. Anawalt, M. R. Blackman, et al (Ed.), *Endotext* [Internet]. MDText.com, Inc. https://www.ncbi.nlm.nih.gov/books/NBK279012/

Dillon, C. (2024, March 22). *Using AI and data science to ReNOURISH food deserts*. SDSC Communications. https://www.sdsc.edu/News%20Items/PR20240320_NOURISH.html

Durán, J. M., & Jongsma, K. R. (2021). Who is afraid of black box algorithms? On the epistemological and ethical basis of trust in medical AI. *Journal of Medical Ethics*, *47*(5), 329–335. https://doi.org/10.1136/medethics-2020-106820

Dwivedi, Y., Pandey, N., Currie, W., & Micu, A. (2023). Leveraging ChatGPT and other generative artificial intelligence (AI)-based applications in the hospitality and tourism industry: Practices, challenges and research agenda. *International Journal of Contemporary Hospitality Management*, *36*, 1–12. https://doi.org/10.1108/IJCHM-05-2023-0686

Eastman, J., Muncy, J., Jain, V., & Iyer, R. (2023). The journal of consumer Behaviour's first 20 years. *Journal of Consumer Behaviour*, *22*, 1282–1295. https://doi.org/10.1002/cb.2206

FENS. (2015). 12th European nutrition conference (FENS), Berlin, Germany, October 20–23, 2015: Abstracts. *Annals of Nutrition & Metabolism*, *67*(Suppl. 1), 1–601. https://doi.org/10.1159/000440895

Ford, J., Jain, V., Wadhwani, K., & Gupta, D. G. (2023). AI advertising: An overview and guidelines. *Journal of Business Research*, *166*, 114124. https://doi.org/10.1016/j.jbusres.2023.114124

Futuredatastats. (2024). Artificial Intelligence in Personalized Nutrition MarketSize, Share, Trends & Competitive Analysis By Type (Machine Learning, Deep Learning, Natural Language Processing, Computer Vision) By Application (MealPlanning and Recommendations, Nutrient Analysis, Personalized Supplementation, Allergen and Sensitivity Detection, Health Monitoring) By End User; By Provider; By Regions, and Industry Forecast, Global Report 2023–2030. Report ID:FDS347. https://www.futuredatastats.com/artificial-intelligence-in-personalized-nutrition-market

Gkikas, D., & Theodoridis, P. (2022). AI in consumer behavior. In M. Virvou, G. A. Tsihrintzis, L. H. Tsoukalas, & L. C. Jain (Eds.), *Advances in artificial intelligence-based technologies. Learning and analytics in intelligent systems* (Vol. 22). Springer. https://doi.org/10.1007/978-3-030-80571-5_10

Golonko, A., Pienkowski, T., & Swislocka, R., Orzechowska, S., Marszalek, K., Szczerbinski, L., Swiergiel, A. H., & Lewandowski, W. (2024). Dietary factors and their influence on immunotherapy strategies in oncology: A comprehensive review. *Cell Death & Disease 15*, 254. https://doi.org/10.1038/s41419-024-06641-6

Guo, Y. (2024, June 28). *The new personalized AI nutritionist*. The Decision Lab. https://thedecisionlab.com/insights/health/the-new-personalized-ai-nutritionist

Gupta, M., Dheekonda, V., & Masum, M. (2024). Genie: Enhancing information management in the restaurant industry through AI-powered chatbot. *International Journal of Information Management Data Insights*, *4*(2), 100255. https://doi.org/10.1016/j.jjimei.2024.100255

Hajishafiee, M., Kapellas, K., Listl, S., Pattamatta, M., Gkekas, A., & Moynihan, P. (2023). Effect of sugar-sweetened beverage taxation on sugars intake and dental caries: An umbrella review of a global perspective. *BMC Public Health*, *23*, 986. https://doi.org/10.1186/s12889-023-15884-5

Haleem, A., Javaid, M., Qadri, M. A., Singh, R. P., & Suman, R. (2022). Artificial intelligence (AI) applications for marketing: A literature-based study. *International Journal of Intelligent Networks*, *3*, 119–132. https://doi.org/10.1016/j.ijin.2022.08.005

Harvard, T. H., & Chan School of Public Health. (2023). Nuitrtion and immunity. *The Nuitrition Source*. https://nutritionsource.hsph.harvard.edu/nutrition-and-immunity/

Hinduja, D. B., Dhanu, A. S., Swamy, G. G., Murugesan, K., Elango, B., Murali, U., Rashid, M., Mathanmohun, M., & Basalingappa, K. M. (2023). Diet and nutrition strategies for cancer prevention: A comprehensive review. *Research in Biotechnology*, *14*, 12–18. https://doi.org/10.25081/rib.2023.v14.8618

Igd.com. (2021, November 3). Consumers increasingly open to adopting healthier and more sustainable diets. https://www.igd.com/Social-Impact/Articles/Consumers-increasingly-open-to-adopting-healthier-and-more-sustainable-diets/16137

Institute of Medicine and National Research Council. (2009). *The public health effects of food deserts: Workshop summary*. The National Academies Press. https://doi.org/10.17226/12623

Jacobs, N., Brewer, S., Craigon, P. J., Frey, J., Gutierrez, A., Kanza, S., Manning, L., Munday, S., Pearson, S., & Sacks, J. (2021). Considering the ethical implications of digital collaboration in the Food Sector. *Patterns*, *2*(11). https://doi.org/10.1016/j.patter.2021.100335

Jain, V., Rai, H., Parvathy, E., & Mogaji, E. (2023). The prospects and challenges of ChatGPT on marketing research and practices. *SSRN Electronic Journal*. https://doi.org/10.2139/ssrn.4398033

Jenna (2020, April 8). What you need to know about the Mediterranean diet. https://www.healthyhappywonderful.com/blog/what-you-need-to-know-about-the-mediterranean-diet

Katsikeas, C., Leonidou, L., & Zeriti, A. (2020). Revisiting international marketing strategy in a digital era: Opportunities, challenges, and research directions. *International Marketing Review*, *37*(3), 405–424. https://doi.org/10.1108/IMR-02-2019-0080

Kaur, J., Mogaji, E., Paliwal, M., Jha, S., Agarwal, S., & Mogaji, S. A. (2023). Consumer behavior in the metaverse. *Journal of Consumer Behaviour*. https://doi.org/10.1002/cb.2298

Kowalska, A., & Manning, L. (2021). Using the rapid alert system for food and feed: Potential benefits and problems on data interpretation. *Critical Reviews in Food Science and Nutrition*, *61*(6), 906–919. https://doi.org/10.1080/10408398.2020.1747978

Kumar, V., Ashraf, A. R., & Nadeem, W. (2024). AI-powered marketing: What, where, and how?. *International Journal of Information Management*, *77*, 102783. https://doi.org/10.1016/j.ijinfomgt.2024.102783

Ley, S. H., Hamdy, O., Mohan, V., & Hu, F. B. (2014). Prevention and management of type 2 diabetes: Dietary components and nutritional strategies. *Lancet (London, England)*, *383*(9933), 1999–2007. https://doi.org/10.1016/S0140-6736(14)60613-9

Lim, W., Kumar, S., Pandey, N., Verma, D., & Kumar, D. (2023). Evolution and trends in consumer behaviour: Insights from journal of consumer behaviour. *Journal of Consumer Behaviour*, *22*(1), 217–232. https://doi.org/10.1002/cb.2118

Lorenzo, P. M., Izquierdo, A. G., Rodriguez-Carnero, G., Fernández-Pombo, A., Iglesias, A., Carreira, M. C., Tejera, C., Bellido, D., Martinez-Olmos, M. A., Leis, R., Casanueva, F. F., & Crujeiras, A. B. (2022). Epigenetic effects of healthy foods and lifestyle habits from the Southern European Atlantic diet pattern: A narrative review. *Advances in Nutrition*, *13*(5), 1725–1747. https://doi.org/10.1093/advances/nmac038

Manning, L., Brewer, S., Craigon, P. J., Frey, J., Gutierrez, A., Jacobs, N., Kanza, S., Munday, S., Sacks, J., & Pearson, S. (2022). Artificial intelligence and ethics within the food sector: Developing a common language for technology adoption across the supply chain. *Trends in Food Science & Technology*, *125*, 33–42. https://doi.org/10.1016/j.tifs.2022.04.025

Mariutti, L. R. B., Rebelo, K. S., Bisconsin-Junior, A., De Morais, J. S., Magnani, M., Maldonade, I. R., Madeira, N. R., Tiengo, A., Maróstica, M. R., & Cazarin, C. B. B. (2021). The use of alternative food sources to improve health and guarantee access and food intake. *Food Research International*, *149*, 110709. https://doi.org/10.1016/j.foodres.2021.110709

Marous, J. (2024). *15 applications for AI and machine learning in financial marketing*. https://thefinancialbrand.com/news/data-analytics-banking/artificial-intelligence-banking/ai-machine-learning-analytics-marketing-banking-trends-71350/

Martin, K. (2019). Ethical implications and accountability of algorithms. *Journal of Business Ethics, 160*(4), 835–850. https://doi.org/10.1007/s10551-018-3921-3

Microsoft. (2024, July 16). Achieve your nutrition goals with the help of AI. https://www.microsoft.com/en-us/microsoft-365-life-hacks/everyday-ai/achieve-your-nutrition-goals-with-the-help-of-ai

Mishra, V. (2022). Analysis of systemic and behavioral barriers to COVID-19 vaccination in rollout phase. *International Journal of Healthcare Management, 17*(1), 131–140. https://doi.org/10.1080/20479700.2022.2157934

Mishra, V., & Singh, J. (2022). Health technology assessment of telemedicine interventions in diabetes management: Evidence from UAE. *FIIB Business Review, 0*(0). https://doi.org/10.1177/23197145221130651

Mittelman, S. D. (2020). The role of diet in cancer prevention and Chemotherapy efficacy. *Annual Review of Nutrition, 40*, 273–297. https://doi.org/10.1146/annurev-nutr-013120-041149

Mogaji, E., Balakrishnan, J., & Kieu, T. (2021). Examining consumer behaviour in the UK energy sector through the sentimental and thematic analysis of tweets. *Journal of Consumer Behaviour, 20*(2), 218–230. https://doi.org/10.1002/cb.1820

Mogaji, E., & Jain, V. (2024). How generative AI is (will) change consumer behaviour: Postulating the potential impact and implications for research, practice, and policy. *Journal of Consumer Behaviour*, 1–11. https://doi.org/10.1002/cb.2345

Namkhah, Z., Fatemi, S. F., Mansoori, A., Nosratabadi, S., Ghayour-Mobarhan, M., & Sobhani, S. R. (2023). Advancing sustainability in the food and nutrition system: A review of artificial intelligence applications. *Frontiers in Nutrition, 10*. https://doi.org/10.3389/fnut.2023.1295241

Narimatsu, H., & Yaguchi, Y. T. (2022). The role of diet and nutrition in cancer: Prevention, treatment, and Survival. *Nutrients, 14*(16), 3329. https://doi.org/10.3390/nu14163329

National Library of Medicine. https://www.ncbi.nlm.nih.gov/books/NBK208016/#

Naz, H., & Kashif, M. (2024). Artificial intelligence and predictive marketing: An ethical framework from managers' perspective. *Spanish Journal of Marketing – ESIC*. https://www.emerald.com/insight/content/doi/10.1108/SJME-06-2023-0154/full/html#sec01

Ngarmwongnoi, C., Oliveira, J., & AbedRabbo, M. (2020). The implications of eWOM adoption on the customer journey. *Journal of Consumer Marketing, 37*(7), 749–759. https://doi.org/10.1108/JCM-10-2019-3450

Niti Aayog, Government of India. (2018). *Transforming nutrition in India: Poshan Abhiyaan*. https://www.niti.gov.in/sites/default/files/2020-02/POSHAN_Abhiyaan_first_progress_report_6_Feb_2019.pdf

Pallazola, V. A., Davis, D. M., Whelton, S. P., Cardoso, R., Latina, J. M., Michos, E. D., Sarkar, S., Blumenthal, R. S., Arnett, D. K., Stone, N. J., & Welty, F. K. (2019). A clinician's guide to healthy eating for cardiovascular disease prevention. *Mayo Clinic Proceedings. Innovations, Quality & Outcomes, 3*(3), 251–267. https://doi.org/10.1016/j.mayocpiqo.2019.05.001

Papastratis. I., Konstantinidis, D., Daras, P., & Dimitropoulos, K.(2024). AI nutrition recommendation using a deep generative model and ChatGPT. *Scientific Reports, 14*, 14620. https://doi.org/10.1038/s41598-024-65438-x

Pascual Fuster, V., Pérez Pérez, A., Carretero Gómez, J., Caixàs Pedragós, A., Gómez-Huelgas, R., & Pérez-Martínez, P. (2021). Executive summary: Update on dietary treatment of prediabetes and diabetes mellitus type 2. *Endocrinología, Diabetes y Nutrición*, *68*, 277–287. https://doi.org/10.1016/j.endien.2020.10.008

Peres, R., Schreier, M., Schweidel, D., & Sorescu, A. (2023). On ChatGPT and beyond: How generative artificial intelligence may affect research, teaching, and practice. *International Journal of Research in Marketing*, *40*, 269–275. https://doi.org/10.1016/j.ijresmar.2023.03.001

Reynolds, A., & Mitri, J. (2024). *Dietary advice for individuals with diabetes.*

Rosário, A. T., & Dias, J. C. (2023). How has data-driven marketing evolved: Challenges and opportunities with emerging technologies. *International Journal of Information Management Data Insights*, *3*(2), 100203. https://doi.org/10.1016/j.jjimei.2023.100203

Rosenfeld, R. M., Kelly, J. H., Agarwal, M., et al (2022). Dietary interventions to treat type 2 diabetes in adults with a goal of remission: An expert consensus statement from the American college of lifestyle medicine. *American Journal of Lifestyle Medicine*, *16*(3), 342–362. https://doi.org/10.1177/15598276221087624

Sacks, F. M., Lichtenstein, A. H., Wu, J. H. Y., Appel, L. J., Creager, M. A., Kris-Etherton, P. M., Miller, M., Rimm, E. B., Rudel, L. L., Robinson, J. G., Stone, N. J., Van Horn, L. V., & Association, American Heart (2017). Dietary fats and cardiovascular disease: A presidential advisory from the American heart association. *Circulation*, *136*(3), e1–e23. https://doi.org/10.1161/CIR.0000000000000510

Samad, S., Ahmed, F., Naher, S., Kabir, M. A., Das, A., Amin, S., & Islam, S. M. S. (2022). Smartphone apps for tracking food consumption and recommendations: Evaluating artificial intelligence-based functionalities, features and quality of current apps. *Intelligent Systems With Applications*, *15*, 200103. https://doi.org/10.1016/j.iswa.2022.200103

Sattarapu, P., Wadera, D., Nguyen, N. P., Kaur, J., Kaur, S., & Mogaji, E. (2023). Tomeito or Tomahto: Exploring consumer's accent and their engagement with artificially intelligent interactive voice assistants. *Journal of Consumer Behaviour*, *23*, 278–298. https://doi.org/10.1002/cb.2195

Setzu, M., Guidotti, R., Monreale, A., Turini, F., Pedreschi, D., & Giannotti, F. (2021). Glocalx-from local to global explanations of black box ai models. *Artificial Intelligence*, *294*, 103457. https://doi.org/10.1016/j.artint.2021.103457

Snetselaar, L. G., DeSilva, D. M., & Stoody, E. E. (2021). Dietary guidelines for Americans, 2020–2025: Understanding the scientific process, guidelines, and key recommendations. *Nutrition Today*, *56*(6), 287–295. https://doi.org/10.1097/NT.0000000000000512

Srivastava, S. (2024, August 14). AI in the food industry – how artificial intelligence and robotics are transforming the sector. *appinventiv.com*. https://appinventiv.com/blog/ai-in-food-industry/

Su, Y., Wang, E., & Berthon, P. (2023, January). Ethical marketing AI? A structured literature review of the ethical challenges posed by artificial intelligence in the domains of marketing and consumer behaviour. In *Proceedings of the 56th Hawaii International Conference on System Sciences* (pp. 4942–4992). https://doi.org/10.24251/HICSS.2023.603

Thaichon, P., Cheah, J., & Ting, H. (2022). The dark and bright side of online consumer behavior. *Journal of Consumer Behaviour*, *21*(3), 445–449. https://doi.org/10.1002/cb.2041

Theodore Armand, T. P., Nfor, K. A., Kim, I., & Kim, C. (2024). Applications of artificial intelligence, machine learning, and deep learning in nutrition: A systematic review. *Nutrients, 16*(7). https://doi.org/10.3390/nu16071073

Tomé-Carneiro, J., & Visioli, F. (2023). Plant-based diets reduce blood pressure: A systematic review of recent evidence. *Current Hypertension Reports, 25*, 127–150. https://doi.org/10.1007/s11906-023-01243-7

Trichopoulou, A., Martínez-González, M. A., Tong, T. Y., Forouhi, N. G., Khandelwal, S., Prabhakaran, D., Mozaffarian, D., & de Lorgeril, M. (2014). Definitions and potential health benefits of the mediterranean diet: Views from experts around the world. *BMC Medicine, 12*, 112. https://doi.org/10.1186/1741-7015-12-112

UNDP. (2021, October 14). *Precision agriculture for smallholder farmers*. https://www.undp.org/publications/precision-agriculture-smallholder-farmers

UNICEF. (2022, March 2). *Sugar sweetened beverage taxation: Policy brief.* https://www.unicef.org/media/116681/file/Sugar-Sweetened%20Beverage%20(SSB)%20Taxation.pdf

United Nation *United nations' 2030 Agenda for sustainable development*. https://sdgs.un.org/goals

Voramontri, D., & Klieb, L. (2019). Impact of social media on consumer behaviour. *International Journal of Information and Decision Sciences, 11*(3), 209–233. https://doi.org/10.1504/IJIDS.2019.101994

Wang, W., Liu, Y., Li, Y., Luo, B., Lin, Z., Chen, K., & Liu, Y. (2023). Dietary patterns and cardiometabolic health: Clinical evidence and mechanism. *MedComm, 4*(1), e212. https://doi.org/10.1002/mco2.212

Yaiprasert, C., & Hidayanto, A. N. (2024). AI-powered in the digital age: Ensemble innovation personalizes the food recommendations. *Journal of Open Innovation: Technology, Market, and Complexity, 10*(2), 100261. https://doi.org/10.1016/j.joitmc.2024.100261

Zupo, R., Castellana, F., Piscitelli, P., Crupi, P., Desantis, A., Greco, E., Severino, F. P., Pulimeno, M., Guazzini, A., Kyriakides, T. C., Vasiliou, V., Trichopoulou, A., Soldati, L., La Vecchia, C., De Gaetano, G., Donati, M. B., Colao, A., Miani, A., Corbo, F., & Clodoveo, M. L. (2023). Scientific evidence supporting the newly developed one-health labeling tool "Med-Index": An umbrella systematic review on health benefits of mediterranean diet principles and adherence in a planeterranean perspective. *Journal of Translational Medicine, 21*(1), 755. https://doi.org/10.1186/s12967-023-04618-1

Printed and bound by CPI Group (UK) Ltd, Croydon, CR0 4YY

13/09/2026

14961028-0003